to
Denise!
Great working
with you — bold
together!

Josh

JUST
DON'T
FALL

HOW I GREW UP,
CONQUERED ILLNESS,
AND MADE IT
DOWN THE MOUNTAIN

JUST DON'T FALL

Josh Sundquist

VIKING

To my parents

VIKING
Published by the Penguin Group
Penguin Group (USA) Inc., 375 Hudson Street,
New York, New York 10014, U.S.A.
Penguin Group (Canada), 90 Eglinton Avenue East, Suite 700,
Toronto, Ontario, Canada M4P 2Y3
(a division of Pearson Penguin Canada Inc.)
Penguin Books Ltd, 80 Strand, London WC2R 0RL, England
Penguin Ireland, 25 St. Stephen's Green, Dublin 2, Ireland
(a division of Penguin Books Ltd)
Penguin Books Australia Ltd, 250 Camberwell Road, Camberwell,
Victoria 3124, Australia
(a division of Pearson Australia Group Pty Ltd)
Penguin Books India Pvt Ltd, 11 Community Centre, Panchsheel Park,
New Delhi – 110 017, India
Penguin Group (NZ), 67 Apollo Drive, Rosedale, North Shore 0632,
New Zealand (a division of Pearson New Zealand Ltd)
Penguin Books (South Africa) (Pty) Ltd, 24 Sturdee Avenue,
Rosebank, Johannesburg 2196, South Africa

Penguin Books Ltd, Registered Offices: 80 Strand, London WC2R 0RL, England

First published in 2010 by Viking Penguin, a member of Penguin Group (USA) Inc.

1   3   5   7   9   10   8   6   4   2

Copyright © Josh Sundquist, 2010
All rights reserved

Library of Congress Cataloging-in-Publication Data
Sundquist, Josh.
Just don't fall : how I grew up, conquered illness, and made it down the mountain / Josh Sundquist.
p. cm.
ISBN 978-0-670-02146-8
1. Sundquist, Josh—Health. 2. Tumors in children—Patients—United States—Biography.
3. Ewing's sarcoma—Patients—United States—Biography. I. Title.
RC281.C4S86 2010
618.92'9940092—dc22
[B]
2009026831

Printed in the United States of America
Set in Adobe Garamond   •   Designed by Nancy Resnick

*Penguin is committed to publishing works of quality and integrity.
In that spirit, we are proud to offer this book to our readers;
however, the story, the experiences, and the words
are the author's alone.*

Editor's Note

These are true stories.

Memoirs, based as they are on memories, are inherently skewed by point of view. That being said, the author of this work has attempted to adhere to the truth of his memories as best he can.

Most dialogue, of course, has been reconstructed, but the author has interviewed many of the people who were present at key moments. In some cases the author has condensed chronology and dialogue for the sake of narrative pacing.

JUST
DON'T
FALL

The physical therapist glues two stickers to my back, to the lower part of my back right above my underwear. There are wires coming out of these stickers, wires that will give me an electric shock—not the kind that electrocutes and kills people, no, don't worry, she says, this is a tiny shock I will barely feel. And this tiny electric shock will send a message to my brain that will block the pain from the thousands of tiny needles that are still stabbing my left foot, even now after the doctor gave me as much morphine as a nine-year-old can get at one time.

But when the physical therapist turns the knob, the stickers with the wires coming out start burning holes through my skin, and my body is bouncing up and down and side to side on the bed. I try to stop bouncing, because you are not supposed to bounce on beds, especially hospital beds. But I can't stop. My body is bouncing . . . automatically, the way my knee does when Dr. Marsh hits it with the orange triangle-shaped hammer. That's how I feel now, except my whole body feels like it has been hit with the hammer, and it's a big, heavy hammer like an orange triangle-shaped sledgehammer, so it's not just my knee but also my head, shoulders, elbows, belly button and everything else in my body that is bouncing on the bed. And I can't hear anything, either, because it sounds like there are bees stuck in both of my ears that are buzzing so loudly they are shaking my brain.

Then the physical therapist presses a button and there is no more burning or bouncing or buzzing. She says that oh, she's so, so sorry and she accidentally started with level fifteen instead of level zero, which happened because she had the knob turned all the way to the right instead of the left, and now she will try again starting at zero and turn it up, very, very slowly. But I tell her I don't want to get shocked by the stickers anymore because instead of stopping the needles from stabbing my foot, the stickers made me bounce up and down and put a buzzing noise in my head and almost burned holes through my skin, and all this hurts even more than the needles.

Well then, the physical therapist says, she has one last idea that might help. The nerves that go to your right foot and the nerves that go to your left foot are connected in your spinal cord, she tells me, so your brain doesn't always know which foot is which. I say that I can always tell my right from my left, but she says this is different, and sometimes if one foot hurts and the other one gets a foot rub, the two signals cancel each other out. She says she will try rubbing my foot for me, but I say no thank you, I don't really want her to touch me right now.

So Mom sits on the end of my bed and puts my right foot in her lap. She starts by rubbing my toes. Her hands are cold. I shiver. But after she rubs my foot for a few minutes, her hands start to feel warm like the heating pad I used to put on my left leg. She rubs my toes and then moves up to the middle where the arch is and then down to my heel, kneading my foot like pizza dough, the kind with the dark brown whole wheat crust and spinach on top that she always makes—the kind that tastes terrible. We always ask her to make pizza with white crust and pepperonis because we don't mind about eating lots of fat and cholesterol and having heart attacks when we grow up, but she still makes her whole wheat crust and spinach-on-top pizza every week.

And today, in the hospital, when she rubs my foot like the whole wheat pizza dough, the needles stabbing my invisible foot start to disappear. First there are a thousand needles, then only a hundred, then just one or two, and then, for the first time since my leg was cut off, I have no pain at all. I fall asleep.

1

Dad is making up a number for me. He's an accountant, so I know he's good at anything to do with numbers, especially making them up.

I asked him for the number—whispered, actually, since we are in church—because of the family sitting in the front row. We are right behind them, in the second row. It's where we always sit.

Sitting in the second row means almost everyone can see you. Last year, when Dad decided he wanted to raise his hands in the air during the singing like they do at Pentecostal churches, he asked Pastor Smuland if it would be all right, even though we are a Presbyterian church, and even though our family sits in the second row, which means the whole congregation would see him do it.

"Go for it," Pastor Smuland said.

It was the same answer Pastor Smuland gave him a few months ago when Dad asked if it was all right to bring a tambourine to church and play it from the second row. *Go for it.* So that next Sunday, Dad brought the tambourine I got for my birthday this year when I turned six. But he kept hitting it on the wrong beats and the piano player would tilt her head around the side of the piano and frown at him. So during the prayer I whispered to Dad that he should probably think about not going for it anymore with the tambourine.

In the front row is the Jacobson family. The Jacobsons—who are what we call a little bit different (actually, they are weird, but Mom doesn't let us call people weird unless they are liberals or feminists)—always sit there, right in front of us. The Jacobsons are a little bit different because, for one thing, they grind their own wheat flour, which they do because they say it is more biblical to eat bread made with stone-ground flour since it contains all the germ and gluten God intended when he created the wheat kernel. They tried to sell us some of their biblical wheat bread, but Mom only buys bread when it is on sale after it has passed its expiration date.

The Jacobsons are the reason I asked Dad to guess the number. Actually, Mrs. Jacobson is. She wrote an article in the church newsletter last month about the Dangerous Levels of Sugar in Soft Drinks. Mrs. Jacobson wanted to share something with the congregation that God had put on her heart and He just really wanted everyone to know about, which was the fact that sugar levels in soft drinks are so high that if you drink one can of Coca-Cola, one third of your immune system shuts down.

Mom made me read the article.

"See, that's why we don't eat sugar in our family," she said.

But I told her I knew the article was wrong, because some of my friends' parents have let them drink three cans of soda, and according to Mrs. Jacobson that would have shut down their whole entire immune system.

"But none of my friends have died," I said.

She frowned.

"Right?" I said.

Mom looked at Dad, because this was a numbers question and he is an accountant.

"It's possible that the effect of the sugar is nonlinear," Dad said.

I knew that I was supposed to ask what *nonlinear* was, but then I would have to listen to one of Dad's math lessons.

"Oh," I said.

God had also wanted Mrs. Jacobson to tell the congregation that cancer tumors are fueled by carbohydrates, and carbohydrates come from sugar, so sugar causes cancer. That's the part of the article I thought about when I saw the Jacobsons sitting on the front row today, and that's why I just asked Dad for the number:

"Dad, how many people get cancer during their life?"

"I guess . . . probably . . . ten percent," he whispers back.

"You mean if there are ten people, one of them will get cancer?"

"That's right."

I count the front row. I count Mr. and Mrs. Jacobson and all six of their weird children and the two other people sitting beside them that I don't know. Ten people. One will get cancer. Maybe it will be Mrs. Jacobson.

We know the Jacobsons because besides going to our church, they are also homeschoolers, like us. One thing about being home-schooled is that when you meet people at the grocery store or the dentist's office or any other place during the middle of the day, the people always ask why you aren't at school like the other kids. You tell them it's because you are homeschooled. Then they always want to know why you are homeschooled, so you tell them it's because your parents want to protect you from the dangerous things in pub-lic schools, like drugs, gangs, and the Theory of Evolution.

One of the best things about being homeschooled is that you get to go to homeschool group potlucks. Each month at the potluck after we finish eating, while all our parents are in the picnic shelter discussing Creation-Based Science Textbooks, we kids have races on the play-ground. I always win because I am the fastest. We also play a game called Boys Against Girls. These are the rules: The boys chase the girls around the playground. If you catch a girl—I always try to catch Keisha because she is the prettiest girl in our homeschool group—you get to give her a kiss. I kiss Keisha even though I know that if you kiss a girl before you are married to her you might get AIDS.

One time last summer at homeschool swimming class, I wrote a love note to Keisha and put it on her towel before class started. After the lesson, while I was still in the water, she walked over to the edge of the pool and held up my note.

"Is this from you?" she asked. I hadn't signed my name on the note because I didn't want her to know it was from me. But I guess she figured it out because, like Mom always says, girls have female intuition. Or maybe because I give her kisses on the lips. Somehow she had figured it out, though, and now she was standing by the side of the pool asking me if I wrote the note. I was trapped. If I said yes, Mom would hear me and I would get in trouble because in our family we are not allowed to date girls until we are sixteen, which won't be for ten more years. But if I said no, that would be a lie, and we are not allowed to lie, either. So I ducked underwater and hid at the bottom of the pool. I waited and waited and waited until my lungs started to burn and my chest felt like it would explode if I didn't open my mouth. Then I pushed off the bottom and launched out of the water—I looked kind of like a dolphin, I think—to gasp for air.

She was still there.

"Is this from you?"

She waited that whole time while I was holding my breath? It seemed like . . . such a long time! I couldn't believe she was still there.

So I decided to try a different plan. I took an even deeper breath and swam underwater along the side of the pool, hoping to confuse her. I surfaced—like a dolphin, again—at least ten feet away from where I'd started.

"Is thiiiis frooooooom yooooou?" she said the words very slow and loud, like the way Dad talks to people who don't speak English.

She really wanted to find out, I realized, if I wrote the note, but I really *really* wanted to not get in trouble for dating or lying, so I ducked under the water again and swam out to the deep end of the pool. Now when I came up for air and she yelled and jumped and waved her arms, I just pretended not to notice her. Eventually she threw her arms up above her head and made a loud grunting noise like she was really mad—I could hear it even out in the deep end—and then she wrapped a towel around her waist and skipped back to the locker rooms, which was strange because usually people don't skip when they are mad.

But she must have just been pretending to be mad because the next week at swimming class, Keisha gave me a piece of paper folded up so it was the size of my Patch the Christian Pirate tapes. She handed it to me—*Handed it to me! Right in front of Mom!*—after class, on the way to the showers. I ran inside the locker room and unfolded it. The paper had a drawing of a bunch of rectangles all fitting inside each other. Every rectangle was made with a different color, so it looked like a rainbow. At the middle of the page was a space where someone—probably Keisha since she was the one who'd handed me the paper—had written in black marker the words "I LOVE YOU!"

I showered and got dressed. All of us homeschool kids wear the same kind of clothes—the boys wear polyester polo shirts, old ones, tucked into dress pants that our moms make us hike up above our belly buttons. The girls wear T-shirts underneath long dresses that reach all the way down to touch their shoes, which are always white sneakers.

The pants I was wearing that day didn't have any pockets, so before I tucked my shirt in, I slipped Keisha's drawing underneath, leaving the paper unfolded so it would be flat against my chest. Bulges would make Mom want to see what was under my shirt, and then she would read the note and I would get in trouble.

"Are you all right?" Mom asked when I walked out of the locker room.

"Yeah of course I'm all right. Why does it look like I'm not all right or something? Because I am all right."

The words were squirting out like the diarrhea I got the time Grandma let me eat lots of French fries and sugary ice cream at McDonald's.

"You are just walking sort of . . . stiffly," Mom said.

That was so the paper wouldn't make crinkly noises, of course. But I couldn't lie, so I just said, "Oh."

When I got home, I folded the paper up again and taped a white string to it. Then I pushed this folded paper all the way back to the wall underneath my bookshelf, with the string sticking out far enough so that I could still reach it. That way, anytime I wanted to see the note again, I could just pull on the string and the note would slide out.

2

I have always been fast. That's why I'm good at soccer. I can beat the other kids in a race to the ball, and then beat them in a race to the goal, too. But even though I've been practicing soccer with the homeschool kids since I was six—three whole years now—there are no other homeschool teams to play against, so I've never played in a real game.

Then one Sunday morning I walk into Sunday school class and see Aaron, a homeschool friend who goes to my church, wearing green shorts, a matching jersey, and knee-high socks. I have on my white collared shirt and scratchy dress pants.

"I can't believe your parents let you wear that to church!" I say.

"Well, my travel soccer team has a game right after Sunday school," Aaron says. "And I won't have time to change clothes before it starts."

A *travel* soccer team! They play games . . . against other teams! They wear uniforms . . . to church! And homeschoolers are allowed to play!

As soon as Sunday school finishes, I run down all three flights of stairs to the hall outside adult Sunday school. I wait while the adults have a final prayer that lasts almost *three hours,* and then I jump in front of Mom as she walks out the door.

"Mommy!" I say. "Can I please, please, please play on a travel soccer team?"

She gives her standard response—"We'll have to think about it"—which really means, "We'll have to think about reasons you can't do it," which really means, "No."

But I want that uniform. I want those shiny shorts and bright socks to wear in games against other soccer teams in other cities around Virginia. I want it more than anything I have ever wanted, even more than I wanted to kiss Keisha before she moved away and stopped coming to homeschool potlucks. So I keep asking Mom.

This is one of the advantages of homeschooling. You are with your mom all day, every day, so if there's something you want, you can ask her over and over again. Of course, you don't want to ask her so much that she gets annoyed—just enough so she doesn't forget. That's why I only ask every fifteen minutes. I did this the time Luke took his first steps and Mom said that he had figured out how to walk because he'd seen us walking all the time. So I asked Mom, "If we all flew around in jet packs all the time, would Luke figure out how to fly?" She said no, he wouldn't, but I thought it would be really, really cool if Luke could learn how to fly, so I kept asking every fifteen minutes for several weeks, hoping she would say yes. But she never did.

The soccer team question turns out differently than the jet pack question, though. I ask Mom about the soccer team all week, and after just five days of asking every fifteen minutes, Mom agrees—*but you can't wear your uniform to church*—to let me play. *Yes!* But try-outs aren't for a few weeks, so I will use those weeks to practice and get good. I will start tomorrow, on Saturday.

It's Saturday morning and I've just woken up. I look at my alarm clock: 7:03. I do a quick calculation: An hour and fifty-seven minutes left. Less than two hours. I feel something warm under my foot. I pull back the covers and see Mom's heating pad, the piece of fabric that heats up when you plug it into the wall. I've been using it for almost four months. I like to put it on my leg to help the growing pains when I am trying to go to sleep. *I must have rolled around and pushed it down to my foot while I was asleep.* I switch it off and climb down the ladder. Matthew, sleeping in the bottom bunk—he gets the bottom because he is seven and I am nine—feels the bed move and wakes up.

"Is it Saturday?" he whispers, like there are other people in the room who might wake up if he talks too loud.

"Yeah," I whisper back.

"Yessss!" he says, scrunching his eyes together and smiling so I can see the gap where his adult teeth haven't poked through. "Sweet cereal!" (*Thweet thereal*).

Matthew jumps out of bed, but I am already halfway down the hall to the kitchen. I beat him there, and when I stop running I slide several inches on my socks across the kitchen floor. I see it on the table: Honey O's, which I will love if I like Honey Nut Cheerios, trademark General Mills. It contains nine essential vitamins, and is a good source of—but while I am still reading the box, Matthew grabs it off the table. He lifts it with two hands and shakes it over his bowl. A couple of Honey O's land in the bottom, *plink, plink.* He shakes the box a few more times, and the cereal comes out like an avalanche into his bowl and pieces are rolling off the table and onto the floor.

"Awwww*wwwwww*!" I say, which is what you say when you see someone break a rule and they are going to be in trouble. The "awwww" starts out in a low voice and then you get higher and higher until you are saying the "*wwwww*" part like a girl.

"Oops," Matthew says.

"That's more than a half bowl of sweet cereal!" I say. "I'm gonna tell Mom."

"No, please"—(*pleath*)—"don't tell Mom," he says. "Watch."

He grabs a fistful of Honey O's from the table and returns them to the box. Twelve more fistfuls, and now the bowl is only half full, and the pieces from the table and on the floor are back in the box.

"There, see?" Matthew says.

7:34 a.m.

"An hour and twenty-six minutes left," I say.

"Yeah," Matthew says.

Saturday is the best day because you don't have to vacuum or wash clothes or mop or dust or sweep or shake out the rugs. We watch Saturday morning cartoons instead—the old kind, like *Bugs Bunny* and *Road Runner*. They're some of the only things we are allowed to watch.

Our TV has a special machine in it that reads the CC (which stands for "Closed Captioning") so it can substitute for bad words. For example, if someone says the word "butt," the machine replaces it with "toe," so people on our TV say things like "I want to kick your toe." Once we watched something called *The Penis Van Homosexual Show*, which made Dad laugh so hard he started crying.

"Linda," he said to Mom. "Look! It's *The Dick Van Dyke Show*!"

Mom did not think this was funny.

After Looney Tunes, Matthew and I run down the hall and wait at the door until my watch reads nine o'clock exactly. Then we push it open so fast it swings around on its hinges and slams against the wall. We run across the bedroom and jump on Dad.

"Wake up! Wake up!"

"It's Saturday morning, Daddy!"

Dad groans.

"Uuuuuuuuuuuuuuuuuuuuuuuuuuuuuuuuuuuuuuuuuuuuuuuuuuuuuuuh."

I always jump on his stomach when he starts groaning like this because it pushes all the air out of his lungs and sounds funny.

"Uuuuu—HUMPH! Uuuuuuh . . ."

We shake him until he opens his eyes.

"Come on Dad. It's nine. You said we could wake you up now," I say. "We are going to play soccer together today, remember?"

"Yes, I know . . . okay, okay, I'm awake," he says.

"Daddy, guess what," Matthew says.

"What?" Dad asks.

"The sweet cereal is Honey O's!" Matthew says. He says it like *oath.*

After Dad and I practice soccer, Mom makes me take a shower. She always makes me take a shower when I get sweaty, even if I just took one the day before. So I take my shower and Dad takes his, and then we all go out to eat. We start with waters all around, please, which we order because water is free. Then the waitress looks at each of us and asks what we will be having and we say the Country Vegetable Buffet, please, which is free for children ten and under. I'm nine, Matthew is seven, and Luke is one, so we are all free. Mom will get charged $3.99 for the adult buffet price, which is strange because actually it's the same buffet as the kids' buffet and Matthew and I eat more than she does even though we are free. But it's good that we are free because our family pays for things like eating at restaurants and playing miniature golf—things that are fun—with the entertainment budget, which is an envelope in the hutch by the front door. On the first day of each month, Dad puts forty dollars in the envelope, and when the money runs out, so does the fun. That's why we always come here to Country Cookin, where kids ten and under eat free and adults eat for $3.99 unless they order steak.

"And for you, sir?" the waitress says to Dad.

Dad likes to read name tags so he can use people's names at least once in every sentence. "Well, Sheri," he says. "I'll have a six-ounce steak, please."

"How would you like that coo—"

"Paaaul," Mom interrupts.

She gives Dad the same frown she gives me when I finish my homeschool assignments for the day in twenty minutes and she knows I rushed through and probably made lots of mistakes on my math problems. The side of her lip dips down inside her left cheek, and she leans her head slightly in the same direction.

"Ummm, actually, Sheri," Dad says, "I will just go with the buffet tonight."

"Okay," Sheri says, stacking our menus. "I'll be right back with those waters."

Matthew asks why Dad didn't get a steak. Mom answers.

"Well, we are trying to save money right now."

"Do you mean there is going to be less money in the entertainment budget?"

"Maybe."

"But—no fair!"

"Yeah," I say. "No fair!"

"Why are we trying to save money?" Matthew asks.

"So we can have more savings."

"I know, but whyyyyyyyyy?"

Dad looks at Mom. "Now's a good time," he says. She nods.

"Boys," Dad says, "we're going to move in a few months, and after we move, I'm not going to have a job anymore."

"Move! Where?"

"What about soccer?"

"Why won't you have a job?"

"Is there a travel soccer team where we're going?"

Matthew and I are asking the questions, and Luke starts crying in his high chair. Mom takes a deep breath and breathes it out.

"I'll go get him some food," she says.

Dad slides out of the booth to let her stand up, and then he sits back down and starts talking again.

"Pastor Smuland has asked me to come work for the church," Dad says.

"Why? Is he leaving?" Matthew asks.

"No, our church is getting so big the elders think we need two pastors."

"And they want you to be the other one?"

"Uh-huh."

"So why do we have to move?"

"Well . . . to be a pastor, you have to go to seminary—do you boys know what seminary is? It's like a school for people who want to be pastors. So we're going to move to Florida for two years . . . so I can go to seminary there."

"Cool!" Matthew says. "Can we go to Disneyworld?"

"We can probably do that, maybe once while we're there."

"Yeeesss!" Matthew says. He reaches up his hand so I will give him a high-five, but I am not sure whether I should give it to him because I don't want to go to Florida. All my friends like Aaron and the other homeschool boys from church are here, and I have known all of them my whole entire life, and we race against each other during homeschool potlucks and play Boys Against Girls on the playground together. Every summer, when I have a birthday, I invite all of the homeschool boys to our house for a sleepover. This year, since I will turn ten, Mom and Dad were going to let me invite ten boys. If I'm in Florida for my birthday, I probably won't even *know* ten boys I can invite. And the worst part about moving is that soccer tryouts are in two weeks, so I will miss most of the season.

But maybe I should give Matthew a high-five anyway, because he is my very best friend, an even better friend than the homeschool boys because I have known him longer. So I lift my hand in front of his, but do it slowly, like I am volunteering to be the one to wash the dishes after dinner.

"Well—" I say. "Can I play on a travel soccer team in Florida?"

"We'll have to think about it," Dad says.

The next day is Sunday and we go to church, like always. Soon, Dad will stand up front and give sermons. That's the only good thing about moving to Florida—when we come back to Harrisonburg and

Dad is Pastor Sundquist, our whole family will become famous because he will tell stories about us in his sermons.

On Sunday night, I can't sleep because my leg hurts and I have the heating pad turned up to high and I still can't sleep. I sit on the top bunk, staring at the ceiling. I'm tired of thinking about how I miss Keisha. I've thought about everything I miss about her. I'm tired of thinking about soccer. I've thought about the uniform I want to wear, the goals I want to score, the position I want to play, and how much everyone in Sunday school will want to talk to me when they find out how good I am. I've thought about all those things at least three times already. Now I'm just tired and I can't sleep because my leg hurts and the heating pad doesn't help.

"Good morning," Mom says the next day.

I frown and don't say anything so she will know it's not a good morning.

"What's wrong?"

"I barely slept. It took *for-ev-er* to fall asleep," I say.

"I'm sorry, pumpkin. Were you worried about something?"

"No, it was the growing pains," I say.

"Did you try the heating pad?"

"Yes, but my skin gets so hot on my thigh, so sometimes I have to turn it off."

Mom squeezes her eyebrows together.

"You always have it on your thigh?" she says.

"Yeah . . ."

"On both thighs?"

"No, just my left."

Mom starts talking faster.

"Only your left leg? Your left thigh is the only place it hurts?"

"Yes, it's the only place that hurts. I told you that, like, *a century ago*."

"I don't think so."

"I did."

"I would've remembered."

"I told you."

"Okay, well, we are going to the doctor."

"Why?"

"To find out what is wrong with your leg."

"When?"

"Today. Right now."

3

I am getting an X ray. I sit up on a cold, flat table while a lady who is dressed like a nurse but is not a nurse, who is actually an *X-Ray technician,* adjusts a machine that looks like a giant overhead transparency projector that has been turned upside down and stuck to the ceiling.

I know what overhead transparency projectors look like because we use them at church so we can read the words to the songs we are singing. After each song, you can see the shadow of a hand on the screen while the fingers pull off the sheet of words for one song and put up the words to another. When I was a little boy, I thought the fingers on the screen looked so gigantic they must be God's fingers, and he had sent his fingers down to earth to switch the words for us just like when he sent down his only begotten son Jesus to die on the cross for us. But now that I am nine years old I know that the hand is just a regular human being hand—the hand of the person operating the projector—and the fingers just look big because everything looks big projected on the screen.

The X-ray technician hands me a blanket—which is the heaviest blanket I've ever lifted—and tells me to lay it across my lap.

"Ta protect yer cheel-drin," she says, followed by the "huh-ha" laugh people make when they want everyone to know they've just told a joke. But Mom doesn't laugh at this joke, so neither do I.

When we get home, the red light on the phone is blinking. "Hi

Linda, it's Mike," a voice says, a voice I can tell is Dr. Marsh's. I can tell it's Dr. Marsh's because I hear his voice every Sunday at church when he plays guitar and leads us in singing the songs that are on the overhead transparency projector. "I have the X-ray results back. Please call me as soon as you get this, we need to—"

Mom picks up the phone before the message is finished playing, and the tiny cassette tape inside makes a screeching noise as it jerks to a stop.

Mom calls Dr. Marsh.

"Hi, this is Linda. Thanks for calling so soon . . . All right . . . Yes . . ."

She listens for a while. Then she opens her mouth to talk, but doesn't say any words.

She closes her eyes and does it again.

Finally, words come out.

"But four of them—four of them thought it was benign? . . . Okay, just a minute . . ." She looks at the calendar. "Ummm . . . yes . . . next Wednesday at two is . . . fine."

She crosses off "Soccer" on the calendar and writes in "CAT scan."

Tryouts for the travel team are in a month. I can't miss homeschool soccer practice!

"But *Mom!*" I say. "*Soccer!* I need to go to soccer practice."

I say this in a whisper so she will be able to hear Dr. Marsh on the phone at the same time she listens to me. But she puts a finger over her lips to shush me.

"What do—what do you think it is, Mike?"

Mom is allowed to call him Mike since she is an adult. When I become an adult—when I turn eighteen—I will start calling him Mike, too.

"Mom? *Mom!* Can't I go to this cat thing another day?"

She slides her hand over the part of the phone where you put your mouth. "Joshua, wait please," she says. "Yes, sorry, go on Mike."

After she finishes talking to Dr. Marsh, she tells me that it might be very serious, but only two of the radiologists thought so, and there were six radiologists, so four of them thought it was benign.

"What's a radiologist?" I ask.

"A doctor who looks at X rays."

"Well what's a benign?"

"Benign. Not 'a benign.' It means not cancer."

"So . . . two people thought I have cancer?"

"Yes," Mom says. "But only two."

The only thing I know about cancer is that Grandpa died from it. I don't want to die, so I don't want to have cancer. But four out of six radiologists thought it was benign. That is the majority, so I will be all right.

Mom picks up the phone again to call the first person on the prayer chain. That person will call the next person on the list and pass the message along that we want God to make my leg benign, and then that second person will call the third person, the third person will call the fourth, and on and on like that. The weird thing about putting something on the prayer chain is that if you are on the list—and Mom is, of course—later that day the phone will ring, and it's someone calling to tell you to pray about *you*. Then you are supposed to pray—for yourself—and call the next person to pass along the message that they should pray for you, too. This happens unless you are lucky, and the person before you in the chain realizes that you are probably praying for yourself already, so she skips you and goes straight to the next person on the list.

The reason for the prayer chain is to get lots of people to pray for you, because the more people who are praying, the more likely it is that God will listen. A long time ago I asked Dad how many people have to pray for something for God to change his mind about it.

"God doesn't change his mind," Dad said. "He's omniscient. Do you know what that means?"—Dad kept talking before I could answer yes, I know what that means because we learned it in Sunday

School—"Omniscient means God knows everything. And since he already knows what's going to happen, he can't change his mind."

"So . . . if he can't change his mind, why do we pray?"

"Because God tells us to."

"But why should we do what God tells us to do?"

"Because God is good."

"Oh," I said.

But I thought about it later and realized that if God can't change his mind, then the prayer chain is very silly, because the only thing it does is share your problems and worries with all your friends from church.

On Wednesday I miss soccer so I can go to my CAT scan. It is the worst day of my life. The whole time I just think about the soccer I am missing. It is even worse than the day that used to be the worst day of my life, which was the day Papa made me pick up rotten crab apples in the grass in his backyard *all day* and only paid me ten cents.

On Friday I go to another doctor, Dr. Blanco. He works at the University of Virginia Children's Hospital an hour away, and he is called a Pediatric Orthopedic Surgeon. Since all three of the words in his title have Greek roots, and those old languages are so important on something called the SATs, Mom wants me to try to figure out what they mean.

"Think about it," she says on the drive to see Dr. Blanco. "Orthopedic. What does 'ortho' mean?"

"Ummm . . . I don't know."

"Think about it."

"Like 'orthodox,' maybe?"

"No . . . sound it out . . . orrrr-thooooo."

"I don't really know, Mom."

"How about . . . like . . . 'ba-ba-ba . . . ba . . . own?' " she says.

"Oh—bone?" I say.

"That's right, bone!" she says. "He's a bone surgeon. You're so smart!"

Dr. Blanco the bone surgeon says that based on my X ray he would like to do a needle biopsy. He will push a needle down through all the muscle in my leg—which is a lot of muscle; he noticed that about me as soon as I walked in today—and take out a sample of my femur to look at it under a microscope. Then he will know whether my bone is benign or not.

"Don't worry about the needle," he says. "We'll give you medicine to put you to sleep."

"Will I have to swallow a pill? I can't swallow pills."

"No, you'll breathe anesthesia through a mask," Dr. Blanco says. "Or if you want, you can get a shot that will make you feel very tired, and then we will put the mask on your face so you can breathe the anesthesia."

This is an easy decision.

"I hate needles."

"That's fine," he says. "You can just start breathing through the mask and you'll go right to sleep."

I have another question.

"When you're asleep for surgery, do you have dreams?"

"Actually, under anesthesia most people don't dream."

That scares me. I do not like the idea that one second I will be falling asleep with a mask over my face, and the next second I will wake up, but that actually two hours will have passed in between. On the drive home, Mom tries to tell me that this happens every night when I sleep, but no, I tell her, when I go to sleep at night, I have dreams. I know how long I have been sleeping based on how many dreams I have. Sometimes I wake up and know exactly what time it is without even looking at the alarm clock.

But when I am asleep for my surgery, I won't know what time it is. My mind will be completely dark, and blank, and empty. Dad says that's what Hell is like. It's not like people think, what with the fire and demons and brimstones. Hell is really just an empty black space where you float by yourself with no other people or thoughts or sounds or movement for all eternity. It's just black.

So surgery is like Hell. Everything is black, and empty, and you can't measure it or know what is going on in the hospital where your body is. Worst of all, you might die there, in that blackness, and all of a sudden God will take you to Heaven, and you'll say, "What's going on? Why am I in Heaven?"

And God will say, "Sorry, you died while you were having surgery."

And then you will be so mad at God—even though you aren't supposed to be mad at God—because you will have died without having time to say goodbye to anyone in your family or play on a travel soccer team or go to college. That's why I am afraid of surgery—because I might go to sleep and never wake up. I might bleed to death during the operation, but since I will be in the blackness of anesthesia, I won't even know it. And then, all of a sudden, I will be dead. That's the worst way to die.

But I wake up from the surgery. I wake up and Mom and Dad are standing there and I am not in Heaven, I am still alive and I am still on earth. I smile.

"Joshua, your leg is benign," Mom says. She hugs me, but she is very careful when she does since I just woke up from surgery.

"So what's wrong with my leg then?" I ask.

"We still don't know," Mom says.

"Dr. Blanco wants to wait six weeks," Dad says. "Then he'll do some more tests."

"So the needle—the bone—it was just, like, normal?" I ask.

"Dr. Blanco found dead cells," Mom says, and then adds, "But no cancer."

Dead? Dead cells? Sounds bad.

So I ask, "What if it's some kind of cancer that just kills the cells and then moves on to someplace else in your body?"

"That's not what cancer does," Mom says.

"Are you sure?"

"Well, I've never heard of anything like that."

4

Since it turns out I don't have cancer in my leg, we are going to visit Nana and Papa, who are Mom's mom and dad, next weekend. Now Papa, he is an expert in everything, especially guns. He always carries a gun in his back pocket—I'm not supposed to know this but once when I hugged him, I felt it there—and he has a gun hidden in every room in their house in case a burglar comes in and Papa can't reach into his pocket fast enough but he has time to reach under the couch cushion (the living room), above the pantry (the kitchen), or behind the books on the second shelf (Nana's sewing room). Papa is also an expert at making things like leather belts and things made out of wood. One time he helped me make a bow and arrow. We found sticks in the backyard and then tied on real arrowheads that he bought for me at an Indian reservation. But Mom doesn't ever let me shoot them with the bow we made, so it was a waste of real arrowheads.

And Nana, she is a great cook. She cooks chicken or beef at all her meals, which is different from Mom, who only lets us have meat when we have Hot Dog Night once per month. Also, Nana can do two things at once. I know this because I asked her, and she said yes, she could do two things at once. I remind Mom about this whenever Mom says she's busy and she can't help me now but she'll help me if I will just wait a few minutes. *Nana* can do two things at once, I tell her.

When we pull into the driveway at Nana and Papa's, I jump out first because I am closest to the sliding door. This gives me a head start in the race against Matthew. I need it, because my leg still hurts from the needle biopsy last week. Halfway between the driveway and the front steps, Matthew catches up, so I stick my arm out to block him. I can hold him behind me and still win the race to the door. Then I hear dogs barking. I look up and see two dogs, both bigger than Matthew and almost as big as me, running faster than I've ever seen dogs run. They are coming toward us across the neighbor's front lawn. *I don't have cancer*, I suddenly think. The dogs have teeth as long as my fingers, and as they run, drool runs through their teeth and spills off their gums. *I don't have cancer.* One of the dogs is looking at me. He is making eye contact with me, just like a person would, but his eyes look angry like Matthew's do when we are fighting. *I don't have cancer*, I think, my mind locking, *but I am going to get killed by a dog.*

I am too scared to run or talk or move. Matthew and I stand still on the sidewalk. I can't stop looking at that dog's eyes. I want to look away but I can't because it keeps looking at me.

I feel a sharp pain in my neck—I am choking! I can't breathe!—and my body flies backward. I am hanging by my shirt collar, and Mom is swinging me behind her. With her other arm, she grabs Matthew. As she pulls us back, she steps forward, in between us and the dogs. And now *Mom* is going to die, right now, she is going to die! Then I hear a whistle, and the dogs stop running and drop their heads at Mom's feet. A man is running across the yard. He is the one whistling.

"Come on, boys," he says. The dogs stop and walk over to him.

"Sorry about that," the man says with a smile, like he is thinking, "Aren't dogs just the funniest animals?"

Later, at dinner, Papa thanks God for protecting Mom from the dogs and protecting me from the cancer. He asks God to help Dad get the job at church. When Papa prays, he talks slowly and quietly, like God is a good friend of his.

"Amen," Papa says.

Everyone else says, "Amen."

"Paul, when do you interview for the job?" Nana asks.

"Tuesday," Dad says.

"I thought Pastor Smuland already said he wants you to have the job?" I ask.

"He wants me to have it, but I still have to interview with the elders," Dad says.

"And then what—if you get it?" Nana says.

Dad tells her we will move to Florida for seminary, and after he graduates seminary, we'll come home so he can work for the church.

Dad takes a bite of food just as Nana asks another question.

"How will you support Linda and the children in seminary?"

Nana always tries to ask Dad hard questions like this right after he puts food in his mouth. But she never does this to Mom, because Mom is Nana's daughter and you shouldn't ask your own daughter hard questions when she is taking a bite of food.

"We have—I mean." Dad catches himself talking with food in his mouth, which is not as bad as chewing with your mouth open but worse than eating with your elbows on the table. "We have been saving."

"Well," Nana says, "have you thought about getting a part-time . . . a . . . ummmm . . . a part-time . . ."

Mom stops drinking her water, and Papa puts his hand on Nana's shoulder. He nods at her very slowly.

"A job?" I suggest. "A part-time job?"

"Yes, that's right, Joshua . . . a . . . well, never mind," Nana says. She takes a deep breath in and out and looks sad. "My memory," she says. "Just hasn't been the same since the diagno—"

But Mom puts her finger over her lips so Nana will stop talking, which is very rude because you should never interrupt your own mother, especially if she doesn't ask you hard questions when you are putting food in your mouth. After Nana stops talking because of Mom's finger, Mom points at Matthew and me, and Nana nods. Matthew probably doesn't understand what it means when Mom points and Nana nods since he is only seven years old, but since *I* am nine years old, I understand. It means Nana is supposed to keep something a secret from us. An early birthday present for me, maybe?

But we finish dinner with no early birthday presents, and put Luke to bed, and then it's bedtime for Matthew and me, too. We lie down on the special bed in Nana's sewing room, the one that unfolds from underneath the cushions on the couch. But we don't go to sleep. We stay awake until eleven o'clock, and then we crawl on hands and knees down the hall and hide behind the coffee table in the living room. Papa is still awake, but he doesn't hear us because he has shot too many guns during his life. From our place behind the coffee table we can see the television where Papa is watching *Star Trek,* which we are not allowed to watch. *Star Trek* is a show about a man who looks silly because his hair is shaved and his head is shiny. People with no hair and shiny heads always look silly. The bald man lives with his friends, like the black man with weird sunglasses, on a spaceship. They shoot lasers at aliens, even though the bald man and his friends know how to disappear and could just disappear instead of wasting the laser power in their guns, which is probably expensive. When I watch them fighting the aliens, my legs and arms start shaking a little and I am not tired at all. It's the same way I used to feel at the start of a soccer game.

The drive home a few days later is terrible because my leg is hurting, aching deep down. It hurts even more than it did a few weeks ago. Mom says that we will go back to the doctor first thing tomorrow and try again to find out what is wrong with it, but I say that doesn't help me feel better now. She gives me a magazine to read to keep my mind off the pain. I read a story about a soccer player who liked to touch certain doorknobs and avoid stepping on cracks in the sidewalk. Sometimes he tried not to do these things, but then he would start sweating and couldn't breathe and would go to the hospital because he thought he was dying. So he just kept touching doorknobs and avoiding cracks, but that got to be all he could think about. He couldn't play soccer or even go outside because of the doorknobs and sidewalk cracks, so he just lay in bed all the time and didn't talk to anyone. I tell Matthew about the soccer player and about the doorknobs that made him stay in bed. We both laugh, but Mom says it isn't nice to laugh at other people, because you can't understand what it's like to have their problems, and if we were like the soccer player and were so sad that we lay in bed and didn't want to talk to anyone, we wouldn't want anyone to laugh at us now would we? And then she says how we won't ever need to worry about having problems like that because we are such happy boys. We are just so cheerful all the time and we bring joy to people like Nana and Papa and Mom and Dad.

5

"This looks like a totally different leg," Dr. Blanco says as he hangs some X rays in front of a light on the wall. "Whatever is in your femur, it's changed, a lot, in the past couple weeks."

Dr. Blanco is going to have to do a full biopsy, which means I will have surgery where he will cut open my leg and look at it. He thinks it's probably a bone infection, and if it is, he will cut out the whole infection while I am still asleep. The surgery will take eight hours, and I will wake up in a body cast. The body cast means I won't be able to get out of bed for a few weeks, and it means I won't be able to play soccer for a few months, maybe a whole year.

So I decide that once we move to Florida, while Matthew is outside playing with his new friends and probably joining a soccer team, I will use my year of recovering from the surgery to do push-ups and sit-ups in my bedroom, getting stronger. By the time the year is over, I will be able to do hundreds of push-ups without stopping, one right after the other, *boom-boom-boom-boom*.

For this operation, I decide I don't want to put on the anesthesia mask. When I had the first biopsy—when I just sat down on the operating table and put on the mask—there were a few seconds just before I fell all the way asleep when my muscles were not obeying my thoughts anymore. I could *see* what was happening—the doctor put his arms around me and laid me on the bed, saying I was doing great—but I couldn't feel anything. And I couldn't move. It was like my whole body was tied up with a bunch of ropes like I was kidnapped. It was very scary. So even though I hate needles, this time I will have a shot with medicine that will help my mind feel sleepy before my muscles stop obeying me.

The night before the operation, Dad takes us to Country Cookin for dinner. You can't eat anything for twelve hours before anesthesia, so Mom wants me to fill up my stomach at the All-U-Can-Eat Country Vegetable Bar. I eat three plates, but by the time we are sitting in a little room at the hospital the next morning, I am hungry again. A nurse finds us. She is carrying some tubes.

"Good morning Joshua," she says. She wears the same clothes all the surgery nurses wear—a green V-neck shirt with matching green pants. It's a uniform, I guess. But not the kind I want to wear.

"Hi," I say.

"How are you feeling?"

"Fine, how are you?"

"I'm . . . good, thanks," she says, picking up a piece of rubber that looks like a very thick rubber band that got cut so now it's a rubber string, not a band. "I'm going to put your IV in now, all right?"

"Okay."

She ties the rubber string around my left arm. I hope she notices how much of the string it takes to fit all the way around my bicep muscles. She tells me to make a fist and squeeze as hard as I can. I squeeze my hand while she wipes my arm with alcohol, which stings a little and then feels cold. My other hand is holding Mom's hand, and I try not to squeeze hers too tight.

"Are you ready?" the nurse asks.

I nod and close my eyes.

"One, two, three."

I feel a sharp pain like someone with very long fingernails has pinched my skin and then twisted it.

"It's all over, Joshua. You can relax your hand."

I open my eyes and see the needle sticking out of my arm. The needle is attached to a syringe, and the nurse is trying to pull blood into it.

"Need to make sure I hit a vein," she says.

But there's no blood.

"I'm really sorry. I'm gonna have to move the needle around just a little bit to try and find a vein."

The nurse grabs my elbow with one hand, holding it firmly against the table. With her other hand, she adjusts the needle underneath my skin the way you would if you were pushing a straw through a plastic lid to locate the last remaining sip of an excellent milkshake. She pulls it out a little bit, then changes the direction of the needle and pushes it all the way in, as far as it will go. Still no blood. She moves the syringe around in several small circles, and it feels like she is shredding the muscles in my arm. A few drops of blood finally flow into the tube. This turns the liquid inside the syringe from clear to cloudy orange, like orange juice mixed with water. She pulls at the syringe, but the blood stops coming.

"Let's . . . uh . . . try that again," she says, pulling the needle out of my arm and smiling briefly at Mom and Dad, who do not smile back. The hole left by the needle starts bleeding, and Mom looks at the nurse, and I can tell Mom is thinking, "Why couldn't you find *that* blood?"

The nurse soaks up the blood with a piece of fluffy fabric and then pushes the needle back through my skin right beside the first hole without counting to three. I clench my teeth together and close my eyes because that is what people always do when they get stuck with needles. This time blood flows into her syringe. I realize that I have been holding my breath ever since the nurse started adjusting the needle, so I let out the air and then let go of Mom's hand. It's over.

The nurse gets another syringe and pushes its liquid into the IV.

"You are going to start feeling sleepy."

Mom gives me a kiss.

"I love you," she says.

Even though you can't have dreams under anesthesia, when I wake up I can tell the surgery did not take eight hours . . . I can just feel it . . . too short . . . and . . . no body cast! There was supposed to be a bone infection, and Dr. Blanco was going to take it out, and I was going to wake up with a body cast! But there's nothing on my leg other than bandages. What happened? Where is the cast?

"Sorry, I am going to need you to sit up."

A different nurse is talking to me. She presses a button so my bed lifts me to a sitting position. It makes me dizzy. Then someone else pushes a giant machine on wheels until it is touching my chest.

"We just need a quick lung X ray," the nurse says.

"Wha—Why? Where are my parents?"

"Just a quick lung X ray," the nurse says.

She gives that same answer to every question, no matter what I ask, so I stop asking questions. Then she lets the bed back down and I am dizzy again and the ceiling is blurry so I close my eyes.

"Joshua," Mom says. Dad and Mom are standing on the left side of my bed. Their eyes are red like they missed their bedtime several days in a row.

Mom looks at Dad.

"Joshua," Dad says. "Dr. Blanco found cancer in your leg."

I have cancer. I have cancer. My life drops out from underneath me and I am falling into blackness through a hole in the bed, but I can't drop off completely because my head and shoulders and chest are so heavy. *I have cancer.* The future, that line I have always seen in my mind that stretches out for eighty years into space and has photos along it like the one of us moving to Florida and another of me playing on a soccer team and one of me watching *Star Wars* when I turn twelve—that line is gone now and I am lying in a hospital bed.

Now the hospital bed is the only thing that exists in the universe. *I have cancer. I am going to die.*

Suddenly, as I continue to feel myself falling backward into the universe, I feel a sharp pain in my neck—I am choking! I can't breathe!—then I snap back to reality and realize it's not pain at all. I open my eyes. Mom is hugging me around the neck.

"I'm so sorry, Joshua," she says. "I am so—I am so sorry. We didn't—I wish there was something—I could help—"

The only time Mom ever cries is when she is very tired and she starts saying things about how no one appreciates anything she does around here. But now she is crying. She looks into my eyes and then at my face and my chest and my left leg, in bandages. She shakes her head and leans into Dad, who is looking out the window, even though there are no windows in this room.

Ewing's sarcoma, which is the kind of cancer I have in my leg, moves like the Vikings in the Middle Ages. It doesn't stay in one place and grow there. Instead, it moves through your body from place to place, fighting and feeding wherever it lands and leaving only dead cells behind.

I know all this because Mom and Dad told me. Some parents of children with cancer, they said, don't tell their children everything about their sickness. Some children don't even know they have cancer at all, because their parents don't want to scare them. But Mom and Dad have promised to always tell me everything.

"Even if you find out I am going to die? Would you tell me that?"

"Yes . . . even if . . . you were going to die."

Before I had cancer the only person I knew who had it was Grandpa, who was the dad of my dad. So when I first woke up from that biopsy and Mom and Dad told me there was cancer in my leg, I knew I was going to die. But then they told me that I have a 50 percent chance to live. I will have chemotherapy treatments that will fight the cancer, like special warriors who were sent in to help the villagers defend against the Vikings. I will have chemotherapy for one year. After that, we will hope the cancer is gone and that it doesn't come back.

My chemotherapy treatments will come through a Port-a-Cath in my chest, which will be like a permanent IV. I will have to have another operation to put in this Port-a-Cath.

"Another operation?"

"Yes, but hopefully this will be the last one."

"Don't they need take it out when I am done with the chemotherapy?"

"Yes, you're right. I guess you will have two more operations."

And there's something else, something called Side Effects, which are bad things that can happen to you from the chemotherapy. If the special warriors accidentally broke some things in the town they were defending, or killed a few villagers with friendly fire from their crossbows, that would be Side Effects.

One Side Effect Mom especially wants me to know about is that I might not be able to help my wife get pregnant if I get married. Then I couldn't become a dad.

"Couldn't I just adopt a baby?"

"Well, yes, of course."

After she says that, I don't mind about not being able to help my wife get pregnant, because I know that you get the same benefits from adopted children as you get from regular children, like having a small person who can sweep and dust and vacuum for you, or play soccer with you on the weekend when you would probably get bored otherwise, or talk to you for free during dinner at Country Cookin, as long as they are ten and under.

Adopted children have all these same benefits. That's why I don't mind if I can't help my wife get pregnant and we have to adopt. But Mom says even if *I* don't mind, a girl would probably still appreciate knowing about this before she marries me. Then I ask Mom why chemo will make my wife not get pregnant, since I am the one on treatment, not her, and Mom looks at Dad and he says he'll tell me when I'm older.

On the way to the hospital for the operation to install my port, I tell Mom and Dad I want to go back to breathing the anesthesia through the mask. I will never, ever, let someone put an IV in my arm again. They look at each other and then Dad says that's fine with them. We get to the hospital and then go back to sit in the room with curtains everywhere. The curtains hang from the ceiling to make little rooms where you can sit and wait with your parents.

A nurse comes into our curtain room.

"We are ready to take you back, Joshua," she says. I am on crutches now because of the cancer, so the nurse has a wheelchair for me. But the nurse is the same one who stabbed me, cut me open with that needle and then sliced up the muscles in my arm before my last operation. No way I am going to leave Mom and Dad and let her take me to the blackness in the operating room. I will not go anywhere with her. I know I am supposed to obey adults, and the nurse is an adult, but I will not listen to her. I hate her.

"Joshua, we need to go now, sweetheart," she says.

Sweetheart? You don't even know me. Don't try to talk like you're my mother.

I lean on Mom—my real mom, not a nurse who is trying to act like my mom so she can trick me into getting stabbed with needles—and wrap my arms around her waist and hold my hands together. It's the same trick I use in the summer when I am wrestling with Dad in the pool. He has never been able to get me off without Matthew's help, because the only way to get my hands apart is to pull back each finger individually. That takes one hand for each finger, and I have ten fingers.

"Joshua?" the nurse says. "Do you want to get better? You want to get better, don't you? You need to have surgery so you can get better."

Do I want to get better? Really? What do I look like, a-three-year-old?

"I'm not going with you."

"Joshua," Mom says. "Maybe you—"

"NO!"

The nurse pulls on my wrists, gently. "Let's go."

But I am not going anywhere. She pulls harder. My arms don't move.

"I'm sorry," she says to Mom, and then she pulls as hard as she can, but it's still not enough. "I will be right back," she says.

The nurse returns with a man, probably a doctor.

"Not too excited about the operation today, huh?" he says, drying off his hands with a paper towel.

"No, I don't want—anymore—" I start to cry. I am trying not to because I am very strong and very brave like Mom always says, but I can't help it, and the crying takes control of me.

The doctor and the nurse each grab one of my arms and pull on them, but they don't know about how they have to pull off my fingers one by one. Dad knows, but he doesn't tell them. Now Mom is crying, too.

"We are going to have to give him a sedative," the doctor says.

"A shot? Does that mean he's giving me a shot?" I say. "No more shots!"

"He doesn't want the sedative," Dad says. "He wants to breathe through the mask."

"If he won't come with us we have no choice," the doctor says. He turns to the nurse. "Get the IV."

"Okay."

The doctor puts on rubber gloves.

"Daddy, don't let them give me a shot!"

"You cannot give my son a shot!"

"Ma'am, will you please hold your son still?"

The nurse returns with another man who is very fat and holds me against the chair.

"No! Do not give him a shot!"

"Sir, I'm sorry. We have no choice here."

The doctor pushes the needle into a small glass bottle and pulls its liquid into the syringe.

"Are you listening to me? He wants the mask!"

"Get away! I don't want a shot!"

I am screaming and kicking against the man who is holding me still.

"Hold still, young man!"

The doctor walks toward me, holding the syringe the way you hold a pencil. Then he puts his thumb on where the eraser would be so he is ready to push the medicine out.

Dad stands in front of him.

"No! *He wants the mask.*"

I am still crying very loudly, but no one else is talking.

"Fine!" the doctor says very loudly, just as another person walks in. Together the four of them yank my arms apart and pull me off Mom. They put me in the wheelchair and hold me there. I am crying so hard I can barely breathe. They wheel me back to the operating room and push the mask against my face, and my eyelids fall and the world is black.

When I wake up, there is an IV in my arm. And my chest hurts where they put in the port. I want to go home now that the operation is done, but I have to have my first chemotherapy treatment. It will last for seven days. Mom has gone home because there is only space for one other person to stay on the couch in my room, and it's the weekend so Dad will stay with me.

Once the chemotherapy begins, a nurse hangs something on my IV pump that looks like a big Ziploc bag filled with water. The nurse says it's actually salt water, like in the ocean. She says I need to have fluids flowing into my body through my port all the time. Otherwise the chemotherapy will get stuck in my bladder and cause bladder cancer.

The fluids make me have to urinate at least once an hour. I am not allowed to use the toilet, though, since the nurse has to test all my urine. So we save it all in plastic jugs. Every hour, I sit up on the side of my bed and Dad holds the jug in place while I fill it up. The same that night.

"Dad," I say, in a whisper. "*Dad!*"

He wakes up, and we do it—side of the bed, hold jug, fill up. Then he falls back asleep. But I don't. My leg hurts too much. Finally, at about three o'clock in the morning, a dream starts playing on the back of my eyelids—which is the place where you watch your dreams, like your own personal TV—but just then a nurse walks in with another Ziploc bag.

"Sorry, did I wake you?" he says, hanging the bag on my IV pump.

"Not really," I say.

Dad wakes up. Since he's awake anyway, he helps me use the jug.

"Dad, my leg hurts so much!"

"I'm sorry, Joshua. Is there anything I can do?"

"No."

"Do you want more medicine?"

"No."

"Do you want anything?"

"I just want to die."

"What?"

"I wish I could just die so my leg wouldn't hurt anymore."

"No, you don't."

"Yes," I say. "I do."

Dad doesn't answer. He puts his lips together, then separates them again.

"Is it all right if I watch TV?" I ask.

Dad blinks, but it takes a long time, like his eyelids are in slow motion. He breathes out the way you do if you are blowing up a balloon.

Then he says, "If you want to."

I start watching a show about a detective investigating a lady's murder. One of the places where he goes to ask a few questions is a restaurant where ladies wearing bikinis are sliding down poles like firemen.

"This is not appropriate," Dad says.

He says this because he thinks girls should always wear modest one-piece bathing suits, not bikinis.

"But Dad, don't you want to know who killed her? It's almost over."

"I guess—since it seems like you really like this show—you can watch the rest. Try to go back to sleep when it's over though, okay?"

It turns out she was murdered by her own son, which shows that even though children give you benefits, sometimes they can give you problems, also. It's too bad her husband never had chemotherapy, because then he would not have been able to help her get pregnant and she would not be dead.

On Sunday morning, during the time when I would normally be going to church if I was not attached to an IV machine, a six-year-old Korean boy moves into the other bed in my room. His name is Johnny. He has cancer, too. But, Dad says, I am not ever supposed to talk about cancer with Johnny because his parents haven't told him that he's sick.

"How long has he had cancer?" I ask Dad.

"About two years."

"And they still haven't told him?"

"No, I guess not."

"Dad?"

"Yeah."

"Thanks for . . . telling me."

Dad looks over at me.

"Of course, Joshua. We could never keep secrets from you."

That night Mom comes to the hospital and Dad goes home because he has to go to work in the morning. Mom brings my schoolbooks, but on Monday she doesn't make me finish my normal amount of work. She says we will just do a light load this week. So I get done early and ask Mom if I can play Nintendo. She says I can—*yes!*—and she brings in the Nintendo machine that sits on a table with wheels so you can roll it into your hospital room. While I play Super Mario Bros. and try to eat mushrooms and get pieces of gold to get 1-ups, Johnny pulls back the curtain between our beds.

"Hi," he says.

"Hello there," Mom says.

Johnny carries a chair from his side of the room and puts it beside my bed. He sits in the chair and watches me play Nintendo. I ask him if he wants to play a turn, but he shakes his head. So he just sits beside Mom and me and watches. He does the same thing all day the next day, too. He never talks. After Johnny goes back to his side of the room and Mom pulls the curtain so he can go to sleep, I whisper to her:

"Where are Johnny's parents?"

"They're at home."

"How do you know?"

"I asked the nurses."

"Why don't they come stay in the hospital with him?"

"Because they don't have enough money—they can't miss work," Mom says. Then she says, "They live in a *mobile home*," like this is an example of how they don't have very much money.

"A mobile home? Like Nana and Papa?"

"No, Nana and Papa live in a regular house—they just use an RV when they're on vacation. Johnny's family lives in a mobile home all the time."

"Oh," I say. "Does he have brothers or sisters?"

"No."

"That's good."

"Why?"

"Because they probably wouldn't all fit in the mobile home."

The next morning, while I am working on my light load, the walls start blinking.

"A fire has been reported," a voice in the ceiling says. "Please evacuate."

"A fire has been reported," the voice says, again. "Please evacuate."

I close my books and start to get out of bed so we don't get burned up in the fire. Mom stands up, too, and walks over to my IV pump. She switches it to battery power. She'll push it for me since I am on crutches and can't push things while I walk. Then, all of a sudden, the fire alarm stops, which is good because I did not really want to have to get out of bed.

Then a nurse walks in with her hand on Johnny's shoulder.

"Don't you ever do that again," she tells him. "I am going to have to call your mommy."

The nurse leaves, and Mom follows her into the hallway. Johnny sits down in his chair beside my bed. We look at each other, and we laugh. Then Mom comes back in and says stop laughing because that was not funny, so we cover our mouths, but laughs keep exploding through our hands.

When my week of chemo is finally over, a nurse comes to take the IV out of my port. I say goodbye to Johnny. Mom and I get in the car and she drives us out of the parking deck. I look back up at the hospital. *Which window was my room?* I can't tell. All the windows look the same from down here.

6

Right beside Country Cookin is the Everything is $1 Store. That's where I buy my LA Looks hair gel. I get the red kind because it has Level Five Most Extreme Hold. I put on huge globs of gel every morning—Mom says it makes my hair look plastic—so that whenever I look in the mirror I will see that my hair looks perfect. Sometime I hope I will be walking around at the mall and someone will come up to me and say, "Hi there, I saw you walking around here at the mall and I think your hair looks perfect, and I hire models for the JCPenney advertisements you get in the newspaper, and would you like to be one of our models?" You never know when this might happen, and that's why I use a lot of gel.

But soon I won't have hair because the chemotherapy will make it all fall out. When I think about this, I think about chunks of gelled-together hair sliding out of the skin in my head and into my hand, staying perfectly stiff even when I hear it bounce off the bottom of an empty trash can. So I ask Mom to shave my hair so I don't have to watch it fall out. She does, and now when I look in the mirror in the bathroom I can see the large bump on my head that has always been covered by my hair. I look stupid. I don't want anyone to see me like this. I want to stay in my room for the whole year of chemotherapy so no one finds out that I am bald like the man on *Star Trek*.

Matthew says he doesn't want me to have to be the only one without any hair. He asks Mom to shave his head, too. One of the home-school boys asks Matthew why his head is shaved, and Matthew tells him it's so I don't feel bad about losing my hair, and the boy asks his mom if he can shave his head, too. Then lots of moms start calling our mom, saying their boys want shaved heads to help me not feel bad. So we set up some stools in the backyard and invite everyone over to our house. Mom runs an extension cord into the backyard and plugs in the electric razor. Eighteen homeschool boys come over and get the Chemo Cut, and it makes me wish I was turning eighteen this summer so I could invite all of them to my birthday sleep-over, because it seems like if people shave their heads for you they should be allowed to your birthday party even if that means you have more than ten people there.

A reporter from the newspaper wants to write a story about the head-shaving party, so that night, after we have gotten all the hair off the grass and put it under the bushes so it can help them grow, the reporter talks to Dad, Mom, and me in the family room.

"That looks annoying," he says.

"What?" I ask.

"That! That brace on your leg!"

"Yeah, it is, a little bit."

"Well . . . are you getting used to walking on crutches?"

"I guess so."

"Let me ask you this: What did you think when you first found out you had cancer?"

"I thought I was going to die."

"What about now? Do you think you are going to beat this disease?"

"Yeah."

Then Mom tells the reporter about how many times God has saved my life. When I was one, I ate a poisonous plant. When I was two, I tumbled down a flight of stairs. When I was six, I climbed up the maple tree in the backyard to the height of a telephone pole, and then a branch broke and I fell fifty feet to the ground. My only injury was a partial break of a bone in my left arm. God has a guardian angel working overtime to protect me, Mom says. He sure must have a special plan for my life.

The reporter asks me if I have always been so optimistic. Was I ever sad about having cancer?

"A little bit," I say.

"Just a little?" he asks.

"What about the first night you had chemotherapy?" Dad interrupts.

"What?" I say.

Don't talk about that, Dad, don't! Stop!

"Don't you remember . . . the night when you first got your port put in your chest?"

"I don't think so."

Of course I remember, but please don't talk about it!

"You said that your leg hurt so much"—I can't *believe* you are telling the reporter—"you wished you could die."

Why, Dad? Why would you ever tell anyone that? That was a conversation between you and me, at three o'clock in the morning just a week after I found out I had cancer, and my leg was throbbing with pain. This reporter, or anyone else, does not need to know about it. I can't believe you told him.

"I did?" I say, pretending to be surprised, like I forgot about that conversation.

"Yes, you did."

Done. It's done. Now the reporter knows I am not brave and inspiring, like he thought I was before.

"Well . . . does it still hurt that much?" the reporter asks.

"No, after about two days of chemotherapy it stopped hurting."

Now the reporter turns to look at Dad, to ask him a question. I don't turn to look at him because I am so mad at him for telling the reporter that I wanted to die. It's too much.

"How has cancer changed your family?"

"It's changed everything," Dad says—Dad, the one who tells reporters about conversations that should be a secret. "We were actually planning to move to Florida so I could go to seminary this summer. But because of Jo—um, because of the cancer, we are staying here."

I look up from the floor, where I am sitting. I have been thinking about my cancer all the time recently and I forgot about Dad's seminary. Florida! The move! But now we're not going? We're staying here? Great! I am very happy about this because I do not want to move. And I'm also kind of glad Dad doesn't get to go to seminary even though he wanted to, because I am mad at him.

"'It's changed everything,'" the reporter repeats Dad's words, writing on his pad. He looks up. "Even your faith?"

"No," Dad says.

"Not even a little?"

"It has not shaken my faith."

"So after Joshua is done with chemotherapy—will you go to seminary then?"

"Well . . . I'll pray about it . . . but the most important thing right now is for me to keep my job so we can keep our health insurance," Dad says. "And even after he's done with the chemotherapy, if his cancer ever relapsed, or if he had major side effects—"

Just then Luke comes in, wearing only a diaper and a T-shirt and walking in that funny way one-year-olds walk. He holds his little hand up in the reporter's face.

"Look!" Luke says.

There's a brown speck on his palm.

"Hey there little guy. What is that?"

"It's a splinter," Mom says. "He got it about two weeks ago. I just . . . haven't had the heart to take it out yet."

Something starts to leak from the bottom of Luke's diaper.

"Oh, Luke!" Mom says, lifting him and carrying him away, holding her arms straight out.

Before I got cancer, Mom was taking Luke across the state, to doctor after doctor, hoping one of them could figure out why Luke had had diarrhea for almost an entire year, or at least prescribe something that helped. But now she only has time to talk to *my* doctors. So Luke still has diarrhea.

Luke's diarrhea was an even bigger problem when he was still a baby, since Mom was feeding him with her nipples, which is called nursing. Dad told her it would be all right not to nurse this time because you can't be expected to nurse a baby with diarrhea, but Mom said no, nursing is the most healthy thing you can do for your baby and it's what God intended and it's how a mother bonds with her baby infant. She will always nurse all her children no matter what, she said.

The reporter asks a few more questions, and then he leaves because it is time for bed. When it is time for bed in our family, we have a rule that you have to tell everyone that you love them, whether you mean it or not. Tonight when I tell Dad I love him, I don't really mean it because I am still mad at him. But when I tell Matthew I love him, I *do* really mean it because he shaved his head for me and got eighteen other boys to shave their heads, too. In fact, tonight I have the most love I have ever had for Matthew.

Two weeks later, I go back to the hospital for another round of chemotherapy. On the third morning I wake up and there is black dust on my pillowcase. I brush it off with the back of my hand and go back to sleep. But the next time I wake up, my pillowcase is covered with it. Then I realize it is the roots of my hair. Mom couldn't shave it close enough. My hair is still falling out.

I look at Mom. She is awake.

"I'm sorry," she says.

I try not to cry—I haven't cried since the doctors pulled me off Mom and took me to surgery—but I can't help it. I start crying, and tears and mucus and drool are running out of my eyes and nose and mouth. Mom sits in my bed and holds me and rocks me back and forth.

"Mom?" I ask once the crying has changed into quick little breaths. "Do you think—do you think if we all flew around in jet packs that Luke would figure out how to fly?"

She smiles at me.

"Yes, sweetheart, I think he would."

We go home two days later and I spend a whole week lying in bed because I am too tired to do anything. Then Mom and Dad say that since I am on crutches, I don't have to wear dress clothes if I come to church on Sunday. In fact, I can wear anything I want . . . any-thing . . . to church! So Sunday is a great day. I decide to wear a T-shirt and my favorite pair of pants. My favorite pair of pants are black and shiny and don't have belt loops because there is a long shoelace sewn inside that you tie around your waist to hold them up. At the bottom, around the ankles, they are stretchy like rubber bands. I put the pants on over my leg brace. I also find a baseball hat with a cross on it. I put it on backward, but I know Jesus won't mind since it has a cross on it.

Before we leave, Mom takes me into her bathroom and uses makeup to draw black lines where my eyebrows used to be.

"Do you think they look like real eyebrows?" I ask.

"Yes, I think so," she says.

"Are you sure?"

"Well, I did my best."

I smile and hug her.

But when I climb into the minivan, Matthew stares at me.

"Hey, what's wrong with your eyebrows?" he says.

I look at Mom and her face is sad because she knows she did not do a good job drawing my eyebrows. I run back inside as fast as I can on my crutches and stare at my reflection in Mom's bathroom mirror.

"Looks like real eyebrows, Mom?" I say.

There's no one in the house, so I yell.

"Real eyebrows, huh? Yeah, right!"

I scream and pound the sink with both of my fists.

"Aaaaaaah!"

I take a piece of toilet paper and wipe it over the fake eyebrows. Some of the makeup comes off. The rest just smears across my forehead. So I splash water from the sink onto my face, and I get more sheets of toilet paper and rub them on my forehead until little balls of dark, wet toilet paper start falling in the sink. When the makeup is finally gone, I throw the whole mess in the toilet.

At church, I have to walk up all three flights of stairs on my crutches, so I am late getting to Sunday school. But when I walk in wearing my black shiny pants over top of my leg brace and my backward hat with a cross on it, everyone claps. Several of them are the homeschool boys who shaved their heads for me—but I notice today that no one shaved their eyebrows for me.

I glance at Aaron. *Soon I'll finish the chemotherapy and get a soccer uniform like his.*

On Monday I am lying on the couch watching a Zorro movie that I am allowed to watch because it is in black and white. Mom comes in and sits beside me. She asks if I can pause it, which I do not want to do because it is very exciting, but I do it anyway because Mom said so. Mom tells me that Dr. Dunsmore called our house.

"Okay," I say.

"Do you remember Johnny, the little Korean boy in the hospital?"

"Yeah."

"Well, he died yesterday."

"Really?"

I am not sure why I ask this, because normally you say, "really?" only if you think the person is lying or joking, and Mom doesn't ever lie or tell jokes.

"Yes, really."

I think about how he was alive just a few weeks ago, and he sat beside me in the hospital, and he watched me play Nintendo, and now I will never see him again.

"Would you like to go to the funeral?" Mom asks.

"Yes."

All that time when he sat beside me in the hospital, I never knew he might die and I would never see him again.

"You don't have to go if you don't want to."

"Okay."

"So do you still want to go?"

"Yes."

It is the first time I've ever been to a funeral. I don't ask Mom and Dad if I can wear a T-shirt and my favorite pants. I wear church clothes. After the service, people are drinking punch (I think it's Hawaiian Punch, which has a lot of sugar in it) and looking at photos of Johnny that are taped to pages in a three-ring binder. His mom is talking to my mom. She doesn't really speak English, so their conversation is short.

I wonder if Johnny's mom is wishing she was my mom instead, because then her son wouldn't be dead. And I wonder if Johnny's mom is also wishing she never had a son named Johnny, because then he wouldn't have died and she wouldn't be at his funeral. This makes me hope that I die after Mom and Dad do. I don't want them to have to go to my funeral and wish they'd never had me.

Then Johnny's mom turns to me and puts her hands on my cheeks.

"You such handsome boy!" she says, and starts to cry. She puts her arms around me, but I don't hug her back. I just stand there, straight and stiff with my hands at my sides, because she never told Johnny that he had cancer. He never knew. He was six years old and had no idea he was dying. They gave him enough medicine that he was never in pain, even though the leukemia was slowly taking over his body. Dr. Dunsmore told Mom that the day before he died, Johnny started telling the nurses that he was getting ready to move out of his mobile home and into a big house.

"What big house?" they asked.

"The big house," he said. "It looks like a castle. It's right there."

And then he would point at the wall, or the sky, and the nurses would just nod at him because he was on so much pain medicine that he was seeing things that weren't really there. And even then, his parents didn't tell him he was dying. Then—poof—the lights went out in his eyes, and he was gone. Gone without a chance to say goodbye or build some blocks or draw another picture or whatever a six-year-old would want to do if he knew he was going to die.

This is the worst way to die. It's just like dying in the middle of an operation. You are there, and then you are not. At least if you are in a car wreck or fall off a tall building, you probably have a second or two to realize it's all about to end, and you can choose a thought that you would like to be your final thought. But if you don't know it's coming, there are no final thoughts. There are just thoughts, and then no thoughts. That's why I don't hug Johnny's mom, because Johnny didn't get a final thought.

It's a month after Johnny's funeral, and we are driving home from Country Cookin. We don't go every week anymore, since I am in the hospital so much and everyone is always tired. We just try to go when we can. And there's no entertainment budget anymore, either. Now, after dinner, Dad just pulls the money out of his wallet and pays for it. As we drive the last block before our house, I say how I can't wait until my leg is better so I can start playing soccer again.

"When will that be, do you think?" I ask.

Mom and Dad don't answer. They are sitting in the front seats of the van. I am behind them with Luke, who is sitting in his car seat beside me, and Matthew, who is in the very back. Mom and Dad keep looking back at each other.

"So when can I get off the crutches?" I ask again as we pull into the driveway.

Dad puts the van in park and hands the keys to Matthew.

"Go inside," he says. "Take Luke with you."

Matthew unbuckles Luke and lifts him—Luke's getting really big, almost too heavy for Matthew to carry—to the driveway. They hold hands and walk up the sidewalk to the front door. We listen as keys jingle, and then we hear the door open, and then shut. And then we hear nothing.

"We need to talk to you about something," Dad says.

"Okay," I say.

Bad news is coming—that's why Dad gave Matthew the keys and told him to go inside. But how bad? Extra chemo treatments? Another surgery?

"The chemotherapy is not shrinking the tumor in your leg."

"Okay . . ."

Not shrinking? What does that mean? What happens when the cancer doesn't shrink?

"We have been talking to the doctors, and it's possible you—your leg might possibly have to be amputated."

I gag, choking on the air in the van. I know what an amputation is, but I can't believe it—No soccer! No running! Might as well be dead!—so I play dumb.

"What does that mean?"

"It would mean . . . the doctors would cut off your leg."

"I don't want them to cut my leg off!"

I bend forward and wrap my arms around my leg. Tears drip onto my pants.

"I'm sorry Joshua," Dad says. "I wish they could amputate mine instead."

"How soon?" I ask.

"A few weeks, maybe."

Usually when my brain remembers sounds, they are things you can hear, like music I listened to or words someone said to me. But even though it's quiet after I stop crying, and even though quiet is not actually a sound, this quiet is so loud that I think I will always be able to remember it in my brain.

Each night, while I lie on the bottom bunk—Matthew and I switched since I have to wear the leg brace and I can't climb up the ladder—I think about how my leg might possibly have to be amputated in a few weeks maybe, and I cry myself to sleep. If I have one leg, all I will be able to do is sit in a chair all day and watch Matthew out the window while he plays soccer in the backyard. What kind of life is that? Why even be alive? I try to cry softly so Matthew can't hear it, but probably he can because sometimes Dad hears me and comes in and rubs my back.

We drive to Baltimore to meet an orthopedic surgeon at Johns Hopkins who will give us his opinion, which is called a second opinion since we already got a first opinion from Dr. Dunsmore. The Johns Hopkins doctor says his second opinion is that I need to do something to get rid of the cancer, but it does not have to be an amputation. *I could keep my leg?* He says he could take out my femur bone with the cancer in it and replace it with a metal rod. It would save my leg, but every six months I would have to have another operation to lengthen the rod to match my normal growth.

"So if I still had my leg, I could play soccer, right?"

"Actually, no, not really. You wouldn't be able to run. Your leg would be too fragile."

"Could I play any sports?"

"You could do things where you stand in one place, like shooting baskets with your friends."

Stand in one place? Shoot baskets? That's not a sport! What is the point of a leg if you can't do anything with it?

He has other ideas. He could replace my bone with a bone from someone who had just died in a car wreck, if they had signed some papers before they died. But that would be just as fragile. He could also take out my femur and move my lower leg bone up, sewing my knee to my hip, with the foot turned around backward. This would allow me to keep half of a leg instead of losing the whole thing.

"Wouldn't that look kind of . . . weird?"

"Yes, well, it is somewhat strange," he replies. "But it's very popular in Europe."

Europe? Europeans are crazy liberals and communists, that's what Mom always says, so I probably don't want to look like them. The only other option is the amputation, which is my best chance at staying alive.

"With an amputation, you will have a harder time getting around in life, but I would not tell you you're not allowed to run or play sports," the surgeon says. "In fact, I know amputees who ride bikes, swim, ski, even a few who play soccer."

"Really? Amputees play soccer?"

"Well yes, but they are a lower level than you would be," he says. "These are people who only lost their foot. You would lose your whole leg from the hip."

"But I could play sports if I wanted to?"

"Sure, you could try."

For the first time since that conversation in the van with my parents, it seems like there may be a good reason to keep fighting the cancer: I can play sports again. I can become fast again. I can be free and I can be fast. Free, because I would no longer be weighed down by the feeling that something inside my body wants to kill me. Fast, because I could do push-ups one right after the other until I got strong again. Then I would get a uniform, a uniform with matching socks and shorts and a shirt, and I would wear it to church every single Sunday over top of my fake leg and no one could tell me that I can't wear on it Sunday and every day of the week, too, because I would be a cancer survivor who is free. So now I know. I have to survive. I have to live. I have to get that uniform.

The night before the operation we do not go to Country Cookin, even though I know I'll be hungry in the morning. I don't feel like going anywhere, or seeing any people.

The next morning as we drive over the mountain to the hospital, I sit in the back of the van and listen to the engine. *Huuuummmmm.* I lean my head against the window and feel it vibrate on my forehead. I look at the people in the other cars and wonder what they are doing today. Probably going to work or to the grocery store or something. I wish I was one of them. Any of them. Dad turns on the radio. The DJ is talking. No, actually he is praying.

"And Lord, we pray that you would comfort Josh and his family as they travel to the hospital this morning . . ."

But I do not feel very comforted, because today the doctors will cut my leg off.

I used to think that after my leg got cut off I would never walk again. Then Mom and Dad said that in Heaven, God will give me a new leg. I asked them how they knew this, because the Bible doesn't say you get extra body parts in Heaven. They told me that there are lots of things we believe that aren't actually in the Bible, but we can figure them out because we know God loves us. Like when Mom had a baby die inside her while she was pregnant, we believed that it went to Heaven even though it hadn't gone to church or been baptized yet. The Bible doesn't say this, but we still believe it. That's the same reason why Mom and Dad think I will get my leg back. We believe it because we know God loves us. Hopefully Mom and Dad are right. It would be fun to be able to run on the gold streets in Heaven.

We listen to the DJ pray until we cross the mountains and lose the signal. Once we are in our private waiting room at the hospital, I take off the leg brace I've worn for three months and lay it on the floor because I won't need to wear it anymore. Then I bend over and wrap both arms around my leg. I sit like that for a long time, and it is very quiet. *I will wake up and my leg will be gone*, I think. Then a nurse comes in and asks me to put on a hospital gown and a pair of brown socks that are made out of fabric like a towel and have rubber strips on the bottom to help you grip the floor. *My leg will be gone, but I will still be here. I will survive.* A few minutes later she returns with a doctor and an empty wheelchair and the fat man who held me down before my last surgery. *I will beat the cancer and I will learn how to run. I will be strong.* The fat man walks over and stands beside me. The doctor looks at my parents, and they nod.

"Joshua, can we take you to the operating room now?" the doctor asks.

And I will be fast.

"Actually," I reply. "I think I will just walk."

"Oh . . . okay," he says. He looks at the fat man, lifting his shoulders and his eyebrows. "Sure, we can do that."

The fat man leaves.

As I follow the doctor and the nurse back to the operating room, I feel the coldness of the hallway floor under my brown socks. I know it will be the last time I do this until I get to Heaven.

When I wake up from the operation, something is wrong. I can feel my leg propped straight up in the air. They . . . they . . . didn't cut it off! There's been a terrible mistake! I lift my head from the pillow to look down at it. Nothing . . . it's gone . . . it's been amputated, sure enough . . . but I still feel it, feel it in my mind, just like I always have . . . in fact, it is throbbing in pain. Not the kind of pain like I had from the cancer, though. No, this pain feels like my foot—the left foot that was just cut off—is being stabbed with thousands of tiny needles every second. They are tearing down through my skin and stabbing the tendons and the muscles and now scraping into the bones.

Someone shows me the morphine button beside my bed, and I press it and feel warm. Doctors come and go, machines beep, and fluids drip into my port.

About ten o'clock that night, a nurse with red hair tells me that she needs me to urinate, because I haven't emptied my bladder since the operation and she is afraid things haven't woken up yet down there. I am too weak to sit up, so Mom holds the jug for me as I lie flat on my back. But nothing comes out.

"Can't go, huh?" the nurse says.

"No."

"Okay, I'm going to have to put in a catheter."

"What's that?"

"It's a tiny tube that we will put in your—" she looks at Mom.

"Penis," Mom says.

"Yes, in your penis. It will drain your bladder for us."

A tube? A tube in my penis?

"Does it hurt?"

"Some people say it stings a little."

A little?

"How do you get it in?"

"We just push it in."

I shiver, even though I am under so many blankets.

"How about—can you please wait a few minutes?" I say. "I will go for you in the jug."

"I'm sorry, I have to."

"Wait, just wait a few more minutes. I will drink tons of water."

"Tell you what," she says. "Midnight. You have until midnight."

Mom fills up a cup of water at the sink, and I drink it down in a few sips. She fills it again and I gulp that one, too. I drink cup after cup. And then we wait. I try to go in the jug at fifteen minutes after eleven. Nothing. At 11:30. Nothing. At 11:45. Still nothing. At 11:57, I make one last attempt.

Come on Joshua, come on! You have always been able to start and stop urinating when you need to! Remember? You can always . . . control . . . it . . . *Yes*! There it is! Done! No catheter for me, thank you very much Miss Nurse with Red Hair.

When the nurse with red hair comes back at midnight, I hold up the jug like a trophy.

"Look!"

She takes the jug and holds it in front of the light.

"Let me see here . . ."

What is there to see? I did it. You said by midnight, I did it by midnight. You can't change your mind now.

"Sorry, that's not quite enough. I am going to have to give you a catheter."

Not enough? Not *enough*! But you said . . . she had said, hadn't she? . . . Yes, she had . . . *midnight* . . . not an amount . . . just midnight. She lied to me, and now . . . now . . . pain is coming! I start punching the morphine button beside my bed like it is the close-the-door button on an elevator and the bad guys chasing me are just down the hall. Hurry! Close the doors! Pump the morphine!

"This will only sting a little, I promise."

Yeah, right. I know how your promises work.

I expect the worst, but it is worse than the worst. It feels like she is stuffing barbed wire in my penis. Stuffing it . . . in . . . and it is shredding the insides of my insides. And just when I think it's over, the barbed wire turns red hot and it burns, burns, burns the same gashes it is carving on the insides of my insides.

"There. That wasn't so bad, was it?"

Wasn't so bad?

"That was . . . the worst pain I have ever felt," I say.

I wake up a few hours later and it hurts even more. My penis is sticking straight out the way it does when I wake up in the morning or when I think about girl nipples for a long time. The tube is stretching and rubbing along the inside of my penis all the way up into my bladder. It hurts so much I can barely breathe.

I watch the second hand on the wall tick around in circles, minute by minute. This will get better. It has to. It can't get worse, right? I will feel better and finish chemotherapy and my hair will grow back. I won't have to go into the hospital anymore and I won't have to have shots all the time and worry about dying. I will learn how to run with a fake leg and I will play sports and I will not wear a hospital gown, which looks like something you wear in a nursing home, a place where people die. But not me, I am going to live.

In the morning, a physical therapist comes to my room to teach me how to walk.

"Would it be all right if you come back tomorrow?" I say. "I have a—I just don't think I can move today."

This is true. I really can't move. There's the catheter, of course—that tube alone should be enough to stop this conversation. But I also have an IV pumping me with a who-knows-what mixture of post-surgery antibiotic things and pain killers, and another pump that has a dark red Ziploc bag that is drip, drip, dripping into my veins to replace what I lost when my leg was cut off and all of that blood that was supposed to flow into my leg started flowing out onto the operating table. And then there's *that* tube, that tube that is stuck inside me, in between the stitches that are holding my skin together across my pelvis where my leg used to be—that tube, it is the one the surgeon *left inside me* when he sewed me up. He wants it there for several days to collect drainage from the incision, and sure enough, there's a constant flow of thick yellowy pus and blood and pieces of flesh-colored clumps the size of crumbs oozing out through *that* tube.

"No, I think we should learn how to walk today. That's very important," the physical therapist says, as if her saying "we" will trick me into thinking we are on a team together.

"I'm sorry. I just can't do it."

"Just try, okay? Please. All you have to do is try."

Her assistant is holding my crutches for me beside the bed. I sit up, and the physical therapist puts her arms around me. It hurts.

"You're squeezing my port."

"Oh, sorry."

I put my foot on the carpet. I'm still wearing that same brown sock with the rubber strips on the bottom that I got when I checked into the hospital. *What did they do with that other sock after the surgery?* When I attempt to stand, I fall straight into the physical therapist. I am nearly twenty pounds lighter than I used to be, so the balance I remember in my mind doesn't work anymore, kind of like when Mom didn't want to spend money to replace our old map and then we got lost because the roads had changed. The assistant shoves the crutches under my arms.

"There you go. Try to take a step."

I do, and a pain shoots through my penis as the catheter rubs against the rawness inside my insides.

"Aaaaah!" I cry. "No more! I'm done! Let me back in bed!"

The next day a doctor comes to examine me. He has short dark hair combed back like mine used to be before it all fell out. He looks under my gown and tells me it is time to remove the drainage tube. I am very afraid of this. It hurts enough to pull a thin little *needle* out of your skin, and I know it will be worse if it is a *drainage tube* that's stuck between differently shaped sections of skin stitched together like pieces from two separate jigsaw puzzles. I ask the doctor to please please please leave it in for a few more days, or to give me anesthesia before he pulls it out, or to just come back later, maybe later today or tonight, and pull it out then. Just don't do it *now*.

"Joshua, it's not going to hurt. I promise."

I've heard that one before.

"Please! Just leave it!"

"How about I just look at it?"

"Okay, but don't pull it out."

"I won't even touch it."

"Promise?"

"Promise."

"All right."

He lifts up my gown and looks at the tube.

"Yeah, I think it's ready to come out," he says, smiling like he thinks this is good news.

"No! You promised!"

"Okay, I won't pull it out. Just let me touch it, and you can tell me if that hurts, all right?"

I look at Mom. She nods that this is a good plan.

"Okay. You promise you won't pull it out?"

He raises his right hand.

"Cross my heart, hope to die."

I wiggle my hand at Mom so she will know I want her to hold it, and she does.

"Are you ready?"

"Yes."

I close my eyes and squeeze Mom's hand. The doctor touches the tube, but he does it so lightly I can barely feel it.

"Did that hurt?"

"No," I say. "It didn't."

He touches it again.

"How about that?"

"Nope," I say, my eyes still squeezed shut.

He touches it once more, a little bit harder, but it still doesn't hurt.

"Did that hurt?"

"No."

"Well guess what?"

"What?"

"It's out."

I open my eyes and see him standing there holding the end of the pus-and-blood-and-other-stuff tube, smiling like he just pulled that tube out of thin air and we should clap for his magic trick.

"I told you it wouldn't hurt!"

"But . . . you raised your . . . you . . . you promised!"

I wish I wasn't still attached to so many other tubes and I knew how to balance on one leg, because if I were I would hop out of bed and pick him up by his white coat and throw him against the wall. "You promised!" I would scream at him. "You broke your promise to me!" But he wouldn't be able to say anything back because I would be choking him.

"I'm sorry, Joshua, I just wanted to get it out for you," he says.

"You promised," I say. *And you kept a secret from me . . .*

He walks out carrying the tube in his hand and shaking his head.

My mind goes back to when I shared a room with Johnny. I think about when his mom hugged me but I didn't hug her back because she kept secrets from Johnny and didn't tell him he was dying. And I think about Mom and how she promised to never be like Johnny's mom. Then I feel Mom's hand, still in mine. I let go of her hand and turn my head to face her, but she looks away before we make eye contact. She looks down at the floor, and then she looks toward the ceiling.

Why do adults make promises and then break them? Why do they lie? When I am an adult, I am going to tell kids the truth about everything, like telling them if they are going to die from cancer, and about how much catheters hurt and about drainage tubes and about Santa Claus, too.

Two days later, while Mom is having a meeting with Dr. Dunsmore, I can tell that my catheter has something wrong with it. I need to urinate, but I feel like I am holding it inside, the way I usually do when I don't have a catheter. I press the nurse button on the side of my bed. It beeps a few times. Then I hear a very loud voice coming out of the speaker right beside my head.

"Yes, Joshua?" the loud voice says.

"Hi, this is Joshua . . . well, my catheter . . . I don't think it's working anymore."

"How do you know?"

"I can feel it. It doesn't feel right anymore. Can you please take it out?"

But the loud voice doesn't believe me.

"Why don't we just leave it in for now?"

"Well . . . I guess . . . it's just that, I have to urinate, and I don't think the catheter works anymore."

"Don't worry, Joshua. Just let it go. The catheter will get it."

Why don't you believe me?

"Okay, I will try," I say. "But I don't think it will work."

I hear a loud click from the speaker, and thirty seconds later my nursing-home-style hospital gown and the hospital sheets and even the crinkly plastic mattress are soaked in warm urine. It feels kind of nice, like being in a hot tub, except that I know it's not a hot tub and it's actually urine and that makes it feel disgusting.

"Uh-oh, did we have a little accident?" the nurse says when she comes to put a new Ziploc back on my IV.

But I don't say anything, because *we* did not have an accident, *she* did. I told her it was not working anymore, and she did not believe me.

"Well, don't you worry about it," she says. "This kind of thing happens all the time around here, Lord knows, especially when I used to work the night shift. So don't feel embarrassed."

Feel embarrassed? Night shift? Do you think I wet the bed? Yes, that must be what you are thinking. Don't you know this is *your* fault, not mine? You should be the person feeling embarrassed, not me. But I *do* feel embarrassed because you think I wet the bed even though I didn't. Don't you remember talking to me on the speaker beside my head? No . . . wait . . . it must have been a different nurse on the speaker. This nurse just thinks I am a bed wetter even though I am nine years old and I don't ever wet the bed anymore.

"Well, I guess it's time for that catheter to come out, huh?"

On the third day after my amputation, Dr. Dunsmore says I am healing fast and I don't need any more blood or antibiotics pumped through my IV. So she pulls out the last tube, the one in my port. They are all gone. I am free. Without the tubes rubbing all my insides and stopping me from moving, I decide to take off my hospital gown and put on a pair of shorts. Mom helps me pull the hospital gown off my shoulders and down my arms, and then I lean back in the bed so I can pull on a pair of shorts. I hold the shorts out to the side so my left leg can go into them, because that's what I do automatically without thinking about how I don't have that leg anymore. That's when I feel my left leg pass through the shorts and then float *inside* the mattress, like a ghost.

I don't like having my leg inside a mattress because that is impossible. So I think about the leg—the imaginary leg—very carefully in my mind, and after a few seconds I am able to straighten the knee so it's not inside the mattress anymore. Now I can feel it sitting on top of the bed like my real leg. This is much better than when it was stuck inside the mattress.

I put on a T-shirt and stand up and lean against the bed. Two days ago when the physical therapist made me stand up, there were so many tubes in my body. I was chained by the IV in the port in my chest, the catheter, the heart monitor on my finger, the drainage tube in the place where my leg used to be—but now I stand and I feel free and light. There are no chains, and there is no cancer hanging off my body. *No cancer.*

When I used to stand with two legs I would put weight on both of them so my belly button was halfway in between my feet. Now when I stand I can only put weight on one leg, so to balance, my belly button has to be above my one foot. This is called a new center of gravity, and I read about it in a brochure of ten tips for people who are thinking about losing their legs. Mom has given me lots of brochures, and some books, too, about people without legs. The first thing we did once I knew my leg might get cut off was Mom took me to the public library and we looked at a microscope that looks like a TV. Then Mom read out loud the numbers that were written beside the titles of the books on black shiny plastic that we put under the microscope and I wrote them down on a piece of paper. Then we walked around the library to find the numbers. And once we found the numbers, we found the books. Mom said this is the best and cheapest way to solve the problems in your life: come to the library and check out all the books about your problem and read them.

Mom hands me my crutches, and I slide them under my shoulders. I put the crutches on the floor in front of my foot and then I lean onto them and swing forward. All my weight seems to be pushing on my left crutch. I feel like I am falling to the left, so I have to tilt my body to the right so I don't fall.

After a few minutes, I learn how to balance. I keep practicing all morning, and by the afternoon I am running laps around the children's wing of the hospital by hopping on my one foot in between each step on my crutches. I am fast because I don't have a heavy leg filled with cancer, and the physical therapist is running after me in her squeaky tennis shoes and hospital uniform with the V-shaped neck hole, saying I need to take it easy.

On the fifth day after my amputation, Dr. Dunsmore comes in and tells me I can go home.

"But it hasn't been three weeks yet," I say.

Three weeks had always been the plan. I brought tons of books and games and drawing pads because three weeks is a very long time to be in the hospital.

"Well, you healed much faster than we anticipated. And your vital signs have stabilized," she says. "We'd like you to go home and rest for two weeks before your next chemo treatment."

A few hours before I leave to go home, Dr. Dunsmore sends a psychologist to examine me for the depression. I knew the psychologist was coming because I heard Dr. Dunsmore telling Mom about it in the hallway.

"People who suffer from limb loss normally experience depression as if they lost a family member or close friend," she told Mom. "Joshua shows no outward symptoms of depression, so we think he may be repressing his feelings."

"Well, a lot of people have been praying for him," Mom says. "Maybe he's just a happy little boy."

"Maybe, but we'd just like to make sure."

The psychologist comes to my hospital room while I am drawing, and she says she would like to draw with me for a few minutes.

"Would you please tell me about what you are drawing?" she asks.

This is a silly question. Anyone can tell what I am drawing.

"Don't you know who it is?" I ask.

I am drawing a picture of Zorro, the secret identity of Don Diego de la Vega. He has a cape and an eye mask and a big, round hat. Everyone knows that.

"Yes, of course I know who that is," she says, smiling. "But I want you to tell me about it. Can you tell me why you decided to draw that picture? Or how it makes you feel?"

But she is just saying this because she can't tell that it's a picture of Zorro, which means she thinks I am not good at drawing realistic drawings, even though I've taken art lessons for three years. So I decide to stop answering her questions.

She gets out a piece of paper and starts coloring a picture of her own. While she is bent over her page, I look at the top of her head and see that she has wavy brown hair that is clumped together the way mine used to be before it fell out, when I used to put lots of gel in it every day. Then I look at her drawing. It's pretty good, but I don't say anything nice to her about it since she was not nice when she talked about mine. Then she says goodbye and leaves.

Later that day, Dr. Dunsmore says I can go home, so I guess the psychologist must have told her I don't have the depression—and of course I don't, because the depression is what happens to people who just lie in bed all day thinking about sad things, like the soccer player I read about in the magazine on the way home from Nana and Papa's. And even if I *did* have the depression, I wouldn't tell the psychologist or anyone else about it. This is because Pastor Smuland once said in a sermon that if you have the depression you should pray about it and God will take it away. And since you would want God to take it away, that must mean it's a bad thing, and you would not want other Christians like your mom and dad to know you were doing a bad thing. So you should not tell anyone if you have the depression. But there wouldn't be much to tell anyway, because by the time you told them you would have already prayed about it and God would've taken it away.

A few days later we get a bill from the psychologist for four hundred dollars. Insurance will pay for it, but four hundred dollars is still a lot of money. It's enough to buy almost anything, really, even expensive things like bikes or Nintendos. I can't believe we have to pay that much to a psychologist who said not-nice things when she talked about my Zorro picture.

"That psychologist missed her calling in life," Mom says. "If she can charge that much for fifteen minutes of drawing, she should have become an artist."

Mom usually doesn't tell funny jokes, but this is very funny.

8

It's the end of July, three weeks after my surgery. That's usually when we go to Lost River State Park for the church-wide vacation. Matthew was really looking forward to going this year, since last year he was only six and wasn't old enough to play with the big kids and adults in the Annual Softball Game. He wanted to play this year, to try to hit a home run even though that's pretty much impossible in softball, especially for a seven-year-old. But it doesn't matter anyway because we can't go this year. I have to get my shots.

When I am not in the hospital I have to have a shot every day so my body will get ready for more chemotherapy. Four months ago when I was first starting the chemo, a nurse came to our house every day to give me the shot. But then our insurance company said they would not pay for the nurse anymore because it was too expensive, so I had two choices: I could either give myself a shot every day, or Mom could do it. But there would be no more free nurses.

The first option would never work. Who could stab a needle through their own skin? I would be too afraid and I would just sit there and look at the needle for an hour or two, and then I would probably throw it away and lie and tell Dr. Dunsmore I had given myself the shot even though I hadn't and even though lying is wrong. So Mom said, okay, she would be willing to give me a shot every day all year since I didn't think I could do it myself.

The night after Mom said she would give me the shots, I had a dream where Mom chased me with needles and threw them at me one after the other like I was a dartboard. I woke up sweating and breathing fast, and walked on my crutches down the hall and got in bed with Mom and Dad. When I told her about the dream where she was throwing needles at me, Mom started crying even though it was just a dream and dreams aren't real.

But the next day a nurse from our church called Mom and said that she would come over every day after work for the whole year to give me a shot—for free. Mom said the nurse was an answer to prayer, which is what you say when something happens that you hoped would happen. So the Answer to Prayer started coming to our house, giving me shots. Before my operation, she gave me a shot in my right arm one day, left arm the next day, right leg after that, and then left leg. It used to be a four-day cycle. Now it's just three days.

I tell Mom and Dad how much I want to go to Lost River, because all my friends from church, which includes a lot of the home-school boys, will be there. And then—another answer to prayer—Mom and Dad tell me I can go to Lost River for two nights! Yes . . . *two nights*! It will be so fun. I will stay with the Montgomerys, who are allowed to watch TV and eat as much candy as they want. (This will be great because Matthew and I are only allowed to eat one piece of candy per week, on Candy Day, which is Friday.) And Dr. Montgomery can give me the shots since he's a doctor. I wish the Montgomerys had invited Matthew, too, but they didn't. And our family can't get our own cabin because all the cabins are already reserved. So I will just have to go by myself and play with the home-school boys.

Lost River is so fun! The Montgomerys let their kids and me stay up really late in the upstairs loft of their cabin, talking and laughing. The next morning, after I eat sweet cereal for breakfast, Dr. Montgomery asks me to come to his bedroom so he can give me my shot.

So I walk into the bedroom on my crutches and one leg and Mrs. Montgomery sits with me on the bed and holds my hand just like Mom does when I get shots at home. And I don't cry because even though it hurts, I get shots every day, so I know how they feel.

That afternoon, after Dr. Montgomery asks me if there is any stuff I want to talk to him about and I say like what and he says anything and I say no, and I thought that was a very strange question because if there was something I needed to talk about, I would've already talked to him about it—we all go to the Annual Softball Game, and I am sorry Matthew won't be here to play in it since he was looking forward to it all year. So I decide I will play for him, and I will tell him about it when I get home.

There are two captains who will pick the teams for the game. I'm sure no one will pick me because I have one leg and they will think I am not good at softball. Or they might not pick me because they don't know I want to play, since they have probably never seen a boy with no hair and no left leg who wants to play in a softball game. So I walk over to the captains. One of them is Pastor Smuland, and the other is Tim, who I know because he is also homeschooled and comes to homeschool potlucks. Tim is pretty old, probably sixteen or seventeen. I used to play homeschool soccer with him and he is the best soccer player I've ever seen. Before my leg was cut off, I wanted to be just like him.

"I'm going to play in the softball game," I tell them.

Pastor Smuland looks confused, like the way he did when I was six years old and I asked him if Jesus, when he was born in a manger in Bethlehem on Christmas Day, knew that he was going to grow up and die for our sins on the cross. Pastor Smuland said that Jesus didn't know about this until he was older, when he was baptized and a special dove from Heaven came down and sat on his shoulder and told him. I thought that was funny, because it's kind of like how parrots come down and sit on pirates' shoulders, but Jesus was not a pirate.

"Softball?" Pastor Smuland asks. "How will you run?"

"Like this," I say, and I take off on my crutches for about twenty feet, then I run back.

Mom always says people want to be Pastor Smuland's friend because he is very enthusiastic, and now I understand what she means.

"Wow, *awesome!*" Pastor Smuland says, slapping me a high-five. "Aaaaaaall right! That's what I'm *talkin'* about, baby! Ha! Can you hit the ball, too?"

I have not thought about this. *Hmmmmm.* For me to swing, I would have to put my crutches down so I could hold the bat. But then, after I hit the ball, I would have to bend over and pick up my crutches before I could start running. This would take so long I would probably get tagged out, so, no, I guess I can't play after all—

"I will run for him," Tim says. "Joshua can hit the ball, and then I'll run to first base."

"Yeah—yeah, okay," Pastor Smuland says.

Tim keeps talking.

". . . And when the next batter gets to the plate, Joshua and I will switch bases and he can run the rest of the way."

I nod. This is a great plan. And Tim will run for me—*Tim!*

"Okay, let's do it!" Pastor Smuland says.

When they are picking teams, Tim points at me.

"Joshua," he says.

In fact, he picks me *second*, so he must have been really impressed by how fast I can run on my crutches. But while I am walking over to Tim—leaving all those people who haven't been picked yet like I have—I see Dad's car drive into the parking lot beside the softball field.

Oh, no, please . . . not *now* . . . I don't want to go home yet! Not right before the Annual Softball Game!

Dad parks and walks over to me while Tim and Pastor Smuland keep picking teams.

"What are you doing here?" I ask Dad, trying to make my voice sound sad, so he will know I don't want to leave yet.

"Hi, Joshua," he says, hugging me. "I just came to visit you."

"Wait . . . visit—so I don't have to go home now?"

"No, you can stay until tomorrow."

"Yessssss!" I say, pumping my fist.

Dad laughs.

"What's so funny?" I ask.

"Oh, nothing," he says.

But I know something was funny. That's why he laughed.

"Okay I have to go play softball now," I say.

"You're playing softball?"

I am afraid Dad will say I am not allowed to.

"Yeah I'm on Tim's team. He's going to run for me."

I tell him this so he knows I am already on a team, which means he can't tell me to drop out because then the teams would be uneven.

"Oh . . . okay," Dad says. "Well . . . I guess . . . I will be rooting for you!"

It's my turn to go to bat. I walk over and lay my crutches on the ground about five feet behind the catcher. Then I hop to home plate and pick up the bat, putting both hands on the white tape of the bat's grip. I stand upright and let the bat lean back against my shoulder. Then I look at Tim, and he is bent over with the tips of his fingers in the dirt, like a runner at the start of a race. He is waiting for me to get a hit.

Pastor Smuland is the pitcher for the other team.

"Ready?" he asks.

I nod.

He throws the ball underhand, a big, high arcing throw. Right as the ball is coming across the plate, I swing the bat as hard as I can.

Wooosh.

I miss the ball, and the force of the swing spins my body around. I lose my balance. The bat goes flying toward the fence behind the catcher, and I land on my hands and then fall onto my side in the yellowish-brownish dirt. The dirt is so thin and dry that when I fall, a cloud of it fills up the air around me and I breathe it in and start coughing.

Pastor Smuland comes running from the pitcher's mound.

"Joshua! You all right?"

"Yes," I say. "I'm fine. Kind of dusty, though."

I try to laugh a little because everyone knows that if you are laughing, you must be all right. People who stop laughing are always the ones who get hurt.

I stand up and brush the dust off my pants and then clap to get it off my hands, too.

"Here you go."

Tim hands me the bat.

"Thanks."

Pastor Smuland throws me another pitch, another high, slow one just like the first, and I swing and miss and fall down again in the dirt. I get back up, and now it's my third pitch. I have to hit this one, or else I will be struck out and Tim will be sorry he picked me because I am not as good as he thought I was.

"Come on, Joshua!"

It's Dad. I turn and see him standing behind the chain-link fence, halfway between home plate and first base. His fingers are poked through the holes in the fence, gripping tight.

"You can do it!" he says.

There are tons of people from church here, all watching the game, but I can easily hear Dad because the other people are not making any noise. They are all just standing along the fence, not talking. I look at them to find out why they are so quiet, and I see that they are all watching me.

When we used to play baseball in the backyard, Dad always said keep your eye on the ball. So that's what I do on the third pitch. I watch carefully as it flies very, very slowly through the air, spinning forward and falling lower and lower as it comes toward me. I can see Pastor Smuland behind the ball, still standing on his front leg with his arm reaching forward. But wait, no, don't look at Pastor Smuland! Keep your eye on the—where *is* it—There! Swing! Now! *Whoosh.* I swing and miss. I fall in the dust. I am out. Tim is sorry he picked me, and Dad feels sad about being my dad and cheering for me.

I get up and hop over to my crutches.

"Hold on, Joshua," Pastor Smuland says. "Keep going."

"But I'm out," I say.

"You're not out yet," he says.

I look at him because I am confused.

He nods. "We are Protestants, brother! We live by grace, not by the law!" he says, with his enthusiasm.

A few of the adults laugh, and I do not understand what's so funny, but I decide that living by grace means I get to keep swinging. I decide this because one time Pastor Smuland said living by grace means that we can do things like smoke cigars, and he pulled out a cigar and put it in his mouth during his sermon. A lot of people thought this was funny—although Mom and Dad were not part of this lot of people.

So if grace means you are allowed to break rules about not smoking, that means I can break rules about how many strikes you are allowed to have. I smile because I know that I will hit it this time. I will hit it and everyone from church will cheer! But Pastor Smuland gives me four more pitches, and I miss and fall in the dirt every time. I am breathing the way you do right before you start crying. I don't want anyone to see me cry, so I put the bat down and hop over to my crutches. I will run away.

"Joshua," Dad says. "You almost *had* that last one!"

I look at him over there, holding the fence, watching me.

"It was *this close*," he says, making a space of about two inches be-tween his thumb and pointer finger, sticking them through one of the links in the fence.

I look back at Pastor Smuland.

"You're still under grace," he says.

There are so many people on the field, people from Covenant Presbyterian Church who pray for me every day, who shaved their heads for me, who made shirts at Vacation Bible School that read, "Covenant Kids for Joshua!" and who come to my house and play computer games with me, since I can't go outside to play. I can't let them see me cry, but I can't let them see me strike out, either. So I hop back to the plate, pick up the bat, and nod at Pastor Smuland.

"Batter up," Tim says, giving me a thumbs-up and bending down like a track runner again.

I miss the next pitch, but this time I don't fall down. Instead, after I swing I put the bat down on the ground, like a cane, to steady my balance. I hear some people behind me whispering. On the next pitch, I stay standing again, and even though I get four more strikes, I don't fall in the dust on any of them. And then, after twelve strikes, I hear a *twink* and feel the metal bat bounce back a little bit as I swing. The ball rolls forward on the ground, straight toward the shortstop, who is one of the boys who shaved his head for me when I first started chemo. The ball is rolling very slowly, so I know the shortstop will run toward it, pick it up, and throw it to first before Tim can run there. But instead, the shortstop bends over and puts his open glove on the ground. Then he slides a few steps to the left to wait for the ball.

He waits there, and by the time the ball gets to him, Tim is al-ready safe at first base. Lots of people, even people on the other team, clap and say things like good job and great hit, all right. But even with all of them cheering and clapping, I can easily hear Dad when he says, "Way to go, Joshua." All this makes me very glad we're under grace, not the law.

It's time for me to be fitted with a fake leg, which is called a prosthesis. I can't wait. I have seen photos of amputees wearing fake legs and playing soccer. I also have a poster on my wall of two amputees who are wearing tight "USA" tank tops and running on a track with their fake legs on. I would like to be on a poster like that.

The doctor at Johns Hopkins told me that I won't be able to run because my amputation is too high. Most amputees, he said, have their legs cut off farther down, so they still have hip muscles to use for running. But my leg was cut off at the very top, right at my hip joint. With an amputation that high, he said, I will never be able to run again.

But I know that he is wrong, because in my whole life, anytime I have ever heard people tell stories like, "Doctors said I would never walk again," or "Doctors said I would never come out of the coma," the next thing the people always say is how they did exactly the opposite of what the doctors said. They walked again. They came out of the coma. So you should not listen to the doctors, because they're always wrong when they tell you "never again."

Getting fitted for a fake leg is very messy. There is a man, called a prosthetist, who wraps your body from below your arms all the way down to your knee (the one that wasn't cut off) with strips of fabric that drip white liquid all over the floor. The strips dry and get very hard, and you can't move. This will be the mold for the socket, he says, which is the part of the leg that attaches to your body. Then the prosthetist gets out something that looks like a chainsaw, except smaller, and he cuts the cast so he can take it off your body and talks about how he will try not to slip with the saw, because you already lost one of your legs, ha ha.

Then the prosthetist has you stand up against a piece of paper on the wall, and he holds a pencil against your skin and traces your whole leg, like at Thanksgiving when you trace your hand on paper to make a drawing of a turkey. Then you hop away from the wall and look at the drawing, and you can see how your thigh is much wider than your knee because there are so many muscles in it.

You also have to decide what color skin you want. The prosthetist has a book with a piece of rubber skin glued to each page, and you flip through it and choose the color you want. It's like the book with little pieces of carpet at the hardware store that you look at when your family is trying to decide what kind of carpet to get in the living room. You ask the prosthetist why there are twelve different kinds of skin for white people and only three for black people. He says "um" a few times, and then says it is because that's the way the skin company makes the skin, which doesn't really answer your question.

My fake leg, when it is finished, is very uncomfortable. This is surprising since the leg costs as much as a fancy car, and fancy cars are very, very comfortable. The leg wraps around the middle of my body like a one-inch-thick diaper made out of hard plastic. The place where my leg was removed (the prosthetist calls it a "stump," but Mom calls it a "residual limb" because she thinks this sounds better) is very sore because it is still healing, so it hurts to have the hard plastic pressing against it.

My fake leg is heavy. The prosthetist said it actually only weighs ten pounds, which he said is half as much as my real leg weighed before it got cut off. But when I still had my real leg, I didn't ever think, "Wow, this leg is really heavy. I would like to take it off." But that's what I think about all the time when I wear my fake one.

I have to learn how to walk again, too. The physical therapist who will teach me is named Bev and she is very old, and you can tell she has grandchildren, because she is very nice. On the first day, she gets out a big book, as big as a dictionary, and sets it down on the table.

"Let's see here," she says, turning the pages in the book. "Hip. *H-H-H-I-I* . . . Okay, here we are: 'hip disarticulation.'" She scans the page. "It says here that you should be able to learn how to walk just fine," she says. "What else? Carrying. Okay, you won't be able to carry anything, especially books, so that might make it hard at school."

"I am homeschooled."

"What?"

"My mom teaches me. I go to school at home."

"So you don't have books?"

"No, I have books, but I don't have to carry them anywhere because they're already on my desk."

"Oh, okay, good," she says. "What about stairs? Do you have any stairs?"

"Yes."

"How many flights?"

"Five or six."

She looks very surprised.

"Five or six flights?" Bev asks.

"No, no," Mom says. "*Stairs.* Five or six stairs, leading up to the front porch. Our house is all on one level; it's a ranch. No flights."

"Perfect!" Bev says with a smile.

"And actually my husband just put a railing on those stairs," Mom says. "To help Joshua."

Whenever Mom is talking about Dad with people who don't know him, she calls him "my husband." But when Dad is talking about Mom with people who don't know *her,* he says "my wife, Linda," like he needs to tell the person which of his wives he is talking about, even though he is only married to Mom.

"A railing, that's great," Bev says.

"What about running?" I ask, thinking about my poster of the amputees running on their fake legs.

"What about running?" Bev repeats my question.

"Yes."

•   "Well, let's see . . ."

She looks at the page.

"Nope."

"What do you mean?"

"You can't run."

"Not at all?"

"Well . . . there's something you can do that is sort of like running. I can teach you on your last day—how many days do you have scheduled right now?"

"Four," Mom says.

"Right, four," Bev says. "So, after your four days, I want you to go home for two weeks and get used to your prosthesis. Then come back and I will teach you how to run the best way you can. Here, I will show you. It will look kind of like this—"

She stands up, this grandmother physical therapist, and does a very weird thing. It's like she is skipping, but only with one of her legs. The other leg is walking. So she takes a normal step with one foot, and then skips one step on the other one, then switches back to normal. Step, skip, step, skip.

"That's the best you will be able to do, because your prosthesis won't swing through fast enough to do a normal run," she says.

Of course I know she is wrong. Probably she just has to run like that because she is a grandmother, and really she means I will run normally, just a little bit slower than I did before.

At the end of the four days of physical therapy, I can walk on my fake leg without a cane or crutches or handrails. I can even walk carrying that big book in my hands, the book that says I won't be able to carry books. So I know the doctors and the book will be wrong and I will be able to run, too. Then I go back to the hospital for another round of chemotherapy. I wear my fake leg, and it looks very realistic since the prosthetist traced my real leg and I chose a good skin color. The only part that doesn't look real is the knee, which • gets wrinkled when it bends. That's why I will only wear really long shorts from now on.

Before my leg got cut off, Mom always made me wear shorts that stopped above my knees. She said long shorts were for hooligans. But now that I have a fake leg that has a wrinkly knee, she cut off some of my old jeans into long shorts that cover up the knee and its wrinkles so you can't tell it's fake. And Mom and Dad let me wear one of these pairs of shorts to church on Sunday! A lot of people at church came over to look at the new leg and talk about how they couldn't tell which one was fake. This made me very happy about the skin color I chose. And people at the hospital like the leg, too. All the nurses come over and nod with their hands on their hips about my skin color being the right choice. Perfect match, they all say.

When you are in the hospital, there are people who come to your room every day. They are called residents, because they live at the hospital. They come to your room and ask you lots of questions about what you ate and how much you've urinated, and they take your temperature and blood pressure and pulse.

On the second day of this trip to the hospital, one of the residents is doing his exam, and he looks at the watch on his wrist, and then, still looking at the watch, he puts two fingers of his other hand on my artificial leg. I know he is trying to get a pulse but he won't get it there because there is no blood in my fake leg. So he will think I am dead. And then he will think it is very strange that I have been talking to him about what I ate and how much I've urinated, even though I'm dead. Maybe he will think I am a ghost, even though ghosts aren't real.

"Did you know that Joshua has a prosthesis?" Mom asks.

"What?" the resident says.

"Joshua has a prosthesis. It looks like you are trying to take a pulse from it," Mom says.

"Oh—what? Prosthesis. Oh—right, of course. Yes, it says it right here," he says, looking at his clipboard. "Yes, right—uh—well, I just remembered I have a meeting I am late for."

Then he walks out of the room very quickly because he is running late for his meeting. But I guess it's good that he made the mistake with my fake leg, because otherwise he might have stayed in my room for a few more minutes and missed the whole meeting. It's like Dad always says: sometimes when bad things happen to us, or when we make mistakes, God can use them for something good, like remembering to go to our meetings.

After I finish the five days of chemo treatments, Mom takes me back to Bev the grandmother physical therapist to learn how to run. Bev shows me that same walk-skip-walk-skip thing she did before.

"Now you try," she says. "Just skip a step on your right foot while you wait for the prosthetic foot to swing through."

I try it. I watch myself in the mirror and I can see that I look stupid and slow. When I had two legs, if I wanted to run, I would just straighten my leg really fast and put it on the ground in front of my body. But with my fake leg, there are no muscles to make the knee straighten out fast. Instead, it hangs from my body and swings underneath me, powered by springs. With each step, I have to wait for it to swing and then for the heel to hit the ground in front of me. It swings soooooo slooooooowly, like the long piece of metal that swings back and forth inside Nana and Papa's big grandfather clock, the one that chimes every fifteen minutes even when you are trying to sleep.

I try very hard and I even pray and ask God to make my fake leg swing faster, but God doesn't help, and it still swings slowly and the only kind of running I can do is the step, skip, step, skip. On the drive home from physical therapy, Mom asks why I am so quiet.

"Aren't you excited? You learned how to run today!" she says.

"Yeah . . . of course," I say, even though I am not excited.

But maybe Mom can tell from my voice that I am not actually excited because she doesn't ask me any more questions for the whole hour-long drive home. Maybe she is thinking what I am thinking: That I am the first person the doctors have ever been right about. They told me that I would never run again, and it's true. I won't.

9

A lot of people come to visit and sometimes they even bring presents. But they don't bring presents for Matthew, so I always give him the ones I don't want.

A couple months after my amputation, a famous person shows up at our house. I know he is famous because when he talks, I recognize his voice right away. It's Brad Huddleston, the Christian DJ who prayed for me on the radio the morning my leg was cut off.

"I come bearing gifts," he says when Mom opens the door.

Brad Huddleston walks into the house with his arms full of the gifts. He drops them all on the kitchen table and a few slide off the top of the pile onto the table and then to the floor. I look at the pile. There is an illustrated kids' Bible, a T-shirt with a cross on it, and CDs. Lots of CDs. They're from all sorts of Christian rock bands and Christian rappers. Of course, I know that Mom and Dad are never going to let me listen to any of them because Mom read about a homeschool family who let their children start listening to Christian rock music, and a few days later the kids started disobeying their parents and not doing their schoolwork, so the family had to have a special ceremony to burn the Christian rock CDs and pray that God would remove Satan's control over their lives. That's why our family has a special list of all the famous Christian musical artists. We can listen to an artist or band only if they're listed in the "Okay" column.

But I don't want Brad Huddleston to feel bad for bringing me all these CDs that I am not allowed to listen to, so I pretend I am excited. Mom, Matthew, and Brad Huddleston watch as I read the cover of each one and open my eyes wide and smile and thank Brad Huddleston for giving it to me.

"Joshua, I was wondering if you'd like to come to the studio and do a show with me?" Brad Huddleston says.

"Really? You mean like be on the radio?"

"Yeah, we'll have you come in the morning—it will be real early when we start. Can you get up real early?"

I look at Mom, because she's the one who says when I am allowed to go to bed and wake up.

"That's fine," she says.

"Great," Brad Huddleston says. "You'll come at five and we'll be on together until I go off at ten. We'll tell jokes, take calls, maybe give away some CDs."

"Wow! Coooooool!" I say.

Now I don't have to pretend to be excited anymore because I *am* excited. I am so excited that I am hopping up and down on my one leg.

I'm excited because I've always wanted to be on the radio. When I was a little boy, I used to crawl under the desk in my room and talk into the air-conditioning vent in the floor. If I talked real loud, everyone in the house would be able to hear me because all the vents are connected. I would read stories from the newspaper and play songs from my *Patch the Christian Pirate* cassette tapes. I called it WJLS Radio. The *W* was because all radio station names start with *W,* and JLS, that's my initials. They stand for Joshua Lee Sundquist.

But now I will get to be on a real radio station, and I won't have to stop broadcasting when the house gets warm and the air-conditioning starts blowing in my face.

"When will it be?" I ask Brad Huddleston, still hopping up and down.

"Next week, if you can," he says.

"Can I come? Can I come?" Matthew says. He is hopping up and down now, too, except on two legs.

Sometimes Matthew does things just because he sees me do them. That's probably the reason he is hopping up and down right now, and the reason he wants to be on the radio—to be like me. Why can't he imitate someone else, like Luke?

"Well . . . let me think," Brad Huddleston says. "There are only two mics in the studio . . . so actually it wouldn't really be possible. I'm sorry. That would've been great to have you, too."

Matthew stops his imitation hopping.

"Tell you what," Brad Huddleston says. "We'll call you during the show and record an interview and play it on the air. How does that sound?"

Matthew smiles.

"Yeah," he says.

I whisper in Mom's ear and ask if, since he's a famous radio DJ, could Brad Huddleston record a new answering machine greeting on our phone?

"What on earth would he say?" she whispers back.

"He would say, 'Hi, this is *Brad Huddleston,* and you've reached the answering machine of *my friends,* the Sundquist family.'"

She whispers back that we will have to think about it. She must not realize how famous he is. I get his autograph before he leaves.

Being on the radio is the most fun thing I've ever done, even more fun than going to Lost River. Brad Huddleston lets me choose the music to play, and I choose all Christian rap songs even though I know they might make me want to disobey my parents and stop doing my schoolwork. We do things together like watch the fax machine while it prints out the news and then read the news on the air. We take the fifth caller and give her a CD. Brad Huddleston asks me what my hobbies are, and I tell him how I like to draw, and also how I like to call pay phones and see who answers and talk to them. He laughs because he thinks I am joking, so then I pull out my Pay Phone Number Notebook from my pocket, the one I carry with me everywhere so that when I walk by a pay phone I can write down the number for it. Brad Huddleston says wow, this is a great hobby and we call the pay phone at the mall and we are recording to play it on the radio, but no one picks up, because it's 6:30 a.m. and the mall is not open yet.

And Brad Huddleston interviews me.

"Joshua, were you ever angry at God for allowing all this to happen to you?"

"No," I say. "But people ask me that a lot."

"They do, huh?"

"Yes."

"But you just aren't angry, are you?"

"No."

"Didn't you ever think it was unfair, though? Like when you see other kids your age who don't have to go into the hospital like you do?"

"Well, I don't like being in the hospital," I say. "But one thing that Dad showed me in the Bible is where it says that 'God works all things for good.' That means that even when bad things happen, God can use them for a good purpose."

"And have you seen anything like that in your life? Good purposes that God has brought out of your experience with cancer?"

"Yeah!" I say. "Last summer, for my birthday, ProPark—have you ever heard of it?"

"The arcade?"

"Yeah. Well, they found out I had cancer, so they gave me a free birthday party and let me invite as many friends as I wanted to even though I was only turning ten, and we got to play video games for *free*. So that's something good that has happened because of my cancer."

"Sounds like you had fun."

"Yeah, it was real fun!"

"Well, I know your life is a great encouragement to many people," Brad Huddleston says. "You are listening to *The Brad Huddleston Morning Show,* and we'll be right back with more from Josh Sundquist after these messages. Don't go away."

He presses a button on one of the machines, and the red light above his desk switches off. That means we can say things and people won't hear them on the radio anymore.

"When are we going to call Matthew? Are you—are you still going to interview him?" I ask.

"We can do it right now," Brad Huddleston says.

He turns a knob so I can hear the call in my headphones, and I tell him the number for our house.

"How old are you?" Brad Huddleston asks Matthew after the interview starts.

"Seven," Matthew says.

"Wow. What grade are you in school?"

"Second."

"Are you homeschooled like your brother Joshua?"

"Yes."

"What are you learning about in homeschool right now?"

"I learned . . . the difference between synonyms and homonyms."

"Wow, that's great!" Brad Huddleston says. "What is it?"

"What?"

"What is the difference between synonyms and homonyms?"

"Synonyms . . . are words . . . that sounds alike but have a different meaning," Matthew says. "Homonyms are words that sounds different but have the same meaning . . . I think."

"Wow, nice job, Matthew," Brad Huddleston says. "We've been talking with Matthew Sundquist, the little brother of Joshua Sundquist. Bye Matthew!"

"Bye."

Brad Huddleston hangs up with Matthew. Then he turns the knob so I can't hear anything in my headphones, and he makes another phone call.

"Beth, could you please look up something for me in the dictionary? . . . Thanks. Please look up *homonym* . . . Yes, *N-Y-M* . . ."

He turns to me.

"I think your brother might've messed up on his definitions," he says.

"Oh, well, I am in fourth grade and I wouldn't know the difference, so that's okay," I say.

"I know," Brad Huddleston says. "But we can't put it on the air if—yes? . . . *Same* sound but *different* meanings? . . . Okay, thanks!"

He hangs up the phone.

"Yep, he messed up. That's too bad . . . Now it's gonna be a pretty short interview."

Brad Huddleston pulls a tape out of a machine. The tape looks like my *Patch the Christian Pirate* tapes, except bigger. Then he shows me how he can cut out part of the interview with sharp, shiny scissors and then attach the two ends of the tape back together. So now, when he plays the interview on the radio, it sounds like Matthew only told Brad Huddleston his age, his grade, that yes, he is homeschooled, and then said goodbye. These are the words Matthew said that got played during his radio interview:

"Seven."

"Second."

"Yes."

"Bye."

A few weeks after my radio interview, I have a TV interview. It's for the hospital, for a show that will be on TV in a few months called

Children's Miracle Network, which will raise money to help buy medicine for families who have a sick child and not much money, like Johnny's parents. A camera person, a sound person, and a director come to our house to film me. The director is from Los Angeles and he wears three-hundred-dollar sunglasses. I know they cost that much because Matthew thought they were really cool, and wanted to buy a pair, and asked how much they cost. But Matthew doesn't have three hundred dollars because he's only seven.

Before the interview, the director and I sit in my bedroom and talk about chemotherapy. I tell him how I go into the hospital one week out of every three weeks, and lie in bed at the hospital because I am too tired to do anything. I tell him how when I am home I lie in bed, too, and how a nurse from church comes to give me a shot every day after she gets off work. I tell him how I am never hungry because chemotherapy makes food taste like metal, and how I lost so much weight that last summer I only weighed sixty-eight pounds. And I tell him how Mom now makes me eat lots of food so I will stop losing weight, even food that I am usually not allowed to eat because it gives you heart attacks, like whole milk.

"And how old are you?" he asks.

"I just turned ten."

"That's a lot for a ten-year-old to deal with."

"I guess."

"What keeps you going?"

"Well . . . my family . . . because they really love me," I say. "Also, different people from our church make dinner for us every night, and they take care of Matthew and Luke whenever I am in the hospital. And some people from church come and clean our house, too, all for free."

"Yeah, well, that's really great," the director says. "But what keeps *you* going? What gets you out of bed in the morning?"

When he asks his question that way, I know the answer. Every morning when I wake up, before I move the sheets off my body, I think about one thing.

"I want to finish."

I want to get done with chemotherapy, get done with hospitals, get done with shots. I want to see my hair grow back, and I want food to taste good again, and I want to have energy. I want to not have cancer. I understand, I know now, that I will never run. I will never play soccer. But at least one day I can wake up and have a normal life like I did before.

After we talk about all this, the director interviews me in front of a camera and two lights that are so bright and hot they make me sweat. After my interview, he interviews Mom and Dad. Dad cries while he says his answer to every question, except the first one, when they ask him how to spell his name. Lately Dad has been crying about everything, even things that aren't sad, like when the director asks him, "How will you feel when Joshua is done with chemotherapy?" which is actually something you should be happy about.

After the interview, when they are turning off the lights, Matthew walks in.

"Hey do you want to interview me, too?" Matthew asks.

"Well, no, I don't think we have time for that today," the director says.

Matthew frowns and his shoulders fall down.

"Hey, kid," the director says, patting Matthew on the back. "Just be glad that you're not the one who might die from cancer, right?"

Matthew nods.

We watch the director and his assistants pack up the lights and cameras and electrical cords into black bags and black boxes. Then they carry it all to the van outside. Dad helps them carry the bags and boxes, but no one asks me to help. That's one thing I've noticed about having one leg: people don't ask you to help them push wheelbarrows of mulch or trim bushes in the backyard anymore. You wish they would, though, because you want them to know you are strong, and soon you'll be as strong as Dad. But no one ever asks.

Mom and Dad and I stand on the porch and wave goodbye to the director and his assistants as they drive away in their van. They wave back at us.

We walk back inside, and I go into my bedroom. Matthew is standing on the edge of my mattress on the bottom bunk. The cloth belt from his bathrobe is tied around the railing of the top bunk, and the other end is tied in a knot that he is tightening around his neck.

"Awwww*wwwww*!" I say. "You're in trouble! I'm gonna tell Mom!"

In our family we are never, ever allowed to tie anything around our necks or point guns at other people—even if it is a toy gun, because you never know when it might be a real gun and it might be loaded—and both of these rules, the no-putting-things-around-your-neck rule and the no-pointing-guns rule, are the most important rules in our house, so if you break them, you get a spanking, which is the worst punishment you can get.

"Mommm!" I yell, stepping back into the hallway. "Matthew is putting a rope around his neck!"

Mom has bad hips from playing softball. That's why she and Dad chose a one-story house with only five stairs on the front porch. Mom doesn't like walking up stairs, and she especially doesn't like running. But when I call her to tell her that Matthew has broken one of the most important rules, she comes running down the hallway and almost knocks me over when she turns the corner into our bedroom.

"Oh, Matthew!" she says. "Oh—*oh*. Paul! *Paul!*"

But Dad is already here, too, because he heard me yell about Matthew breaking the rule. I have never seen Dad's face look the way it does when he sees Matthew standing on the edge of the bed with the fabric belt tied around his neck. I can tell he has the same feelings I had when I thought the dogs were going to kill Matthew and me at Nana and Papa's house. Then Dad makes a noise. It's a noise like he is in pain, like he just stepped barefoot on a sharp rock in the backyard.

"Yaaa—*aaaaah*!"

Dad scoops up Matthew from the bottom bunk and holds him like a baby.

"Get it off! Get it off, Linda!" Dad says.

"I'm trying!" Mom says.

Mom is trying to untie the knot around Matthew's neck, but her hands are shaking so she can't grab hold of it. Finally she gets one of her fingers inside the knot and loosens it so she can slide it off Matthew, and Dad bends his knees very fast and falls beside the bunk bed and holds Matthew's head against his shoulder. Mom is trying to hold Matthew, too, and she falls against Dad and they all tip back until they are lying on the floor.

Mom and Dad and Matthew are all crying, and now Luke walks in and starts crying, too. I am the only one who is not crying, and I don't understand why Matthew isn't getting a spanking. He broke the *most important rule,* and he almost hanged himself, which means he could have *died.* That means he is supposed to get spanked. But I can tell from the way Mom and Dad are crying that he will not get in trouble for this, and that I should not ask why not.

I sit on the edge of my bed and pull the end of my shorts up so I can feel the wrinkles in the rubber skin around my fake knee. I rub the wrinkles for a long time while everyone lies on the floor and cries, and Luke walks in and out of the room, still crying, too.

"Matthew, we love you so much," Mom says. "You are *so special* to us."

"Matthew . . ." Dad starts to speak, but then he starts crying again and can't talk.

Mom strokes Matthew's hair, which is still very short since he still shaves it to help me not feel bad.

"Sweetheart," she says. "Can you tell us why you did that?"

Matthew looks at her, and then he looks over at me.

"Because," Matthew says. "If Joshua is going to die, I don't want to live anymore."

Going to die? He thinks I am going to *die*? He thinks the cancer will kill me? No way! Not a chance! I am going to *finish*!

I slide off the bed and grab Matthew's hand.

"Don't worry," I say. "I am not going to die."

"You're not?" he asks.

"No, I'm not."

"Promise?"

"Yeah, I promise."

If I want people to think I'm asleep when I'm actually awake, I lower my eyelids almost all the way, so it looks like my eyes are closed. Then I start breathing slowly and loudly and don't move any part of my body.

One afternoon while I am in my hospital room pretending to be asleep so I don't have to take a homeschooling test, Mom makes a phone call. Mom talks to the person on the phone about how things are hard right now because, besides me having cancer, her own mom has been having memory problems. Then Mom stops talking for a second and looks at me—I can see her do this because my eyes are just barely open so I can watch her through my eyelashes—before she starts talking again.

"And we just got that . . . that . . . recent *diagnosis*," Mom says quietly.

A diagnosis is when the doctors tell you that something's wrong with your body, like you have cancer in your left leg. But Mom doesn't say what the diagnosis is for Nana, so the person on the phone is probably wondering, like I am: What is wrong with Nana's body?

Mom is still talking: "And I am just so *tired* all the time."

She listens to the phone for a second.

"For Joshua's chemo? Nine so far. Only three months left to go."

Only three months.

Five chemo cycles! Then I will be done . . . done! . . . Finished with chemotherapy! I will start using LA Looks Gel, Level Five Most Extreme Hold, again! I will play outside again! I will have eyebrows! I will get the top bunk bed back from Matthew! . . . Or, actually, maybe I will let him keep it, since he has been very sad recently and now he has to go to Purcell Park with a man from church who is trying to help him feel happy. So maybe he can sleep on the top bunk bed and I'll stay on the bottom for a while. But even if I stay on the bottom, at least it is a real bed, not a hospital bed with a crinkly plastic mattress and a speaker beside your head where nurses say loud things to you.

After I finish, I will never ever have to sleep in a hospital bed again. I will still have to *go inside* the hospital every three months to get X rays and CAT scans but these will never be overnight visits. And even if someday I have scans and Dr. Dunsmore looks at them and says the cancer has come back, I still won't have to spend the night in the hospital because I will tell her I don't want to start chemotherapy again.

I will tell her I don't want to start chemotherapy again because nine months ago, when food started tasting like metal and my eyebrows fell out and I was too tired to play with Matthew in the backyard, I didn't think I could make it through a whole year of chemo. It was just too hard and a year was just too long—one tenth of my life, since I am ten now. Then I decided I could get through one year of chemotherapy if every day for that year I just thought about finishing, about when food would taste spicy or sweet or sour like it's supposed to, and about when my eyebrows would grow back and about when I could play outside again. Thinking about that made me feel strong. *Finishing.* That's what made me decide I could make it through the year, and that's why I told the director of the TV show with the three-hundred-dollar sunglasses that finishing is what keeps me going.

But I also promised myself that I would only do chemotherapy once, because that's as much as I can do. Doing it more times would be too terrible.

Only once.

Mom listens to the person on the phone for a few seconds before she starts talking again. It's hard to see her with my eyes just barely open, but I can tell that she looks really tired.

"That's right, only three months left to go, so almost. I think . . . actually, I think the only way I've made it this far is by taking Joshua's cancer one day at a time. I can't think about anything beyond that one day. I mean, three hundred and sixty-five days? That's just too . . . overwhelming," she says. "But now . . . with just three months left . . . now I am starting to see that light at the end of the tunnel."

I have always thought this wouldn't happen to me, that my immune system would never get tired. But today when Mom and I go to the hospital for chemo, a nurse draws blood and comes back with lab results that say my immune system has not grown back enough.

"Your blood counts are just too low, Joshua," she says. "Wait a week. Then come see us again."

Dr. Dunsmore told us a long time ago that after about nine months of chemotherapy, your body starts to get tired. And when your body starts to get tired, you have to rest more in between chemo treatments. This happens because chemotherapy kills all fast-growing cells. Cancer is fast growing, so it kills cancer. But your hair is fast growing, too, and that's why it all falls out. And there are also fast-growing cells in your immune system, which is the part of your body that Mrs. Jacobson thinks can get shut down by the Dangerous Levels of Sugar in Soft Drinks. Even though Mrs. Jacobson is wrong about the soft drinks, I know that your immune system *does* get shut down by chemotherapy. In fact, your immune system gets killed by it.

When you first start chemo, your immune system can grow back in just a few days after it is killed by the chemotherapy. But after those nine months, that's when it starts getting the tiredness. Then you have to wait longer for your immune system to grow back before you come to the hospital for more chemo, which means it will take longer to finish your treatments. In fact, Dr. Dunsmore said some kids' immune systems get so tired they end up being on chemotherapy for an extra year.

Dr. Dunsmore—her full name is Dr. Kimberly Dunsmore—is my main doctor. There are lots of other doctors at the hospital who do things for me—doctors who do my surgeries, doctors who look at my CAT scans—but Dr. Dunsmore is the one who is officially in charge of my treatment. It's like how lots of people do different things to help on Sunday morning, but Pastor Smuland is the one who is officially in charge of running our church. Dr. Dunsmore has wavy brown hair, and she wears lipstick, which I notice because Mom never wears lipstick unless she's going to a wedding. Dr. Dunsmore always carries a clipboard, and when she writes on it she leans her head to one side so her hair falls in that direction. I know that she has kids of her own at home because Mom and Dad always ask how they are doing. And they are always doing well. I think Dr. Dunsmore must be really happy about her kids doing well since she sees so many sick kids at her job every day. One time Dr. Dunsmore said she hopes her kids grow up to be just like me, which is a strange thing to say since I am not actually grown up yet, and also because she knows that I might never grow up, since I have cancer and might die.

I don't think I will die, of course, but now we know that my body is sicker than we thought before because my immune system is tired. Since I can't get chemo today, we will have to drive an hour back home to Harrisonburg. It will be a very sad drive because now we know I might not finish in one year. I might not finish for a very long time. And the reason that is sad is because when I knew exactly how long I had until I was done with chemo, I could always be looking forward to the day when it would all be over. But now I don't know when that day is going to be anymore. Now it might be many extra months. Now there's nothing for me to look forward to.

While Mom and I ride the elevator down from the children's floor to the lobby, I read a sign on the wall about how there is going to be adaptive ski instruction on Saturday at Massanutten, which is the mountain you can see from the window in the family room at home. Today is Friday, so that means the adaptive ski instruction is tomorrow. At the bottom of the sign is a phone number and a person's name: Bev Gryth.

"Hey Mom," I say, pointing at the poster. "Is this the same Bev that is a grandmother? Like the one who showed me how to walk with my fake leg?"

Mom looks at the poster.

"Yes it is."

"Well can I go so she could teach me how to ski?"

I expect Mom to say, "We'll have to think about it," but she doesn't.

"I guess . . . you can go," she says. "If Dad is willing to drive you."

I can't believe it! She said yes! I can go skiing! Tomorrow!

Mom has never let us go skiing since it is expensive and we are saving for college so we can have opportunities in life, and besides, you spend most of your time skiing sitting on the lift anyway. I've been asking her if I could ski for five or six years, and she's always said no. I am not sure what changed her mind all of the sudden, but whatever it is, I am very glad it happened!

If I can learn how to ski, that would be great, because there aren't any other sports I can play anymore. I can't play soccer since I don't have hip muscles to make my fake leg swing fast. I tried to ride a bike once, but I couldn't do it because my balance is different now. And even though I got a hit when I played softball at Lost River, I had to have Tim run for me, which means that I can't really play softball, either. But if I can ski, then I will have a sport to play again. So the drive home from the hospital turns out to be very happy even though we just found out my immune system is tired.

If you have the kind of amputation I do that takes off your whole leg, you can't ski with a fake leg on, so at Massanutten I walk on crutches. But with my crutches I can't carry anything and that's why Dad carries my ski for me. He brings it from the rental shop to the bottom of the trails and lays it down on the snow. Then he hands me the warm hat made out of wool. The hat shakes in my hand because I am so excited about skiing. I look around. There are happy skiers everywhere. I look up the mountain, see them ski, see how fast they are going. *I* want to ski that fast! I can't wait to ski that fast!

Before we left this morning, Mom said make sure you wear this hat. I don't want you catching a cold. You know what will happen if you get sick, right? I said yes.

What will happen is I will have to go to the hospital. Whenever I have a fever, I have to go to the hospital since I'm on chemo and my body can't make itself get better like a normal body can. Same thing if I get a scrape on my skin. Last summer, when I tried to ride a bike with one leg, I scratched my leg and had to stay in the hospital for three days.

"Also, be very, very careful," Mom said. "Try not to fall or get hurt. You don't need to ski fast on your first day, okay? Just go very slow and—"

Dad nodded and put his hand up which made Mom stop talking.

"You'll do great," Dad said.

"Yes . . . great," Mom said.

I am at Massanutten, thinking about all this when Dad says, "You ready to switch?"

"Uh-huh," I say.

"One, two, three—"

When he gets to three, he lifts the baseball cap off my head, and I pull on the warm wool hat before anyone can look over and see that I am bald. The wool feels scratchy against the skin on my head.

Bev brings Dad and me over to meet an instructor named Mark who will teach me to ski. Mark has gray hair even though he is not old like Bev is. He also has a gray mustache. Mark is a very nice person. He says he will leave one of his skis at the bottom of the mountain so I can watch him ski on one leg during the lesson.

"Won't your leg get tired?" Dad asks.

"Joshua has to be on one leg the whole time," Mark says. "So I should be able to do it, too, right?"

He is looking at me when he says this, so I nod.

Mark shows me how to balance on my ski by leaning on my outriggers, which are like forearm crutches with ski tips on the end. On the back of these ski tips are pieces of metal that look like teeth, so whenever you want to slow down, all you have to do is push those outriggers farther in front of your body until the teeth dig into the snow.

Mark takes me to a building called the Lift House, where you get on the ski lift. But there is a long line there with tons of people in it.

"Here, come this way," Mark says. He points at a sign that has a plus symbol on it, colored bright red. It says, "Ski Patrol Only."

"I don't think I am ski patrol," I say.

"No, but I am," he says with a smile that stretches his gray mustache. "See, look."

He pulls out a plastic card from his jacket that has that same red plus symbol and says, "Ski Patrol."

So we skip the line and go inside the Lift House, where there are moving benches hanging from a rope. The hanging benches spin around in a half-circle and then run into people from behind. I watch this happen a few times. Whenever the benches run into people from behind, the people bend their knees, and then the benches scoop them off the ground and carry them up in the air.

"How do you know when to sit down on the bench?" I ask Mark.

"Just wait till you feel it hit your leg," he says.

But this is very scary and makes my stomach feel hot inside, because I am afraid I won't bend my knee fast enough and then the bench will knock me over. Or, if I sit down too early, I will fall on the snow and the bench will smack me in the back of my head.

"Can we get a slow, please?" Mark says.

A man wearing a coat that says "Massanutten" on it presses a yellow button and the benches start moving more slowly.

"You need a hand?" the man asks.

"Yes, please," Mark says.

Mark and the man each grab one of my elbows and slide me on my ski up to a red line in the snow.

"Okay, here we go," Mark says.

I wait for the bench, and my heart is beating very fast. I can't turn around and watch for it, because I might lose my balance if I do. So I have to look straight ahead and wait for it to hit my leg from behind. I wait and wait and my heart keeps beating fast. All of a sudden, Mark grabs my shoulders and pushes me down.

Why is he pushing me down? I am going to fall in the snow!

But when my knee bends, instead of falling down, I sit down on a bench, and then we are flying up in the air. I am happy Mark made me sit down on the bench at the right time, but I don't thank him for his help, because it scared me when he pushed me down without telling me why.

Once we are very high up, I look down. I watch the people on the beginner trail below us falling in the snow. If *I* fall, everyone will stare at me because I have one leg, and they will feel sorry for me.

They will tell their children, "See, look. Be glad that you have two legs, not like that poor little boy there who only has one leg and falls down in the snow." They won't know that I fell because it is my first day skiing and I am just learning. They'll just think it's just because I have one leg. So I decide that I can't fall. I won't. Instead, I will ski fast and ski right past all of those parents and they will say to their children, "See, look at that boy who skis faster than you even though he only has one leg and you have two. You should stop falling so much and be a fast skier like he is."

There are many, many skiers here. It is more crowded than I thought it would be when I imagined skiing in my mind. There's a big crowd of people wearing colorful hats and puffy coats. And a lot of the people are standing still on the ski trail, not skiing. They are standing around on the snow talking to other people who are also standing. The people who are skiing have to go around the people who are standing. But all the people, both the standers and the skiers, they all seem really happy to be here.

Another thing about when I've imagined skiing in my mind is that I've always thought skis would slide on snow the way my socks did when I used to run down the hall and slide on the kitchen floor when I had two legs. But it turns out that my ski doesn't slide like that. My ski slides faster than my socks did, much faster. When I get off the lift at the top, the ski slides on the snow so fast that I fall on my back. The lift—the whole entire lift, which has hundreds of people on it and more people standing in line for it at the bottom—gets turned off when I fall. The hundreds of people are all looking at me while Mark puts his arms around my waist and picks me up off the snow. I wish I had a microphone so I could say to all of them, "I did not fall because I have one leg. I fell because it is my first time skiing and I thought the ski would slide like my socks used to slide on the kitchen floor."

After Mark helps me stand up, he asks me if I am ready. I tell him I am.

"You see that snow blower over there?" he asks.

"What?"

"The snow blower. The big blue thing right there."

"What's a snow blower?"

"A machine that makes snow . . . we don't get much natural snow in Virginia, you know."

"So this is all fake snow?"

"Yup."

I look around. On the sides of the trail the snow ends, and you can see grass growing right beside it. The green grass right beside the white snow is kind of like the rubber skin that wrinkles all wrong and rubber-like on the knee of my fake leg—that's the part where if you look at it, you can figure out it's fake.

"Okay, I want you to ski over to the snow blower," Mark says.

"How?"

"Just lean on your outriggers and let your ski slide."

I am very afraid that I will fall, and my heart is beating fast again. I lean on my outriggers. But nothing happens.

"Push off a little with the riggers," he says.

So I push the outriggers into the snow the way I do when I am taking a step with my crutches. As I start to move, the ski makes a soft noise on the snow like the sound of breathing out through your nose. I notice again how slippery the ski is. It wants to slide down the hill instead of across it to the snow blower. The ski slides more and more down the hill, and I try to stop it by leaning on my outriggers. But that just makes the ski go more the wrong way, and I start to feel my body falling over. As I am falling, my hat gets caught on one of the outriggers. I have to grab the hat with my hand and hold it onto my head so no one will see I am bald.

When I hit the ground—and the fake snow is not soft like real snow is, so it hurts to fall and it knocks the wind out of me so I can't breathe—my ski pops off. I try to catch my breath. I feel sick, like I might throw up, the way I do after chemotherapy. *I wish I hadn't come here today.* I look at the snow and sit still, trying to breathe normally and not cry. *I have one leg. I can't play sports anymore.* Mark comes over.

"Let's try again," he says.

When he says this it reminds me of the physical therapist, the one who glued those stickers on my back that made my body bounce up and down. She always used to say things like "let's try this" or "we need to try that." I did not like it when she said these things because *we* weren't going to try anything. *I* was always the one who had to try it. But when Mark says, "Let's try again," I don't mind because he is skiing on one ski just like me. So we are doing it together.

I stand up. He holds the ski in place while I balance on the outriggers and step back into the binding part that holds the ski onto my boot. I push off on my outriggers again and let my ski slide. This time I try to balance my body right above my ski. I'm moving fast enough to feel the air hit my face like wind and to feel my body going faster and faster the way I used to feel when I was roller-skating down a hill. I slide all the way to the snow blower, and then I push the teeth on the outriggers into the snow to slow down and stop. I don't fall! I skied faster and faster without falling! Even though I only have one leg! I can ski! I can ski.

"You did it!" Mark says.

I notice that he says, "You did it," even though actually *we* did it, together.

The next thing we have to learn how to do is make turns. Mark tells me that making turns is like using the brakes on the bike I used to ride. If you want to go fast you just ski straight down toward the Lift House. That's like pedaling. But if you want to ski slower, you just make bigger turns across the hill. That's like brakes. If you can learn how to put on the brakes by turning, you can ski any part of the mountain, because all ski trails are really the same as this one, it's just that when it's steeper, you make more turns.

Mark says the most important part of turning is where your eyes are looking. "Your body follows your vision," he says. "So here is what we'll do. We'll ski across the hill, like we did to get to this snow blower, but then instead of using the teeth in the outriggers to stop, we will look back at a *different* snow blower on the other side of the trail. Then our bodies will follow our eyes and our skis will turn."

So Mark slides across the beginner trail, and then he turns his head and yells back at me, "See, now I am turning my head and looking at the other side of the hill so that . . . see . . . now my ski is turning in that direction?" But really he is looking at me when he says this, not the next snow blower. So I am not sure if this idea really works.

I decide to try it anyway. I slide across the hill on my ski and outriggers, watching the snow blower very carefully. I slide to the place where Mark turned, and then I move my head so I am looking back at the first side of the hill, where Mark is standing now. I look at the snow blower that's a little down the hill from where he is standing. And then . . . my ski . . . starts to *turn,* just like Mark said it would . . . and that makes my whole body turn, like I am standing in the center of a slow-moving merry-go-round. The ski turns so that instead of going *across* the hill, it is now going *down* the hill . . . *straight down* . . . toward the Lift House! Now I am pedaling faster, because I am going straight instead of making a big turn! Looking at the snow blower is not working! I am going faster and faster, and now way too fast!

So I turn my head to Mark, who is about ten feet up the hill from the snow blower. And I think in my mind about my ski turning and pretend my mind is like a magnet that can move things the way the North Pole can. Skis have metal in them, right? And when I look at Mark, I feel my toes and ankle turning sideways, so I know my ski is going sideways, too, since it is attached to my toes and ankle. Then . . . I *turn* and I slide across the trail to where Mark is standing.

"Good skiing," he says.

"Thanks," I say.

I look around at the other skiers. They are all wearing dark goggles, so I can't tell if they are staring at me or not. But usually people stare at me wherever I go since I have one leg, so I bet they are looking at me here, too, only this time maybe they are staring because they are amazed by my skiing. I hope so. I would rather have people look at me because I am good at something than because I lost something to cancer.

We start again. Every time Mark skis out in front of me, he adds another turn. I know this because I count them. The first time there was one turn, then two, then three, then four. I can't believe that I can make four turns in a row! Then we are back at the Lift House. I smile at the man in the Massanutten jacket. He presses the yellow button and grabs my elbow and Mark pushes me into the chair again, but I'm not scared this time because I know he will push me right at the exact second the chair is behind my knee.

"How old are you?" Mark asks after we are flying high again.

"Ten."

"My son is eight."

"Oh."

"He's one of the fastest skiers on the mountain."

"Oh, okay."

Finding out about Mark's fast-skiing son makes me wonder why Mark is with me, instead of with him, since it is Saturday and Saturday is the day that dads play with their sons. But Mark is playing with *me*. It's like I have two dads—my real Dad and Mark—for today, and Mark's son doesn't have any dads at all. I guess I got lucky.

By the end of my day of skiing, I don't fall anymore when I get off the lift, and I can ski straight down the hill, right past all of the people who thought I fell because I have one leg. I am a faster skier than all of them, and it's the first time I have been fast since last year, when I had two legs and I could run. It's the exact opposite of how I always feel in the hospital when I sit in the children's terrace attached to chemotherapy tubes and look out of the windows that go from the floor to the ceiling so you have a very nice view of the cars and people free to go wherever they want, as fast as they want, seven floors below you on the earth.

I have my second ski lesson a month later. Mark is my instructor again. After he takes me on all the easy trails and I don't fall even once, he says that since none of these runs is challenging for me anymore I am ready to ski the hardest trail on the mountain, which is called a black diamond. I tell him I am not sure I can do it, but he says it is not as hard as it looks from the bottom. So we get on the lift for the black diamond trail.

When we are riding up the ski lift, Mark usually tells me stories about ski patrol. Most of his stories are about people who skied too fast and got hurt.

"You see that blower?" he asks, pointing his outrigger toward the side of the black diamond trail that we are riding the lift for.

"Yeah," I say.

"You're ready for this trail. You know that, right? But there're always other people on this trail who shouldn't be here," he says. "Once last year when I was out on patrol, a fellow came flying down here with so much speed that he ran right into that snow blower."

"Oh," I say. "Was he all right?"

"No . . . unfortunately he didn't make it."

I am about to ask Mark what it was exactly this fellow didn't make, but then I think maybe he means the fellow got hurt, and I would rather not hear about that since I am already very afraid of this trail.

After we get off the lift, I look down. It is much steeper than it looked at the bottom. It is so steep that it's almost straight down, like a cliff. I am sure I will fall off and die, and at my funeral people will feel sorry for me because I had one leg and they'll think that's why I fell off the steep trail and died. And they will be surprised that I died from skiing, not from cancer, like they thought might happen. But no one will want to say this because they will not want to admit they were expecting me to die from the cancer. When you have cancer, everyone is supposed to act like God is going to heal you and you are going to live, even if that's not what they really think inside. And Mom would be mad at me at my funeral because I wasn't careful when I was skiing like she told me to be. And Matthew would be mad, too, because I promised him I wasn't going to die, but then I broke my promise and did it anyway. But while I am thinking about people at my funeral, Mark says to not be afraid, to just ski like I did on the beginner trail. Just make really big turns.

"Are you sure I can do this?" I ask.

"Definitely."

"Maybe we should ride back down on the lift," I say.

"Trust me, Joshua. I've taught a lot of skiers. You are a natural."

Then he skis away from me, holding his left foot up in the air. He makes a big, slow turn across the hill on his one ski and outriggers and then stops. So I take a deep breath and hold it and then I lean forward so my ski starts to slide in the track he's just made, and I follow it all the way to where he is standing.

"See, that wasn't so hard, was it?" he asks.

"No, I guess not," I say.

I make it down the whole black diamond trail without falling or running into any snow blowers and not making it, and Mark tells me I should come back the next week to a race for handicapped skiers. I have a chemo treatment starting that day, but I ask Mom and Dad if I can please please please skip the chemo and go to the race, because I want to win first place. Mom and Dad say no, I can't skip chemotherapy. But I keep asking until Mom says she will reschedule the chemo for one day later.

At the race, Mark says that I will be competing in a category called "Three-Trackers," since I make three tracks in the snow with my two outriggers and one ski.

"How many other three-trackers are there in the race?" I ask.

"You're the only one," he says.

"So . . . who am I racing against?"

"The clock," he says.

The clock? That doesn't make sense! A clock is not a three-tracker, and it doesn't even ski. I can't *believe* this! I spent this whole week, this *whole week*, looking forward to winning today. I even did push-ups to get in shape so I could win. But now . . . there is no one to race against. I can't win first place anymore, because to win first place, someone else always has to get second.

But . . . I guess even if I can't win, I do like skiing fast. Skiing is the only time I get to go fast anymore. So I will still ski today, just for fun.

I ski through the race course eight times. Afterward, there is an awards ceremony where Mark gives out medals for each category—blind skiers, skiers with one arm, skiers in wheelchairs, skiers who drool and can't talk right, skiers who walk funny and can't move their left arm, and of course, three-trackers. Since I am the only three-tracker, I get eight gold medals.

After people clap for me, I tell Mom and Dad the eight medals are stupid since I was last place, and they say, no, I was first place, and I say that, no, I was last place, and we keep arguing until an old man walks over and puts his hand on my shoulder.

"Son, I watched you ski today," he says.

"Okay," I say.

"I want to tell you something."

"Okay."

He looks at Mom and Dad, and then back at me.

"I used to coach the United States Paralympic ski team. Have you ever heard of that?"

"No, sir," I say.

"The Paralympics is the Olympics for people with disabilities," he says. "Ski racing is one of the sports in the Paralympics. Like I said, I saw you ski today, and I want you to know that you have great potential."

I look down from his face to his jacket, which is shiny and has a zipper down the middle and is red, white, and blue. On his chest, right in the middle, there are three big patches sewn on. They spell "USA." The patches are big and white and strong looking. Then I look down from his jacket to his pants, and I see that they are made out of the same red, white, and blue shiny material, and they have the same USA patches, just smaller, near the top of the left pant leg.

"Did you—did you get that jacket at the Paralympics?" I ask.

"Yes," he says.

"What about your pants?"

"Yes. And a hat and a few other things, too. Whole uniform, I got there."

From skiing? A uniform? Really? *Could I wear it to church?*

"If I went to the Paralympics to ski race," I ask, "do you think I would get a whole uniform like that?"

"Of course," he says, patting me on the back. "Of course."

Then he winks at me, nods to Mom and Dad, and walks away before I can ask him where I sign up for the Paralympics, because that's what I want to do as soon as I finish this chemotherapy. I want to finish chemo, let my hair grow back, then sign up for the Paralympics and get a uniform. It will be even better than the uniform Aaron wore to church, because his is just plain green. Mine will have three different colors and it will say "USA" on it. And it will be shinier than his, too. If I wear my uniform to church, everyone will want to be friends with me and Keisha will want to kiss me, even though she moved away, so I will have to mail her a picture of it. But I will get the uniform and I will win ski races, maybe even ski races that have other three-trackers in them so I don't get first place and last place at the same time like I did today. Then my life will be perfect.

I have my last chemotherapy treatment two months later, almost exactly one year after I started. Right on time. My immune system didn't get really tired like Dr. Kimberly Dunsmore, my main doctor who always carries a clipboard, warned us about. In fact, my immune system got tired and delayed my chemo treatments only once in the entire year, which was the time I was sent home and then got to learn how to ski the next day. So I guess if I hadn't been delayed that one time, I wouldn't have gotten to learn how to ski. It's one of those bad things that God uses for good purposes like Dad always talks about.

To celebrate the end of chemo, we have a big party on the playground behind the church where all the people who helped our family by cooking, cleaning, giving me presents, taking Matthew to Purcell Park to make him feel happy, shaving their heads for me, and mowing our lawn for free—they all come to talk about how great it is that I finished. I beat the cancer! I won! Praise God! High-five!

We all smile and eat a cake that says, "No Mo' Chemo," and talk about whether my hair will still be brown when it grows back, or if it might be a different color now. I tell people that I hope it doesn't come back red because I don't want red hair, and if it does come back red, I will dye it bright green. Mom hears me say this, and I think she will tell me I am not allowed to have green hair, but instead she laughs louder than she has laughed in a long, long time and hugs me. Since she doesn't say no about the green hair, that means yes, I am allowed to, so I start praying every day that God will let my hair grow back red so I can dye it green.

11

"So, the doctors and nurses at the hospital," Steve Young says, "they must be wonderful people, huh?"

Steve Young—I know he is famous because he's the quarterback for the San Francisco 49ers—wants me to say that the doctors and nurses at the hospital were wonderful people. He wants me to say this because we are on *Children's Miracle Network Telethon,* and people need to call the number on their screen and make a donation to help the children.

The problem is, the doctors and nurses were *not* always wonderful people. There was the nurse who dug the needle around in my arm to find a vein—and she was there when the doctors pulled me off Mom to take me to surgery, too. And there was the doctor who lied about pulling the drainage tube out of the place where my leg was cut off. Also, there was the nurse with red hair who put in the barbed-wire catheter, which is not something a wonderful person would ever do.

But I am almost eleven years old now, so I am old enough to know that people like the nurses and doctors are not like people in movies. People in movies are always either good guys or bad guys. And you always know which one is which, because the good guys have white teeth and they don't laugh really loud when they talk about taking over the world. But real people are not like people in movies. Real people do some good things and some bad things. They are in between. So even though there were times when the doctors and nurses were not wonderful, I know they *were* wonderful sometimes, too. Like when Mom gave Dr. Dunsmore a picture of me skiing, and Dr. Dunsmore said I looked like a very fast skier and hung the picture on the wall in her office.

So I decide it's all right to tell Steve Young that yes, the doctors and the nurses were wonderful, and people should pick up the phone and make a donation. Besides, this is just a rehearsal. The live broadcast that will be on TV won't start for another two hours.

After the rehearsal, Dad and I go to a big room down the hall where you can eat free sandwiches. Since I am going to be on TV soon, I try not to spill any mustard on my shirt, which is a Mickey Mouse shirt because *Children's Miracle Network* broadcasts from Disneyworld. This morning I also put lots of Level Five Most Extreme Hold Gel in my hair to make sure it looked perfect. My hair has had nine months to grow back—brown, same as before, too bad—so now it looks like normal hair and you would never know I used to be bald.

After Dad and I eat our sandwiches, we are walking back down a hallway to the studio for my interview with Steve Young when a door opens and out walks a man who I know is famous because I have seen him on TV. He is Coach K, the coach of the Duke Blue Devils basketball team.

"Hi, Joshua!"

Are there other people named Joshua in this hallway?

I look around.

Nope. Just Dad, me, Coach K. No one else named Joshua.

So how does he know me?

"I saw you on the practice of the broadcast," he says, like he could read the question in my mind. "You did great!"

"Thanks," I say.

"How're you doing? You ready to be on national TV?"

"Yeah, I guess . . . but I'm nervous," I say.

Coach K smiles.

"I'm going to tell you what I tell my players," he says. "When someone does great in practice, I know that they can be amazing when it comes to game time because they can use the excitement of the game to help them play even better."

I nod. "Okay," I say.

"Joshua, you did well in practice," Coach K says. "You'll be amazing when you're on the real thing."

"Thanks," I say.

"Of course. Nice to meet you."

Coach K puts out his hand, and I shake it.

"Hey while you're here," Dad says. "Can we—can Joshua have your autograph?"

I look at Dad and try to make the half-frowning look Mom gives him when she doesn't like something he's just said. I do this because the rule at *Children's Miracle Network* is that you are not allowed to ask for autographs because the famous people are busy, and afterward they will all mail autographed pictures to your house. But my frown doesn't really matter since Dad's already said it.

"Oh—uh—sure," Coach K says, smiling.

"Go ahead, give him your autograph book, Joshua," Dad says.

I have an autograph book in my pocket because I bought it before I knew there was a rule about not asking for autographs. I hand it to Coach K.

"Do you have—" Coach K starts to ask.

"A pen?" Dad says. "Yeah, here. Just a second."

Dad unzips the bag he wears around his waist. He bends his neck, touching his chin to his chest so he can look for a pen inside while he digs around in the bag with his fingers.

"There it is."

He puts the pen in his mouth and bites down on the cap. Then he pulls on the pen and it slides out, leaving the cap between his teeth. His other hand is still digging in the bag, and it comes out holding a map of Disneyworld. Dad scribbles on the map.

"No, this one's dry," he says, and his voice sounds funny since there is a cap in his mouth.

He pushes the pen back into the cap in his teeth—he has to do this slowly and carefully so that he doesn't miss the cap and stick the ink part of the pen on his tongue, which would be bad because ink is poisonous if you eat it. He puts the pen back in the bag and pulls out another one. This pen doesn't have a cap. It has a button on the end that you push, which he does, with his thumb, to make the ink part pop out, *click*. Dad tests this second pen on the map.

"This one seems to be working," he says

Dad hands the pen to Coach K, but he holds the side of the pen with the button on it so that the ink part is facing Coach K. Coach K turns his hand around sideways and grabs the pen in the middle so he doesn't get ink on the palm of his hand.

"To Joshua," he scribbles on my pad. "Mike 'Coach K' Krzyzewski."

"Here you go," he says, handing me the autograph book and Dad the pen.

We thank him and shake his hand again, and then we hurry to the studio because it is almost time for my interview. I sit in a tall chair beside Steve Young, and he holds a microphone. There are so many lights I have to squint, and the only things I can see clearly are the microphone and Steve Young standing beside me. I look down, and there is a TV on the ground facing up toward us that I can barely see because of the lights. The TV is playing the video that the director with the three-hundred-dollar sunglasses made at our house. Dad is on the screen, and even though the sound is turned off, I can tell that he is crying whenever he answers a question. And then my part of the video comes on the screen, and I know that I am probably answering a question about *finishing*—

which, I can now say, I did. I finished. I am done with chemotherapy and hospitals forever.

Then I see a red light flash on top of one of the cameras. Steve Young starts talking about how he's Steve Young and you're watching *Children's Miracle Network*.

"We are joined right now by cancer survivor Joshua Sundquist, who just won eight gold medals in the recent Rainbow Games. Joshua, how did you win eight gold medals with one leg?"

Why does Steve Young have to keep asking me such hard questions? Why can't he just ask me what I want to be when I grow up, like all the other adults in the world do? His question is an impossible question to answer, because the real answer, the true answer, is that I won the medals because I was the only person in my category. I didn't win. I just went through the finish line. I would've gotten the medals even if I had gone through the course backward, or if I had stopped halfway down the hill and done all my homeschooling for the entire year before I finished the race. But I can't tell Steve Young this, because we are on TV and that wouldn't make people want to give money to the hospitals. So instead of saying that I won eight gold medals because I wasn't racing against anyone, I laugh a little—so it sounds like I am surprised I won so many medals—and say, "A lot of hard training."

Children's Miracle Network has a party for all the famous people and for the people who operated the cameras and for the kids like me and their families. At the party, there are seven different tables with food on them, and you are allowed to go back to the tables as many times as you want to get more. It's like the All-U-Can-Eat Country Vegetable Bar at Country Cookin, except instead of spinach and green beans, this party has food like pies filled with eggs and cheese that are so small you can put the whole thing in your mouth at once, strawberries covered with chocolate that breaks into pieces and falls on the floor when you bite it, and rolled-up crunchy things with spicy chicken inside. Mom says this kind of food is called or-durvz. Or-durvz is my new favorite food.

There is a man at the party who stands behind a tall table and has a hose that squirts out Sprite. He will use the hose to fill up your cup with Sprite as many times as you want, so I drink cup after cup. Adults also come to his tall table, and he gives them drinks in glass bottles that I know are beer because I have seen beer commercials on TV even though Mom tries to turn off the TV when they come on. Other adults, mostly the girl adults, drink a red drink from cups that have a long, thin piece of glass connecting the part of the cup that holds the red drink to another part, a circle-shaped flat part that sits on the table. Dad says the red drink in the cups is wine, and the cups are special cups called wineglasses.

I know that Mom and Dad won't drink the beer or wine because beer and wine are alcohol, and it is a sin to drink alcohol. One time I asked Dad why, if it is a sin to drink alcohol, Jesus turned water into wine at someone's wedding. Dad said lots of Christians believe that the wine wasn't really wine at all, and it was actually water, and the miracle was that Jesus tricked everyone into *thinking* that it was wine. I thought it was very strange that Jesus would trick people into thinking they were sinning, and maybe people just believe this because it would be too hard for them to believe that some parts of the Bible say it's a sin to drink alcohol and other parts don't.

I am surprised that people at this party, the ones who are drinking alcohol, are not hitting each other with their fists, like Mom and Dad told me people do when they drink too much wine or beer. In fact, they look very, very happy. They are the happiest group of people I have ever seen. Everyone is sipping alcohol and smiling, and the women in black dresses are all laughing at the jokes the men tell. The women hold their wine cups with one hand and put their other hand on the men's forearms.

"Ha! Ha Ha!" they say. "That is just . . . *soooooo* funny."

The people who drink alcohol also dance. But they don't dance the way people dance at the weddings I've been to for homeschoolers, where everyone takes steps at the same time and the couples hold one set of hands together and put the other set on each other's shoulders. The people at this party, who drink alcohol, they dance the way Luke dances when we are watching TV and a song comes on. Luke—he's two years old now—jumps up off the floor and starts jumping around, flapping his arms. We all laugh, and as long as we keep laughing, he keeps dancing.

Maybe he dances because he is happy that he doesn't have diarrhea anymore, now that Mom took him to Dr. Speckhart, who is different from other doctors because he is a Homeopathic Doctor. (He is called "homeopathic" because instead of going to see him at the hospital, you go to see him at his home.)

"Do you want to dance?"

I look up from the pyramid of chocolate-covered strawberries on my plate and see that a very pretty girl with a sparkly crown in her hair is standing in front of me. She is Miss America. I know this because she has a sign hanging from her shoulder that says, "Miss America." I do not want to dance with her because I have a fake leg and I don't know how to dance with a fake leg. But I also don't want to say no, because I don't want to hurt her feelings and make her think she's not pretty, even though she is Miss America which means she is the prettiest girl in America.

So I don't say anything, and I look back down at my chocolate-covered strawberries.

"I'll dance!" Matthew says.

Miss America smiles.

"Great!" she says.

Matthew takes her hand and they walk to the part of the room that has a big square of wood on the floor, wood so shiny it almost looks wet, and they dance on it. Everyone in our family—Mom,

Dad, Luke, and me—we all sit and watch Matthew dance, and we are happy because Matthew is happy. We watch Miss America put her hand on Matthew's shoulder while she laughs, bent over, at his jokes. He laughs, too. Matthew laughs and dances just like all the drunk people. It's like all the music and all the people flow into his blood and make him seem drunk even though he hasn't had any beer or wine.

"I'm really hot!" Matthew says as he throws Mom his jacket, which is sweaty.

Now he is just wearing the parts of his suit that match the jacket—gray pants and a gray vest that has buttons down the front and no sleeves. He has on a black clip-on tie, like I do, because neither of us knows how to tie a real tie like Dad does before work every morning.

After he gets done dancing with Miss America, Matthew walks up to the stage in between songs and taps the singer of the band on her leg.

"Um—Paul? Paul? Matthew is . . . doing something," Mom says to Dad.

We watch as the singer bends her knees so Matthew can whisper something in her ear. She nods, and he climbs up onstage.

"We have a special request," the singer says into the microphone. "For the YMCA."

People cheer.

"Yay!"

"YMCA!"

I am confused because I don't know what the YMCA is, but Matthew just special-requested it, and he is only eight and I am ten, almost eleven. How does he know a song that I don't know?

"Come on, let's dance!" Dad says, grabbing Mom's hand so she will stand up. "You, too, Joshua. Luke! Luke, come over here! There you go, stand up!"

"But I don't know how to dance with a fake leg," I say.

"The YMCA is easy," Dad says. "Here, I will teach you."

Dad shows me how to make arm motions that are like the letters *Y-M-C-A,* except that the *M* looks more like a heart with your head in the middle, and the *A* is pretty much an *O.*

Matthew is still up front, dancing like a crazy person, and people are cheering for him. When the chorus comes, the singer holds the microphone in front of Matthew's mouth so he can sing and do the dance motions at the same time.

"*Y-M-C-A!*" Matthew yells, waving his arms and jumping from side to side.

Mom, Dad, and I all do the motions, too, standing on the shiny wooden floor. Everyone in the room—all the famous people, Miss America, everyone—they all follow Matthew's lead. Even Luke lifts his two-year-old hands up in the air every time he sees us make the *Y.*

12

I have scans every three months. The day before, Mom always calls the prayer chain, asking for no sign of cancer. Then, the next morning, we go to the hospital. I have all the scans, and then we go home and wait around by the phone until Dr. Dunsmore calls to say that there is no cancer. Dad orders pizza, the kind with white dough and pepperonis on it, from Pizza Hut. Then we eat it together and wait three more months.

It's been one year since I finished chemotherapy, and I am at the hospital for scans again. Mom and I are at the front desk, ready to check out, go home, and order pizza. But the receptionist says, "Oh, there's a note here . . . Dr. Dunsmore wants to see you before you leave."

"Before we leave? Are you sure?" Mom asks.

"Yes, ma'am."

"Usually she just calls after we get home—but the note—she wants to see us now?"

"That's what it says."

A nurse comes out and says they have a room ready for us. So we leave the crowded, noisy waiting area and she leads us to one of the rooms where I had chemotherapy eighteen times in one year, where I spent one hundred nights of my life. I will never spend another night here no matter what this meeting is about, even if it is—could it be? No, no way, not me, not after I've come this far and after so many people have prayed . . . No. I can feel my heart. I can feel it because it is beating so fast.

"I'm going to go to the bathroom," I say to Mom.

"Okay," she says.

I walk on my crutches into the bathroom and urinate, which feels strange because I've hardly ever urinated in a toilet here at the hospital. When I was on chemotherapy I always had to use that jug, with Mom or Dad holding it in front of me.

I stand at the sink and wash my hands, looking at myself in the mirror above the sink. Hair. With gel in it. And eyebrows, real eyebrows, right above my eyes. When I was on chemo, people always said my face looked pale.

I wipe my hands on a brown paper towel and throw it in the trash can. Then I go back to the room and sit on the bed, waiting. Mom is looking at a book, but I can tell she is not really reading it because her eyes aren't moving. They stay focused on one spot behind the page. I know she is sad, and this makes me sad, too.

There is a knock on the door as it opens. That's how doctors enter your room. They knock and open the door at the same time.

"Hey guys," says Dr. Dunsmore.

"Hi," Mom says.

This is the part when Mom usually asks Dr. Dunsmore how her kids are doing, and Dr. Dunsmore says they are well. But Mom doesn't ask about Dr. Dunsmore's kids today.

"Sorry to keep you waiting," Dr. Dunsmore says.

She looks at her clipboard and leans her head to the left. Her hair falls to that side. Dr. Dunsmore has blond hair now. When I had cancer it was brown, so she must have dyed it recently. Or maybe she was dying it before, and blond is actually her natural color.

"I wanted to let you know before you leave today—"

This is bad news. If she had good news she would smile and say "good news," not "I wanted to let you know." This cannot be good news. Well . . . maybe . . . maybe it is not bad or good, it is just . . .

news. Something like, I wanted to let you know that . . . I got a new job at a different hospital . . . we are expanding the children's wing next year . . . I've decided to go back to my natural hair color . . .

"—that we've reviewed your CT scan, and the preliminary results show—"

No, it is bad news. She looks sad. She doesn't want to tell me this news.

"—there are three small spots on your lungs. Two in one, one in the other."

I look down at her shoes, which are red.

"Now, we don't know what the spots are, and there's—there's certainly no reason to think they are cancer yet. But unfortunately they are too small to biopsy right now."

No reason to think they are cancer? What else could they be? Just random spots on my lungs? Yeah, right. Of course they are cancer. Why else would you be telling us about this before we go home? Why else would you be getting us a private room where you can tell us about spots and biopsies and unfortunately they are too small to biopsy right now? It's cancer.

"What do we do?" asks Mom.

"Wait. Six weeks. Then come back for another CT scan. If they are bigger, then we operate."

Her shoes are red, shiny red, so they reflect the lights from the ceiling.

"Joshua, do you have any questions for me?"

I don't talk because I know if I talk I might cry, and Dr. Dunsmore has never seen me cry.

"Joshua?"

"No!"

I say it fast so I can close my throat before crying sounds come out. I keep my throat closed until we are alone in the minivan, and then I start crying, wailing uncontrollably.

I tried so hard! I thought I had finished! *Finished!* But I hadn't, really. Really, I lost. I lost the battle. And those people who prayed for me and *are praying* for me . . . right now, on the prayer chain . . . They will be crushed. I let them down. They came to my party and ate "No Mo' Chemo" cake and gave me high-fives because they thought I beat the cancer, but I didn't. I didn't beat anything. I just sat through a year of no hair and shots every day and sickness and sitting in hospital beds for . . . for . . . nothing! I lost my leg . . . for nothing! Now I am going to die and I *wasted* one of my two legs. I could still be playing soccer right now, right this very minute while people are praying for me, I could be playing soccer with two legs, and the cancer would be in my body just the same as it is now. I gave up everything and gained nothing.

And I thought . . . I hoped, I prayed . . . that I would be able to ski, be able to ski on the Paralympic ski team. I would not be able to play soccer, but at least I could ski and wear a Paralympic team uniform, a USA one. That was what I saw in my future, ever since that old man told me I had great potential. That was the photo I saw for my life. A picture of me in the future wearing the USA, the red, white, and blue with matching pants and jacket. But now skiing is gone, too. That photo, and the whole line of photos in my mind for my whole life, are gone. It's all gone. Everything. Gone.

We are back home in the family room and I sit on the floor in between the rocking chair and the window. I curl up on my side and wrap my arms around my leg.

Why would You do this, God? *How* could You do this? After I tried to be so happy for so long even though I had one leg, and I always said such *nice things* about You to other people? I always told them You were great, and You had a plan, so they should trust You. And now—*this*?

I see Dad's car drive up the block and park on the street in front of the house. He walks up the yard, and then I hear the *pop* of the deadbolt unlocking, and then the knob turns and the door swings. I don't hear Dad put his coat on the coat rack or slide his shoes off.

Instead, I hear his footsteps straight through the dining room, across the kitchen floor, and into the family room. Mom is sitting on the couch, and I am curled up behind the rocking chair, staring out the window. This is the window you can look through and see the backside of Massanutten, where I learned to ski. I hear Mom stand up.

"She called me at work," says Dad.

And then I hear a sound like when you take a coat out of your closet, because Dad's coat is brushing against Mom's sweater as they hug.

"She said"—Dad's voice cracks. "She said it might not be cancer," he says. His voice sounds muffled. His face must be pressed against Mom's neck.

Mom doesn't say anything, but I know they are still hugging, because I haven't heard their clothes brush against each other again.

"But when she told me"—Dad's voice cracks again—"she was crying."

And when Dad says that word, "crying," he starts crying himself. His cry is muffled against Mom's neck, but I can still hear it.

"Who? Dr. Dunsmore?" Mom asks.

"Yes," says Dad. "I asked her why she was crying, because she must see so many kids, and she said it was because . . . because Joshua has gotten to be pretty special to her."

I hear the sound of Mom and Dad's clothes moving, but it is the sound of them hugging tighter, not letting go.

I am still watching out the window. I see another car drive up the street and park behind Dad's car. Pastor Smuland gets out and walks to the front door. He comes in the house without knocking. Now I hear Dad hug Pastor Smuland.

It is quiet while I count one, two, three cars going by our house, which means a long time has passed because there aren't ever many cars on our street. That's why Mom and Dad wanted to move here. It's a quiet neighborhood, they said, so they wouldn't have to worry about our getting hit by a car if we played in the street. It would be such a safe place to raise a family, they thought. Such a safe place.

"How long?" asks Pastor Smuland, finally.

"Six weeks, then another CAT scan," Dad replies.

"No . . . I mean . . . how *long*?" asks Pastor Smuland.

When he says this, he and Dad and Mom leave the room and shut the door so I can't hear them talking anymore.

I keep looking out the window until it gets dark outside. Luke walks in and tries to give me a shoulder massage. He gives shoulder massages now because he's seen Matthew give them, only the ones Matthew gives are real shoulder rubs that go on for a few minutes and feel good. Luke's massage lasts about five seconds, and his hands are so small that it feels like a pinch, not a massage.

I smile at Luke because he is little and he doesn't understand. He doesn't know that I am dying, that the cancer has come back and I am dying. He also doesn't know that I am never going back on chemo. He leaves, and Mom and Dad walk back in and sit on the couch. I turn away from the window and look at them for the first time.

"I am not going to have any more chemo treatments," I say.

"What?" Mom asks.

"I said, I'm not having any more chemo."

"What will you do instead?" she asks.

"Not have them," I say.

"What—and just—*die*?" Mom asks.

Dad gives Mom a look.

"We don't know if it's cancer yet," he says.

"Don't know?" I say. "Come on! Dr. Dunsmore was *crying* when she told you."

"Well, your mother is right, if it is cancer you will need to have more chemotherapy," says Dad.

"Why?"

"Because we want you with us as long—we want you to live, Joshua," says Dad. "We love you."

But Mom and Dad don't understand. Chemo is just too hard, too terrible. I am not going to go through it again to get rid of the cancer and then have it come back a year later like it did this time. No. Cancer has already taken my leg and a year of my life, and now, today, it has taken something else—I don't know what, but I can feel that something is gone, cut out from inside me, like my leg was. The part that was cut out today was a part of something else, though, something I can't see or touch.

"I am done with chemo," I say.

"But if it's cancer—" says Dad.

"It's my life."

"We are your parents."

"So?" I say. "You can't make me—"

"Actually, since you are still a minor—"

"I can do whatever I want."

"We can . . . well . . . technically we can . . . *require* you to have treatment," Dad says. As soon as he says this, I can tell from his face that he wishes he hadn't.

"*Require me?* You are going to force me to have chemo?"

"We don't want to do that, Joshua."

"But you would?"

"We would do what's best for you."

"Which is forcing me to have treatment?'

"We love—"

"What, like the police would come and put me in handcuffs and stick an IV in my arm?" I ask. "You would just let them do it, let them drag me away in a wheelchair? Like you did when I had surgery? Just sit there and watch while they hold me down and pull my hands apart and drag me away?"

Mom starts crying when I say this, and seeing her cry makes me want to cry, but I don't cry because I hate Mom and Dad. They want to make me have more chemo while they just sit there on the couch and watch me lose my hair and my eyebrows and the color in my face.

I wait for Mom or Dad to say something else so I can argue more with them. Yelling at them like this makes me forget how sad I am. I spent all afternoon looking out the window, feeling like I couldn't move because my body was so heavy. But now that I am looking at Mom and Dad instead of looking out the window, it's like they have taken away my sadness and just made me angry, and now that I am mad my body isn't so heavy anymore.

Can they actually force me to have chemo? Probably, but only until I am sixteen. Then I can do what I want, because that's when people are allowed to drop out of school even if their parents don't want them to. So I will just stay on chemotherapy for five years, and then drop out of treatment when I turn sixteen . . . no . . . that won't work . . . five years is too long to be on chemo; no one could live through that. What will I do? I will go to the bank and get all my savings, and then buy a bus ticket and ride the bus to somewhere far away, like Kansas, and then use the rest of the money to buy food. Or I could tell people in Kansas I was an orphan and my parents died, and some other parents would adopt me, foster parents who would love me so much that they'd let me do whatever I wanted and would never make rules I had to follow.

I will wait six weeks. The day before Mom and Dad are going to make me have more chemotherapy, I will walk to the bank and get my money and then walk to the bus station and go to Kansas, or Nana and Papa's house, or maybe wherever Keisha lives now, and wait until Mom and Dad call and say all right, they are sorry, they won't make me have chemotherapy. If they don't say that, then I will just stay wherever I am forever. But at least I won't die in a hospital bed.

After I run away, Mom and Dad will feel bad for making me go on chemotherapy. Pastor Smuland and their friends will all ask, "Why did Joshua run away?" and Mom and Dad will have to say, "Because we tried to make him have another terrible year of chemotherapy treatments even though he didn't want to." And Pastor Smuland and their friends will nod and say, "Yeah, I guess you should've loved him enough to let him do what he wanted, huh?" And Mom and Dad will say, "Yes, we learned our lesson."

And Luke will be confused, because he won't understand why I don't live at our house anymore. Even if Mom and Dad try to explain it to him it won't make sense, because he is too young to have real thoughts. I wonder if he'll miss me? I will send him birthday presents and Christmas presents every year. It will be like he has a new uncle.

But if I run away Matthew might start breaking Mom and Dad's rules, because they always say that I am an example and Matthew does what I do. Hopefully he wouldn't actually run away just to be like me. He's only nine. That's too young to run away.

It will be hard to live by myself—even though I am eleven instead of nine—because there are a lot of things I still don't know how to do yet, like paying taxes and driving a car. And my friends from church will probably think it was a bad idea for me to run away, but that's because none of them has ever had chemotherapy, so they don't know how horrible it is, how tiring it is, how much it ruins your life, how you can't even really call it "a life" because being on chemotherapy is not the same as being alive.

On Sunday I decide to stay home from church by myself. Mom and Dad say I should come, because going to church is important. But I say no and then I don't say anything else even though they say lots of other things about why they want me to go. I'm not listening to the other things because I am totally sure that I am going to stay home no matter what. It's not because I am mad at God. Actually I *am* kind of mad at Him, but that's not why. I am staying home because of the people there, at church. I can't see them. And I can't let them see me. It's just too terrible. Those people spent an entire year helping my family. They mowed our lawn, cleaned our house, weeded our garden, and they took care of Matthew and Luke, too, on days when I was in the hospital. And almost every single night for the entire year, someone in the church made dinner and brought it over for us.

And this is why I can't go to church today. The people there gave so much to help my family when I had cancer. Besides making the meals, the taking care of Matthew and Luke, and the cleaning, they also shaved their heads for me, got T-shirts for me, and made a big quilt for me that everyone in the church signed. At the end of that year, they all came to my No Mo' Chemo party. They praised God because God had saved me, He had made me victorious over the disease, hallelujah.

But God—or maybe me, I'm not sure which—failed. The battle

with cancer has been lost. I can't go to church because I can't see the sadness that would be on their faces, sadness like they just lost the Most Important Annual Softball Game Ever, in extra innings. They would look at me with my family in the second row at the front of the church and know that God did not make me victorious.

I am not sure if I will ever be able to go to our church again, actually. Six weeks from now, when we know the cancer has come back, and I run away, I will have to find a new church somewhere else. But at my new church it will be good because there won't be people there who shaved their heads for me or made meals for our family. So at my new church, they won't be sad when they see me.

The next Sunday Mom and Dad say that I have to go to church since people there care about me and if I don't get out of bed and put on church clothes I won't be allowed to use the computer for the rest of the day. So I go. When I walk up the stairs to Sunday school, I stare down at my fake leg so I don't have to look at anyone. They all probably already know about the spots on my lungs because of the prayer chain. And no one claps for me when I walk in the room like they did right after I had my leg cut off. Today they are booing. They are booing to themselves, without making any noise.

"Boo!" they are thinking. "We shaved our heads for you! We prayed for you every night at bedtime! We came over to play with you when you had cancer, and we pretended it wasn't weird that you had one leg! We did all this for you, and now you are going to make us do it again because you couldn't beat the cancer the first time?"

Mrs. Marsh, my Sunday school teacher, is married to Dr. Mike Marsh, the doctor whom I first went to see when my leg started hurting almost two and a half years ago. Mrs. Marsh is also the one who plans the Lost River trip every summer, and she organizes the annual softball game there, too. She's a very good Sunday school teacher, because she makes jokes. But today I don't laugh at her jokes. I sit still and quiet and think about that Lost River trip, about when I went there and everyone was so happy, and it seemed like I was going to be able to beat the cancer and do things like learn to play softball and live my life like a normal person. Everything was so perfect.

Sunday school ends and we go home. I go to my room and sit on the floor and think about running away. Mom and Dad will be sad if I run away. But they shouldn't have decided to make me go back on chemotherapy. And Matthew will be sad, too. Maybe I should tell him my plan? Maybe he'd like to run away with me? No, he would probably tattletale and then Mom and Dad would watch me all the time to make sure I couldn't escape. So it will have to stay a secret for a few more weeks.

The days pass slowly. Sometimes I forget about the spots on my lungs for a few minutes. Sometimes I am doing schoolwork or playing on the computer and I just think thoughts like a normal person would, like "What is the answer to this math problem?" or "I like playing flight simulator and I am going to fly to Chicago." But then I remember these are the last six weeks that I will live at home and I get sad again. And even though I am sad, it's good to always remember like this because the more often you look at your watch, the slower time passes. I want time to pass so slowly that it almost stops, because I don't want to get to the day when I have go back and see Dr. Dunsmore again.

Usually when you get really bad news, you aren't expecting it. Like when I found out I had cancer the first time. I didn't expect that. Nobody did. But today, when the phone rings and it's Dr. Dunsmore, we *are* expecting it. We are ready. It's been six weeks, and this morning I had my X ray to look at the spots, and we've been sitting at home waiting to get the bad news that they've grown. Dr. Dunsmore will want me to have a biopsy right away to confirm that they are cancer, and then she will want me to start on chemotherapy. But none of that will happen, of course, because I'll be gone before tomorrow morning.

The good part about times like this, times when you know the bad news is coming, is that you can choose the person who will listen to the bad news from the doctor and then tell everyone else about it. You should always choose someone who is brave, because they have to be able to listen to the really bad news and still be able to ask important questions right afterward, to find out the facts. And you should also choose someone who is good at explaining things using nice words, so they can share the bad news with everyone else in the best way that the bad news can be shared. In our family, this person is Dad, because he is brave and good at explaining things. And I know this because even though he used to cry a lot the first time I had cancer, he was still brave. I could look at his face when he was crying and tell that he was brave and he would never be afraid, even with tears coming out of his eyes. Nothing could ever make him afraid because Dad believed in God, and God was in control.

But today, when he picks up the phone to listen to the results from Dr. Dunsmore, Dad looks like he is trying to be brave on the outside even though on the inside he is actually a little bit afraid. What is different this time that would make him afraid? What has changed? But maybe Dad hasn't changed at all. Maybe *I* have changed. Maybe he was always a little bit afraid inside before, but when I was nine, I could only see the brave parts.

Earlier today, while I was lying on the X-ray table, I prayed that maybe the news would be good and I wouldn't have to run away. I prayed that maybe the machine was broken or maybe the spots would disappear for a second and then not reappear until after the X ray was done taking the picture of my lungs. I knew that was a silly thing to pray for, because it would mean the cancer was actually still there, growing, taking over, even though the X ray couldn't see it.

But at least if the X rays came back negative, I wouldn't have to run away.

The news from Dr. Dunsmore, when Dad tells it to us, is not any of the types of news I would've expected—not what I had been afraid of and also not what I had been hoping for. It's not even news I thought about as something that might happen. It's totally surprising. It flows over my body, slowly, like someone poured a bucket of paint on my head—gray paint, because this news is not all the way black or white. It is both. It is gray.

What will this mean for my life? What now? I guess I won't run away, no, I guess I don't have to do that anymore. But what will I do later? Will I have to run away later? Will I keep going to tests like this?

"What do we do now?" I ask.

"Wait another six weeks."

"Then what—just get more tests?"

Dad nods.

"I don't understand," I ask. "Why haven't they changed?"

"She said she doesn't know."

"But they could still change?"

"Yes."

"Slow-growing cancer, probably," I say, hoping that Mom or Dad will argue with me, say no, no, Joshua, it's probably not cancer. Probably just something you breathed in the air.

But they don't say this. They look at each other and at the floor. Finally Mom says something. Not what I wish she would say, but something.

"We still don't know it's cancer, Joshua."

14

I am lying in my bed feeling much worse than just sick to my stomach. I feel lightheaded, like I am going to faint. It's like there's a rope attached to the inside of my head and someone in the ceiling keeps pulling on it, trying to lift my brain right out of my body.

It's pretty annoying. But it's not a dangerous symptom, really. It's only serious if the lightheadedness is combined with something else, like . . . oh, no! My chest hurts, too! Think for a second. Where does my chest hurt exactly? Center your thoughts. It hurts . . . on the left side . . . exactly where my heart is! Directly over my heart at the beating center of my life, there is pain right there, and I am lightheaded, too, which means only one thing: heart attack! The only other symptoms would be if my left hand got . . . oh, no! . . . my left hand is tingling . . . almost *numb*! Make a fist, touch fingertips against palms. Sweaty. Sweaty palms. All the major warning signs. All of them! Happening to me, right now!

I feel like I do when I am about to take a fall on the ski slopes, when I can see the snow coming up toward my face, when I have a final thought, like "Wow, this is really happening." That's how I feel tonight, but it's so much worse than crashing at Massanutten. This is a heart attack! I have all the symptoms so it must be a heart attack!

I know these symptoms because ever since I finished chemotherapy two years ago, I have tried to learn everything I can about the diseases and problems that can kill you unexpectedly: Heart attacks, strokes, blood clots that start in your leg and move up into your heart, brain tumors, aneurisms . . . If I learn about these diseases, if I know enough about the chances of getting them and about their symptoms, then they can't kill me. This is because these things are always unexpected, so if I am expecting them, they won't happen to me.

But why am I having a heart attack right now even though I knew all about it *and* expected it? What's going on? What caused this? Why? Could be a side effect, maybe—of one of the chemo drugs? Or maybe it's . . . the spots! The spots on my lungs! Of course! They haven't been growing on any of the X rays I have every six weeks, but now they've finally started getting bigger and they've jumped straight from my lungs over to . . . my heart! The cancer has taken over my heart, and now it is barely beating and barely able to pump blood into my brain! Soon I won't even be able to think anymore, because my brain will shut down! Got to . . . get help! Tell someone! Before it's too late!

I skip down the hall on my crutches and into Mom and Dad's room.

I grab Dad by the shoulders.

"Dad! Dad! Wake up!" I whisper.

Dad groans.

"Uuuuuuuuuuuuuuuuuuuuuuuuuuuuuuuuuuuuuuuuuuuuuuuuh."

I shake him until he opens his eyes.

"Dad, I think I am having a heart attack!" I whisper.

His eyes open all the way.

"What?" he asks, in a normal voice.

"I am having heart attack . . . symptoms."

Dad removes his covers and jumps out of bed in one motion. He steps into a pair of sneakers and drops his keys and wallet in the flannel pocket of his pajamas.

"Come on!" he says, and I know that he means to the hospital. He tells Mom that we'll be back soon.

I've been to the emergency room before, back when I fell out of the tree five years ago when I was seven. The main thing I remember about that trip to the emergency room was that we had to wait *forever*, almost all day it seemed like, to get called out of the waiting area. Tonight I learn that the way to get helped fast in the emergency room is to tell the lady at the front desk that you're having a heart attack. She doesn't tell you to sit down and wait for your name to be called. She doesn't even make you fill out any forms or ask to see your Dad's insurance card.

"Follow me," she says.

She gets up and walks fast—sort of like running, but not quite—down a hallway. She tells me to wait in a little room. I hate waiting in little rooms.

In just thirty seconds, a nurse comes in—"Take off your shirt"—and glues stickers all over my chest. They are like the ones the physical therapist put on my back right after my leg was cut off, the ones she used to shock me with level-fifteen electricity. The stickers on my chest are attached to wires coming out of a machine. This machine has a screen on it that shows lines for my heartbeat, up and down, up and down, like a little kid drawing a picture of Massanutten over and over.

I know that I will probably not live long enough to get on the United States Paralympic team like that old coach said I could at my first ski race. I won't get a uniform that has "USA" on it. I've known this ever since the spots showed up on my lungs, actually. The cancer will come back, and I will only have a few years left—not enough time to get good at ski racing. But tonight, it's not a few years anymore, not even a few months. I have a few hours, at the most. I'm not ever going to get old and married and have sex. I'm never going to turn thirteen and be a teenager, or turn sixteen and be allowed to watch PG-13 movies! I won't even be around at the start of next year to see my new brother or sister when Mom has her baby!

After some papers print off the machine, the nurse leaves, carrying them in her hand. And then we wait. We wait and wait and wait, until a doctor comes in to say that my heart looks normal.

"Normal?" I ask.

"Yes, completely."

"Could it be something that wouldn't show up on that test?"

"No."

I look at Dad. I want him to yell at the doctor and tell him that there is definitely something wrong with me, and that he'd better find out what it is because we are going to stay right here until he does. But Dad looks worried, like he's not sure what he should say.

The doctor starts talking again.

"Joshua, do you have any history of panic attacks?"

"Panic what?"

"Panic attacks."

"What's that?"

"He doesn't," Dad says.

"Panic attacks are when—" the doctor says.

"He has no histor—"

"—you become anxious—that is, really worried about something," the doctor says, loudly, so Dad stops talking. "And it translates into physical—the worries that you have make your body feel things, like shortness of breath, feeling like you are going to faint, sweaty palms."

The doctor stops talking so I can think about this. He wants me to notice that these things he is talking about are the same things that I felt tonight. And I do notice. I see that they are the same symptoms. But I don't want to admit it because I don't want to be having a panic attack. That would mean that I got really worried for nothing. That would be stupid.

The doctor starts talking again.

"That may have been the case here," the doctor says. "So I'd like you to go home and attempt to acquire some rest. If these symptoms persist for twenty-four hours, then return to the ER."

I frown and I clench my teeth together so hard it makes my jaw hurt. This doctor is so wrong! He is so wrong, and because of him I am going to die at home, in my bed, attempting to acquire some rest. I only hope afterward Mom and Dad sue him, so he feels really stupid.

"All right, thanks, Doctor," I say, but with a type of voice that sounds like I am saying, "You're wrong, and you are going to feel stupid when I die and you get sued."

But I guess he was right. A few months go by, and I'm still alive. And I guess he was also right the other times I went back to the emergency room thinking I was having a heart attack, or that my lungs were collapsing, or that I had a brain aneurism, and he rolled his eyes when he thought I wasn't looking. But yeah, I guess he was always right, because I keep staying alive. And the spots haven't grown, either. I still go back and get X rays every six weeks, and Dad is still the one who picks up the phone when Dr. Dunsmore calls, in case it is Bad News. So far, though, only Good News.

And then . . . I get some *really* good news. One Sunday afternoon when we are driving home from church, Mom says, "Joshua, I heard about something you might be interested in."

"What?"

"I think it was called . . . 'Mountain Cruisers.' It's a ski racing development program at Massanutten."

"Wow! Really? Can I be in it?"

"Yes, Dad and I have talked about it, and you can join this winter . . . *if* you would like."

She looks at Dad and smiles when she says "if."

"Yeah! That would be awesome! Wait. Who will pay for it?"

"We will, as long as you go to the practice every week."

"Awesome, thank you!" I say. I would give Mom a hug, but I am not supposed to take off my seatbelt while the car is moving.

"You're welcome," Mom says. Her voice sounds happy. Normally Mom's voice does not sound happy when she is thinking about spending money on something expensive, but skiing is the one expensive thing that Mom and Dad usually seem happy to pay for. And that's really lucky for me, since now that I have one leg, skiing is the only sport I can really play.

And I am *so* happy about this Mountain Cruisers program, because ever since I met that old man at that race when I had cancer, I have been wanting to become a ski racer and get a Paralympic uniform. Hopefully the Mountain Cruisers will help me with this. Hopefully. But I'm not sure.

See, that's the difference between the Paralympics and travel soccer teams. When you have two legs and you want to play on a travel soccer team, it's easy, because all you do is tell your mom you want to sign up, and then she calls the coach and tells him that you will be coming to tryouts. Then your mom puts the date on the calendar, and you go try out for the team. If you are good enough, the coach gives you a green uniform and a schedule for the season. If you aren't, you go home and try again next year. That's how you get on a travel soccer team. But I don't know how you get on the Paralympic team. I don't know the number to call. I don't know when the sign-ups are. And I don't know where the tryouts are, either.

That's why I am so happy about Mountain Cruisers. Hopefully it's the answer I have been looking for. I can go up to Massanutten for Mountain Cruiser practice, learn how to race, and then maybe the Paralympic team coaches will hear about me somehow, or see me at one of the race practices, and then they will call Mom and Dad and ask if it would be all right if I went to the Paralympics. Maybe that's how you get on the U.S. team.

I am *finally* going to ski race!

15

It takes forever for winter to come. When it finally does, I am so excited in the van on the way to the first Mountain Cruiser practice that I am shaking in the backseat. I look out the window. It's starting to get dark. Skiing in Virginia is best at night, under the lights, because that's when the temperature goes below freezing so the slush freezes over into ice and you can go fast. Actually, it doesn't even have to be quite at freezing—which is thirty-two degrees Fahrenheit, zero degrees Celsius, and I can't remember what it is in Kelvin—because Massanutten treats their snow with chemicals to raise the freezing point. I know this because Mom made me write a four-page paper about it in homeschool science class.

On the first lift ride up the mountain—it's the same lift I rode with Mark Andrews the very first time I came skiing—I sit beside another boy in the Mountain Cruisers program. His name is Lee.

"How old are you?" I ask him.

"Thirteen. How old are you?"

"Thirteen."

"What school do you go to?"

"I am homeschooled."

"That sucks."

"What do you mean 'that stinks'?"

"Sucks," he corrects me.

But I said "stinks" on purpose because I am not allowed to use the word "sucks." I am also not allowed to use words like "gosh," "golly," "gee," "dang," "darn," or "shoot." This is because all of these words are euphemisms, which is a type of word that sounds like a cuss word even though it isn't one. Using euphemisms, Mom and Dad say, is a way of cussing without actually using the cuss words, which means it is just as bad, if not worse. So anytime someone in our family says a euphemism, they have to pay a ten-cent fine to Mom and Dad. But it turns out the only person who ever uses euphemisms is Dad, who says, "Oh golly!"—a euphemism for saying, "Oh my God," which is taking the Lord's name in vain, which is one of the Ten Commandments—whenever he is really surprised about something. Dad used to pay himself a dime whenever he said a euphemism, but then Matthew said this wasn't fair, because it was still Dad's money after he paid. So now Dad pays Matthew and me each a nickel whenever we catch him using a euphemism.

Another thing I learned about recently in homeschool is Venn diagrams. Here is a Venn diagram of (1) things Dad says a lot, and (2) euphemisms:

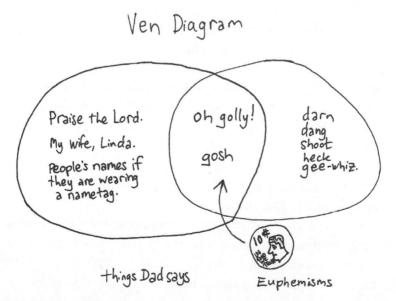

Ven Diagram

Praise the Lord.
My wife, Linda.
People's names if they are wearing a nametag.

Oh golly!
gosh

darn
dang
shoot
heck
gee-whiz.

things Dad says   Euphemisms

But most people aren't homeschooled and Christian, so they use euphemisms and say other words we aren't allowed to say, like "sucks," like Lee does when I tell him I am homeschooled.

"So if you are homeschooled, do you have any friends?" he asks.

"Yeah, of course."

"How many?"

"I don't know, a lot."

"Like how many?"

"Maybe twenty-five."

"Well at my school there are eight hundred people, and I know almost all of them."

"Wow," I say. "That's a lot of people."

"Do you have a girlfriend?"

"No, I am not allowed to date until I am sixteen."

"What the! Sixteen?"

"Yeah."

"Man that *really* sucks," he says. "At my school there are tons of girls who like me. At the last dance, I danced with seven girls."

"You have dances?"

"Yeah, two of them every year."

"And you get to dance with girls?"

"Duh."

I would like to dance with girls. I would also like to meet the *four hundred girls* at his middle school. That would be so awesome.

"But don't you have a lot of homework?" I ask.

Homework is the big problem with going to public school. Kids at public school get five or six hours of homework every day. They start working as soon as they get home in the afternoon and don't stop until they go to bed.

"No . . . like . . . we have tests sometimes," he says. "And I had to write a two-page paper last month. And I guess in math I get a problem set every day, but I just copy my friend's during lunch . . . except on pizza day because I eat for most of the period and don't have time to copy."

Copying homework? That's cheating. But of course he cheats because that's what people do at public school, where there are gangs who stab people with knives and deal drugs and probably cheat on tests all the time, too. And, wait . . . he doesn't spend five or six hours per night on his homework? And did he say . . . *pizza day*?

"What's pizza day?" I ask.

He looks at me like I just asked him a stupid question that everyone knows the answer to, like "what are the atoms in a molecule of water?" or something.

"Duh," he says. "It's when we have pizza for lunch."

"You get pizza for lunch?"

"Duh."

"How often?"

"Once a week."

"Is the crust . . . in that pizza . . . white bread or wheat bread?"

"Huh?"

"The crust. On the pizza. What color is it?"

"Usually it's burnt, and it's black."

"What about the not-burnt parts?"

"White, duh, the same color as pizza crust always is."

I guess you have never had to eat whole-wheat pizza crust.

I think about the things Lee has told me. White-bread pizza once per week! Lunch periods where you can talk to eight hundred friends, every day! Dances where you can dance with four hundred girls, twice per year! I know that there are gangs and drugs and violence at public school, but I could probably avoid all those things. I could tell the gangs I didn't want to join them, I could just say no to the drugs, and as for the violence, well, I guess I would just have to take my chances.

At the top of the lift, all of us in Mountain Cruiser get off and stand in a circle. Everyone else has a newer, nicer coat than I do. Better skis as well. And two legs. That's the most noticeable thing, I guess. I am the only disabled one. I hope I am as good a skier as they are.

Our coach is the last one off the lift. He is tall and skinny—you can tell he's skinny even with his ski jacket on—and his face bones stick out underneath his goggles.

He stops in the middle of the circle and looks at each one of us. Then he swings his ski pole up in the air and points down the hill.

"Let's go!" he says.

"Yeah!"

"Let's go!"

"Skiing!"

Everyone cheers, and then they skate on their two skis—like the way you might do on roller skates—to get going fast and head straight down the hill, faster and faster. I can't skate since I only have one ski. But I can tuck. So I bend my knee as far as it will go and pull my elbows into my body. I lower my head in between my arms, which are sticking straight out in front of me. My outriggers are pointed forward, too, three feet above the snow, level with the hill, cutting the wind. I balance on my one ski. The night skiing lights on the side of the trail make shadows of everyone on the snow, and I guess mine looks sort of like an ostrich bending over so its head stretches out in front. This is how I tuck. I hope the coach is impressed.

I'm the last one to the lift, but Lee is waiting. We ride up together again, and he tells me stories about pranks his friends do while teachers are turned around at the chalk board . . . about girls he has kissed in the stairwell . . . about his substitute teacher in English, who is like totally banging, which does not mean she hits things, but that she is really pretty. Soon it's nine o'clock—I get to stay up late on Mountain Cruisers night, Mom and Dad said—and practice is over. That's when I realize that we haven't actually practiced ski racing

Dad used to read Bible stories to Matthew and me before bed each night. *(Courtesy of the author)*

Mom, Dad, Matthew, and me at our cabin at Lost River. This is the last time we ever went there together as a family. *(Courtesy of the author)*

When we were kids, Matt and I used to have sleepovers on my top bunk. Later I had to move to the bottom because I couldn't climb the ladder anymore. *(Courtesy of the author)*

Matthew and me with Nana and Papa. We went to visit them after my first biopsy, when the doctors mistakenly diagnosed my tumor as benign. *(Courtesy of the author)*

When I started losing my hair, my home-school friends came over and had a head shaving party in the backyard. *(Courtesy of the author)*

My friends came to visit in the hospital, too. *(Courtesy of the author)*

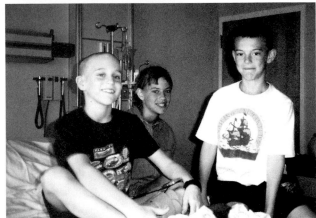

Brad Huddleston, the DJ who prayed for me on the radio the day of the operation, invited me to the studio. We made prank calls together on the air. *(Courtesy of the author)*

Mark taught me by skiing on one ski just like me. Here I am following in his track. This is the first time I ever skied. *(Courtesy of the author)*

Here I am at my first ski race, the day a former Paralympic coach spoke the words that changed my life forever. *(Courtesy of the author)*

When Steve Young interviewed me on national television, he kept asking questions I didn't want to answer. *(Courtesy of the author)*

This is why I love my brother.
(Courtesy of the author)

In moments like this, I didn't miss Mom and Dad at all.
(Gary Caskey Photography)

During college, I traveled to England to get a chance to play soccer with other amputees. It was during my bleached-hair phase.
(Courtesy of Dave Tweed)

Ralph taught me everything I needed to know about confidence, girls, and swearing. Here we are at Closing Ceremonies at the Paralympics in Turino, Italy. *(Photo by Elitsa Storey)*

In the gate for my first race at the Paralympics. I was so nervous. *(Photo by Deborah Laurenti)*

Coming down the mountain in giant slalom at the Paralympics. Mom and Dad were watching from the stands at the bottom. Mom told me later she kept whispering, "Just don't fall, Joshua, just don't fall." *(Photo by Ken Watson)*

Mom, Dad, and me in Italy at the Paralympic Village. *(Courtesy of the author)*

How do I feel right before I give a speech? Exactly like I did in the gate at the Paralympics. *(Photo by Dana Bowden)*

Sharing my story. *(Photo by Dana Bowden)*

As a professional speaker, you might say that auditoriums like this one are my office. *(Photo by Dana Bowden)*

At home with the family. *(Courtesy of the author)*

yet. All we've done is play follow-the-leader in big turns down the mountain and do drills like sliding sideways on steep sections. We never actually practiced *racing*.

"Excuse me," I say to our coach, the skinny one. "When will we start racing?"

"What?"

"When will we start racing?"

"You mean like competitive drills?"

"Is that like a ski race?"

"Sort of."

"Yeah, when will we do that?"

"Next week."

"Great!"

But the next week, it turns out that competitive drills is just a stupid relay race on the flat part of the snow at the bottom of the mountain.

So I talk to the coach again after practice.

"Are we ever going to practice ski racing?"

"What do you mean?"

"I mean, you know, like going around red and blue gates in the snow. Ski racing."

"This is just a racing development program."

"Yeah I know. So when will we do the *racing* part?"

But I can see from the coach's face that there's not really a "racing" part at all. This is just one big "development" program. Mountain Cruisers is just a fancy name for a bunch of ski lessons, and they probably just call it "racing development" so they can charge more money.

So now I am back where I was before, back to not having a plan to get on the Paralympic team. I thought Mountain Cruisers was the answer, that it would teach me how to ski race and help me meet people who could tell me when the Paralympic tryouts are, but I was wrong. I was wrong, and it's very annoying, because the only thing

I can do now is just come here to Massanutten to my Mountain Cruiser ski-lesson-not-race-lesson every week and hope that I see that old man again sometime, because if I do, I am going to ask him and make sure he tells me exactly how I can get on the Paralympic team and get a uniform like the one he was wearing. That's all I can do now: wait.

So I keep going to Mountain Cruisers practice twice per week. The first three weeks of the season go by and now it's a Thursday night at the end of January. I go to practice, and when I tell Lee what's happening—"Guess where my mom is right now?"—he is surprised.

"Your mom's having a baby? Why are you here?" he asks.

"I like skiing," I say.

That's why. I like skiing. I want to become a ski racer. I can't miss the chance to ski just because my mom is having a baby.

Matthew came tonight, too, but not because he wants to become a ski racer. He's just following me around, the way he always does, even now that I am thirteen and he is eleven, and even now that he pretends he isn't part of our family anymore. On Thursday nights he comes to Massanutten with me and takes ski lessons in a class with a friend from church, while I ski with the Mountain Cruisers. Afterward, we all three meet—Matthew, friend, and I—at the wood deck in front of the General Store. We get Ramen noodles for twenty-five cents and make them in the Styrofoam cups and hot water they have for making hot chocolate. Then we go outside to eat the noodles and watch the steam float out of the cups while we wait for Dad to pull up in the van.

But tonight Dad doesn't pull up in the van, because he's at the hospital with Mom. So we are getting a ride with our friend's dad. He will drop us off at the hospital. By the time we get there, I think, Mom is supposed to have delivered Anna or Seth. We don't know which one it will be—an Anna or a Seth—since Mom told her doctor she wanted it to be a surprise. But I am pretty sure she would like an Anna since we already have three boys, and Mom says boys are so uncouth because we think it's funny when people have gas.

Me, though, I am not sure I want an Anna *or* a Seth, because our house is already so crowded. Because of the baby, Matthew is going to have to move out into the sunroom, which is the room with the cement floor where we keep our shoes and baseball bats and tools. I am also not sure I want an Anna or a Seth because I know that one out of every three people gets cancer, and the new baby will mean we will have six people, so someone else in our family will probably get cancer. But hopefully that won't be for a long time, when we are all really old.

Our ride pulls up, and I get in the backseat with Matthew—or, actually, Matt. That's what he wants everyone to call him now. I notice a smell like the smoke smell in some of the neighborhood boys' houses and I turn my head a little. The smell is coming from Matt. I guess he has been playing with the neighborhood boys so much that the smoke smell has even gotten on his ski clothes. Matt does play with them most every day, though. They ride skateboards together and watch TV and spend the night. Mom and Dad don't like him spending the night there, but Dad says they have to choose their battles, which means that they have to let Matt do some of the things he wants to. They have to do this because whenever they tell Matt he can't do something, he starts yelling and screaming, and says that he is going to call Child Protective Services and tell them his parents are beating him, so he can go live somewhere else. This makes Mom cry, and then Dad gets mad because Mom is crying.

Everyone knows that some of the neighborhood boys Matt plays with take drugs, and even though Matt says he never takes drugs, and I believe him, I wonder if his clothes might smell like drugs, too, whatever *they* smell like. Especially his blue pants, the ones he always wears. The blue pants are dress pants, made out of cotton, but Matt likes them because they're ten sizes too big in the waist—he wears a belt—so they're baggy like the jeans his skateboarder friends have. He wears the blue pants every single day, because they are the only baggy pants he has. On days when Mom does laundry, he wears just his underwear all morning until the blue pants come of out the dryer.

But what Matt and I have in common is that we both want to go to public school. Matt wants to be with his skateboarder friends. I want to go to the dances, eat the white-bread pizza, and meet the girls—all four hundred of them. So we always argue with Mom and Dad about homeschooling. They say how good it is for us, because we are getting Christian values and scoring so high on all our achievement tests, and we tell them we hate it, we don't care about Christian values or achievement tests. We just want to go to public school. We tell them this every single day, every chance we get. But they won't listen. They don't care.

We stop suddenly, and this interrupts my thoughts about public school. I look around. We are at the hospital. Matt and I say thank you for the ride and take our ski equipment out of the trunk. We carry it all—Matt carries my one ski and his pair, I carry his poles—up the elevator to the baby floor, which is called "Maternity." We walk down the shiny hospital floor, Matt walking in his pair of ski boots, *clunk clunk clunk clunk,* and me walking on one boot and then slapping the ski tips at the end of my outriggers on the floor like crutches, *clunk smat clunk smat,* until we find a room labeled "Sundquist, Linda." We open the door and see Dad and Luke standing beside Mom's bed. Mom looks up at us when we walk in. She looks tired. She is holding a little baby in her arms. It has a pink hat on. I guess it's an Anna.

"Want to hold her?" she asks.

"Yes," Matt and I both say at the same time. We put all the ski stuff in the corner of the room, and I sit down in a chair and hold baby Anna and decide that for the rest of the night I won't remind Mom how much I hate homeschooling.

On my first day of public school, Dad drops me off forty minutes before class starts because I don't want to be late. If you are late ten times in a semester, you get after-school suspension, which is where you have to stay an extra two hours after seventh period. I know this because I read The Student Handbook three times to make sure I knew all of the rules at Harrisonburg High School. I know, for example, that students are required to walk on the right side of the hallway on their way to class, kind of like how cars go in the street. And you aren't allowed to cuss. And you aren't allowed to wear tank tops if the strap is thinner than the width of two fingers . . . although The Student Handbook did not say *whose fingers* we are talking about here. This seems like a problem to me. If we measured with, say, Anna's fingers, you could wear almost any kind of tank top you wanted, because she's tiny, only eight months old.

Arriving early to Public School, like I do on my first day, means you are required to sit in the cafeteria and wait until 7:42 a.m. Then you get twenty minutes to walk from the cafeteria to your locker and from your locker to your class, which starts at 8:02 a.m. To make sure I make it to class on time, I have three pieces of paper in my pockets. Two are in my right shorts pocket, one in my left. In my right pocket I have a map of the school, so I don't get lost, and a list of my classes, so I know where to go. The third paper, the one in my left pocket, is where I wrote my locker combination. I added an extra number at the end so that if any gang members steal the paper from me, they won't be able to open the locker.

I sit and wait in the back of the cafeteria, which is almost totally empty. Most people, I guess, don't come early to Public School. My heart is pounding as fast as it has ever pounded in my life. I can't believe it! I've made it to Public School! This is amazing! I can't wait to meet all of the girls and to eat lunch in the cafeteria, where the lunches of white-bread pizza and other wonderful things cost only $2.32, which is a pretty good price for a lunch of one entrée *and* two sides *and* a milk carton.

It took Matt and me an entire year of begging and arguing to persuade Mom and Dad to let us go to public school. But we made it. Or at least, I did. Mom and Dad wouldn't let Matt go to Public School because they were afraid he would join a gang or become addicted to drugs. So he's going to a private Christian school. But at least he's not homeschooled anymore.

Mom still thinks it's a bad idea for me to be at Public School, but Dad has the final word in our family, and he thought it would give me good opportunities to take advanced placement classes. So that was that. When Dad told Mom what he had decided, she called all the mothers at church who have children in Public School, and told them that they would be having a prayer meeting on Tuesday afternoons at our house to pray for their children. They started these prayer meetings in mid-August—I guess they wanted to store up some extra prayers before school started. During the first meeting, I peeked around the corner and into the living room. I knew most of those moms. They were mostly former homeschoolers who, like my mom, had children that had begged and pleaded and eventually convinced their fathers . . . like we did. All those moms in our living room reminded me of how mothers look on the news when their child has gone missing and they are crying and asking anyone with any information to please, please call the authorities.

Now it's 7:41 a.m., almost time to walk to my locker. I am so happy and excited to be here at public school, but I've also never been so afraid of anything in my whole life—except for cancer, of course. I am afraid of all the gangs here, afraid of all the drug dealers, and afraid of the students who carry knives and guns in their pockets. I am afraid that I might step on someone's foot with my fake leg by accident, and then she'll want to fight me with her knife. And I am afraid of what people will think when they find out my leg is fake. That's why I am wearing a pair of shorts so long you can see only my ankles. I don't want people to know. Not yet.

And I am also afraid for my Christianity, afraid that I might lose it here because of the worldly influences of Public School, afraid I might lose my faith and die and go to Hell. There are so many ways this could happen. I might be taught the Theory of Evolution in my science class, and if I have a really smart teacher, he might convince me that God didn't actually create the earth in seven days. I might have an English teacher who will make me read pornographic novels that will give me sexual thoughts. And I might come into contact with immoral students who could make me lose my faith, too, like girls who might try to convince me to have sex outside of marriage.

The bell rings—it's called a "tone," actually—and I walk to my locker. I have memorized the combination, so I don't have to waste time reading it off the paper. I enter it, and the locker pops open. Unzip backpack, notebook out of backpack, backpack in locker. Okay, we are doing good here; 7:44, eighteen minutes to go—and that's when I see him. Shawn. Shawn lives in my neighborhood, and he's friends with the boys who smoke cigarettes.

Shawn raises his eyebrows at me and glances down. He's looking at the locker below mine. Oh, I get it. Must be his locker.

I say excuse me and take one step to the right.

Shawn opens his locker and starts pulling a notepad out of his backpack on the floor. Should I look in that locker? I'm pretty sure students keep their drugs in their lockers. But what do drugs look like? How would I recognize them? Drugs are confusing because when you hear people talk about the Drug Problem in America, sometimes they are talking about smoking drugs, but sometimes they might actually be talking about injecting drugs with a needle, or even breathing drugs into your nose through a straw like people do with wasabi when they are playing Truth or Dare on church youth group retreats. So I have no idea what drugs look like, and if I saw them in Shawn's locker, I am not sure I'd recognize them. But I have to at least take a peek, a quick look.

I step away from the wall of lockers, leaning back on my real foot. I reach my arms up in the air and bend backward a little so it looks like I am stretching. This will give me a clear view inside the locker.

Okay, here we go, don't be afraid. If there is a gun or a knife, it's all right, he has no reason to hurt me. Take a quick look on three. One . . . two . . . three—

I look right in and see that it contains . . . nothing! All I see is his backpack, which he has hung on a hook. And then, as I am peering in, Shawn looks up at me. *Yikes!* I throw my head back toward the ceiling and yawn, making it really clear that I am stretching, look-ing up and away, *definitely not* looking in your locker, no sirree. (*No need to fight me, Shawn.*) I'm not sure if he buys this. But I really don't need to be afraid anymore, because I didn't see a gun or a knife in there. On the other hand . . . he might have one in his back-pack . . . or maybe he has a secret compartment in the bottom of his locker! Of course! A secret compartment!

Oh no—wait—I forgot about the time! I look at my watch: 7:46! Time is running out! Only sixteen minutes left!

I rush to my first class and make it with just 13 minutes to spare. It's Algebra II, and we spend 108 minutes hearing a teacher talk about really easy things that I learned three years ago. After class, at 10:05, my lunch period starts. This is a very early lunch, but that's all right, because I am going to eat *school cafeteria* food! Today! Finally! I will be eating a hamburger and a side of French fries—I know because I have a calendar hung on the wall at home with the lunch menu for September—and it will be *so good*!

Dad said he and Mom will buy my lunch twice per week, and the other days I can pay for it myself or pack a sandwich from home. Today I buy it with the $2.32 he gave me. After paying the lunch lady, I stand at the front of the cafeteria holding my tray and wondering where to sit. There are so many tables, so many people. Hundreds and hundreds of people. And they all know one another. In fact, it seems like all of them, even the freshmen, already know *who they are going to sit with,* like they planned it out ahead of time. Did they arrange this over the summer? I stand still for nearly a minute, watching the groups of people gather around tables automatically, as if there were some sort of seating chart that I never got a copy of.

It's not as if I don't know anyone in here. In fact, I know the names of all of the freshmen, all 306 of them, both first and last names. This is because I borrowed an eighth-grade yearbook from a friend at church and went through and memorized it. I figured this would help me make friends, because I would already know everyone before I got to school. And it *has* helped . . . sort of. On the way to Algebra II, for example, I saw a boy named Carroll Hill, whom I recognized from the yearbook.

"Carroll! Carroll Hill!" I shouted. "What's up?"

I raised my hand to give him a high-five.

"Ummmm . . . it's CJ," he said.

"Oh sorry," I said. "I'm Josh." I almost said "Joshua," but then I remembered I'd shortened my name to sound cooler. Like Matt did.

So far I've high-fived about fifteen people I recognized from the yearbook. A few of them seemed to be thinking that they were supposed to know me, that they had just forgotten my name over the summer or something. They were the ones who said, "Hey there . . . *dude* . . . how was your summer?" And there were a few people who looked at me very strangely and didn't say anything at all. But most of them have been friendly. Surprisingly friendly, in fact. I thought everyone here would be rude, uncaring . . . un-*Christian*. But most people apologize if they bump into someone, and they smile (or at least nod) as they pass other students in the hallway, and ask, "How you doing?" or "What's up?" or "'Sup?" in a friendly sort of way.

That is, except for one boy who, while I was walking to the cafeteria before lunch, stuck out his leg and tripped me. Then he and his friend laughed.

"That'll teach you to try and limp around this school," he said. "You ain't no pimp! So don't try and walk like one!"

I didn't know what to say to him, since I *always* try not to limp when I walk. I do my very best, but it's impossible for me to walk perfectly normal. So I said nothing. I just stood back up and kept walking with a limp.

Fortunately I don't see the boy who tripped me as I look around the cafeteria. But I do see Lee, my friend from Mountain Cruisers! He's sitting in the corner at a table with two other boys. I walk over to him.

"Lee, what's up?" I say.

"Hey, what are you doing here?"

"You convinced me to come," I say. I tell him this because over the summer I read a book called *How to Win Friends and Influence People,* and it said the number-one rule for getting people to like you is to make them feel important. I figure it will make Lee feel important to know he was the original reason I wanted to come to Public School.

"Oh, okay," Lee says.

I am hoping he will introduce me to his friends and invite me to sit down. But he doesn't.

"Can I sit with you all?" I ask, eventually.

"Oh sure, if you want to," Lee says.

I sit down and look at my hamburger. It doesn't look as . . . *tasty* as I thought it would. The meat is a strange color, not normal meat color—definitely not—and the bun is smooshed flat. I take a bite. I can tell immediately, before I even start chewing, that it is by far the worst-tasting hamburger I've ever had in my life. I can't believe it! I've been looking forward to this cafeteria food for *so long*. I spent so many hours reading over the menu at home, imagining how good the food was going to taste, but when I finally make it to school, I chew and swallow this hamburger feeling like . . . like . . . like I woke up early on December 25 only to find out Christmas had been canceled.

I look around the table. The other two boys have faces I don't recognize, so they must be in an older grade. Why is Lee sitting at a table of just three people, even though he knows all eight hundred freshmen? And why are there no girls sitting with him, even though he has kissed more girls than any other boy in the whole grade level?

No one at the table talks during the entire twenty-two-minute lunch period.

"See you later, Lee," I say, when I hear the tone.

"Yup, see you," he says.

Then, as I start to walk away, he says, "Hey."

"Yeah?"

"Are you doing Mountain Cruisers again this year?"

"No . . . you?"

"No."

"Yeah . . . I want to learn how to race," I say. "But Mountain Cruisers wasn't a racing program like I thought it would be."

He nods.

"This year," I continue, "I am going to find a real ski racing team and join it. That's my plan."

Lee nods, speaks. "I can't wait for the winter," he says.

"Me neither."

I walk to my next class noticing that people walk on both the right *and* left side of the hallway, a direct violation of The Student

Handbook. In fact, the hallway is nothing short of total chaos, no order to it at all. People walk wherever they want, walk and cuss, walk and cuss and wear spaghetti-strap tank tops.

After the last class period finishes, I walk outside. Hundreds of students are standing on the sidewalk, gathered in little circles. And just like the tables at lunch, everyone knows exactly which circle to stand in. No student ever switches circles or even talks to anyone from another circle. I look over at the parent pick-up curb to see if Mom is there. Not yet. That means unless I want to be the only person waiting alone, I'm going to need to choose one of these circles to join. But which one? How do you figure out which circle you belong to? That's when I see a circle, no, *the* circle, the circle that includes Samantha Morris, Megan Murphy, Kathryn Saint-Ours, and Diana Stuhmiller, four of the prettiest girls in our grade. In one of the yearbook photos that I studied quite carefully this past summer, these four girls were side by side, on one knee, with pom-poms in their hands. Yes. I have found my circle.

"Hi Kathryn Saint-Ours, I'm Josh Sundquist," I say. I work my way around the circle introducing myself like this, and the girls smile at me and return my high-five. While I'm talking to them I try to use their names a lot—something else I learned in *How to Win Friends and Influence People*.

Just then Justin Burchill walks by. I met him earlier.

"What's up Justin Burchill?" I say.

"Look at the new guy!" he says. "A total *mac!*"

A mac, I know, is a boy that girls really like. The same as a pimp. A pimp is boy who always has girls around him. But even though a mac is similar to a pimp, Justin Burchill doesn't try to trip me, which is nice.

After Mom takes me home, she sits down in the family room, in the big blue chair. I follow her into the room, still talking about my day.

". . . and Spanish class is going to be really easy," I say.

"Really?"

"Yeah, it's all stuff you taught me last year."

Mom starts to pull her shirt up. So I look away until everything is covered by Anna's head.

Mom nursed all of us like this when we were babies. She thinks it's very important, very *healthy,* for babies to be nursed by their mothers. That's what God intended, she always says.

I keep talking. When I tell her about the boy who stuck out his leg and tripped me, the bottoms of her eyes turn red and I wish I hadn't told her. So I try to make it sound like it was all, you know, kind of funny, kind of a practical joke that every freshman has to go through on his first day of public high school.

17

D ad drives us home from church today. After second service.
When I was a kid, we always went to the first service, the
early one, so we could get home sooner and play with Dad all afternoon. After I went on chemo, we started going to the second service
because I wanted to sleep later. When I finished treatment, though,
we never switched back.

"I heard that women are more safer drivers than men," says
Luke.

"Yes, that's probably true," Dad says.

"So why isn't Mom driving us?" Luke asks.

Dad laughs with the three-part laugh he always does, the laugh
where the middle part is the loudest: *Huh-HAH-huh.*

"Mom is very tired, so I offered to drive today," says Dad. "But
don't worry, I'm a pretty safe driver, too."

Mom hardly ever comes to church anymore. She rests at home,
waiting for us to bring back a bulletin so she can read the announce-
ments. But today is the Sunday before Christmas. So she decided to
come. She's wearing her gloves, of course, same as she always does
when she goes to the supermarket or anywhere else, to avoid germs
since her immune system is weakened. And Dad came to church
today, too, because even though he has to finish the accounting system, he never ever works on Sunday, because that's one of the Ten
Commandments.

There is a pause, and then Dad speaks again.

"Joshua and Matthew," he says, with a bit of loudness and on-purpose-ness so we know that this is the start of a Family Meeting. "We were thinking that this might be a good time for you to stop going to Boy Scouts."

"Why?" I ask.

"Well, we just think . . . well, it's hard to drive you places like that all the time, and we think—"

"Mr. Barnes takes me every week," I say.

I say "me" because Matt doesn't usually go anymore. He's too busy skateboarding or rollerblading or whatever he does with his friends.

"Right, that's kind of the problem. We don't want you getting rides from everyone if we can't help with the carpool," he says.

And then I understand. Mom is sick. Dad has to work. We all have to make some sacrifices. I get it.

"Okay . . ." I say. And because I am part of the family: "Actually ever since I got Eagle I've been thinking there isn't much point to going anymore anyway."

"Aren't you assistant senior patrol leader now?" says Mom.

I am surprised she says this, because it seems like she is arguing that I *should* stay in Scouts, but Dad is arguing I should quit, and parents are not supposed to disagree.

"Yeah, I am. But it's kind of boring," I say. "I lead the Pledge of Allegiance every week, and that's pretty much it."

Pause. I add: "Getting my Eagle was always the main thing."

"Is it okay with you, Matthew?" Dad says.

"Yeah."

No more Boy Scouts? All right, I can do that. But this probably also means . . . if we can't go to Scouts, which is ten minutes away . . . then no way we'll be able to ski, since it's a half hour. *Another year without racing.* I thought this was the year, the year I would some-how find a ski team and start racing in real races and compete against real competitors and train and figure out how to make the Paralympics. But I guess not. We all have to make—*next year, maybe*—some sacrifices.

I look out the window at the passing cars and buildings. It's cold today, but it feels hot inside the van, I guess because it's so packed with people and stress. That's how life has been—packed with stress—since last month, when Mom was diagnosed with non-Hodgkin's lymphoma, stage four, the worst stage. They thought it was probably malignant even before the biopsy. Ever since Dr. Mike Marsh looked at the X ray and saw the tumor, which was the size of a grapefruit or a small cantaloupe. He actually said, "grapefruit or a small cantaloupe." Why do doctors always have to ruin perfectly good fruit by comparing it to life-threatening malignancies? Before last week, I liked cantaloupe. It's juicy. It's sweet. It tastes good. But not anymore, thanks to this association. Doctors should compare cancer to things that are *not* juicy and sweet, things you wouldn't otherwise think of *eating*. "It's the size of a dead mouse" or maybe "about as big as one of those pickled pig's feet that float in jars of vinegar at sketchy gas stations." That would be way better.

She started chemo right away. Dad told me it would last for five months. But her treatments themselves, the time in the hospital, would be only one day for each visit.

"No overnights?" I asked.

"No overnights."

And when he told me this, I thought: No overnights? One day? Outpatient? When *I* was in the hospital, I spent five days there at a time, four nights, almost a full week! And I did that not for five months, but for an entire year! Why is everyone so worried about Mom now, with her fast-food drive-thru chemo, her Jiffy Lube, her in-and-out, her treatments-while-U-wait chemo? Five months. That's nothing.

But then I thought: Hold on, stop. No, no, no, this is not right, Josh. No, Josh*ua* (because that's what Mom calls you). Joshua, how can you think such thoughts about your own mother? How can you be so arrogant, so self-centered? Your mother has *cancer.*

Everything is quiet in the van for the rest of the drive home, and the air inside gets hotter, stuffier, the closer we get. When we are a few houses away, I notice a bunch of people in our front yard. *Are we being robbed?* Then I recognize them. It's Dr. Mike Marsh, the doctor who I first went to for my cancer, who Mom first went to for *her* cancer. It's Mrs. Jane Marsh, too, who plans Lost River every summer and who used to be my Sunday school teacher. And their son Seth is with them—Seth Marsh, who shaved his head for me five years ago when I was first diagnosed. *Why aren't they at church?* As Dad turns the van into the driveway, I see that Dr. Marsh is standing on a ladder propped against the bricks on the front of our house. He is holding a little piece of pine tree, setting it on the windowsill. *First service. They must've gone to first service.* Jane Marsh is at our front door, hanging a wreath that has ribbons on it. Seth is digging through a box on the sidewalk, pulling out more of the pine tree pieces.

Dad parks the car and cuts the engine. But he does not open his door. So we don't move, either. We just sit in the backseats. Matt and I look at each other. We smile, because we never decorate our house like this for Christmas. The only real decoration we put up—besides the plastic Christmas tree, which we *still* haven't put up yet, and it's already the Sunday before Christmas—is a light bulb. Most years around this time Dad carries a chair from the kitchen table to the porch. Then he unscrews the regular white light bulb and puts in the Christmas one. It makes the whole porch glow green.

Last year Luke asked if we could get a red light bulb instead and put that on the porch since red is the other Christmas color, but Dad said no, absolutely not. I was thirteen, so I knew Dad said this because red lights mean you have prostitutes, who are people you can pay to have sex with you if you don't have a wife to have sex with and you don't want to masturbate. But this is illegal, so I've always thought it was strange that you can put a certain color out to let everyone know there are prostitutes inside. You wouldn't put a light on your house to tell people you had murderers inside, say, or thieves, because then the police would just come arrest them. Weird. Anyway, that's why we still use a green light, not a red one. But no green light this year, because . . . well, everything is a little bit different this year.

Dad finally opens his door, so we feel like we can get out. We unbuckle our seatbelts. Matt grabs the handle and lets the gravity of the driveway slide open our door. He jumps out, goes to talk to Seth. Luke unfastens Anna and lifts her down from her car seat. I hold my fake leg with my left hand and hop out onto the driveway, landing on my right foot.

Dad surveys our house.

"Wow!" he says. Whatever it was that made him quiet in the car, it's gone now. He is enthusiastic. Cheerful. But I don't think he really feels that way inside.

"Merry Christmas, Sundquists!" Dr. Marsh says, with his very, very southern accent. He's still standing on the ladder.

"It's beautiful!" Dad says.

"Yes, beautiful!" Mom says. She sounds enthusiastic, like Dad.

"These are the most Christmas trees we've ever had!" Luke says when he notices the little pieces of pine on the windowsills. "Mom, how come you never put up so many Christmas trees?"

Everyone laughs. Luke isn't old enough to know that you are not supposed to say unkind things, even if they are funny, to people who have lost their hair from chemotherapy. Or maybe he's just not old enough to know that was an unkind thing in the first place.

Dad walks up the porch steps to Mrs. Marsh. Mom and I follow. He looks at the wreath on our front door, with its ribbons and little unbloomed pine cones and brass bells and a big red bow hanging off the bottom. He hugs Mrs. Marsh.

"Thank you," he says. He is not enthusiastic anymore. He is very serious. After the hug, he nods. "Thank you."

"Merry Christmas," Mrs. Marsh says.

Mom doesn't say anything, but she hugs her, too.

"You're family has been through so much," Mrs. Marsh says.

Mom and Dad don't say anything.

Then Mrs. Marsh says, "I want you to know that if I could have the cancer instead of Linda . . . I would."

And we all know Mrs. Marsh really means this, because pretty much anyone can say nice things like that to you, but not many of them will come and decorate your house on a really cold morning the Sunday before Christmas.

That night, Matt, Dad, and I go out in the front yard to look at our house. You can still see the pine branches on the windowsills, even in the dark, because the Marshes also gave us electric candles to put inside the windows, and the light comes through the glass and makes silhouettes of all the pine needles.

It's even colder now, definitely below freezing. So they are probably blowing fake snow at Massanutten tonight, getting ready to open for the season. I wish I was there.

"When are we going to put up the green light bulb?" Matt asks.

I think Matt was asking Dad, but I want Dad to know that I am mature enough to realize we have enough decorations already this year, so I answer.

"Maybe we should just save it for next year," I say.

"That sounds good, Joshua," Dad says.

I smile.

"Dad," I ask. "Remember when I had cancer, and I had a fifty percent chance to live?"

"Yes, I remember."

"What chance does Mom have?"

"What do you mean?"

"What percent chance does Mom have to live?"

Dad looks at Matt and me, thinking.

What is Dad thinking about?

"Mom's cancer . . . is considered . . . incurable."

"Incurable?"

"Yes."

"So what chance is it?"

"It's incurable."

"I know, but what percent chance?"

"None. There *is* no chance."

"You mean Mom is going to die?" Matt asks.

"Eventually we are all going to die," Dad says.

"But she's going to die now?" I ask.

"Not now."

"When?"

"The doctor says people with her cancer get eight to ten years, on average."

"Mom is going to *die*?" Matt says. "Why didn't you tell us?"

"We were waiting for the right time."

"The right time?" I say. "What if I had never asked?"

Dad doesn't answer.

"Were you just not going to tell us?"

And he still doesn't answer, but then I forget to keep asking because I realize that Mom is going to die. No, not just going to die she *is dying* like, as in right now. Right now she is inside and she is dying in our house. I am crying and Matthew is crying and even though we are covering our faces, our cries keep exploding through our hands and freezing the way breaths do when it is cold out.

It's Tuesday, three days before Christmas. Someone from church brought us dinner tonight. It was a quiet meal, just four of us— Mom, Luke, me, baby Anna. Dad's boss said they could wait to install that new computer system until Mom's chemo is over, just upgrade next year, but Dad wanted to get it finished. They hired him specifically to do this, he said. So he won't be home until late. And Matt—you never know with Matt—isn't here, either.

Now that dinner is over, Mom is resting on the couch, where she always rests. I am drinking a cup of water in the kitchen.

"Luke?" Mom asks. Luke's sitting at the table drawing a picture, probably a snowman. That's what he wants to be when he grows up. A snowman. Dad once suggested he come up with a backup plan—in case he melts—and Luke said he'd like to be a mommy.

"Let's just stick with snowman," Dad said. He said it really serious, looking at Mom, both of them frowning, like they would not like the idea of any of *their* three boys wanting to be a mommy.

I look at Luke's drawing, to see what it is. Hard to say. Could be a snowman, I guess.

Luke answers Mom. "What?"

"Could you help me please?" Mom asks.

This makes me wonder: Why did she ask for Luke's help, and not mine? Does she know my secret—that I think her chemotherapy is easy compared to mine—and resent me for it? (*I try not to think this way, Mom! I really do!*) Or does she think I am just too busy with school? Why ask for a six-year-old's help when there's a fourteen-year-old in the same room?

"What Mommy?" Luke says.

"Could you please pick up Anna for me?" she asks.

Of course. That's why. She still thinks I can't carry anything since I have only one leg. Can't pick up Anna. That's why she asked Luke.

Luke frowns.

"What do you say?" Mom asks.

"Yes, Mommy."

"That's my big helper."

Luke puts down his marker beside his drawing on the kitchen table and walks through the open doorway to the family room. Anna is sitting on the floor wearing pink. Mom loves finding pink things for Anna. Pink clothes, pink toys, pink sheets.

I watch Luke dangle Anna from under her arms and carry her to the couch in quick little steps. Because of Mom's operation, a very deep biopsy that involved all sorts of muscle wall stuff and intestinal this or that, she is not allowed to lift Anna for six weeks. So each night, when it's time for bed, Luke has to put Anna in the crib. In the morning, Dad scoops her up and puts her on the floor before work. Mom set up a changing station—plastic sheet, wipes, spare diapers—beside the crib, on the carpet. And she can hold Anna only if someone else does the initial lifting from the floor to the couch.

"Thank you, Luke," Mom says.

She holds the baby bottle to Anna's lips, but Anna pushes it away with her tiny hand and presses her face into Mom's chest, into Mom's long-sleeve T-shirt, sucking on it until drool runs down the fabric. Luke comes back into the kitchen, picks up his marker, and gets back to drawing. Anna grabs a fistful of fabric and tugs on it, stretching the T-shirt's collar. Luke adds what appears to be a carrot nose and a top hat. Or maybe those are charcoal eyes. You never know. Anna turns her face back up toward Mom and cries. I look away, just like I always used to back when Mom was getting ready to nurse. When she still could.

18

Mom's doctor says it's just a waiting game now. The chemo is over, and she's in remission. Her hair is returning. (*How long will it be allowed to grow before . . . ?*) The cancer might come back next month or next year, or maybe not for five years. But it will come back.

My freshman year of public high school is over now, too. I never got offered drugs—not once in the entire year—and was never invited to join a gang. It turns out most kids at public school are more similar to me than they are different. A lot of them even like skiing at Massanutten. That's why this morning, after I wake up and see an inch of snow on the ground—the first snow of my sophomore year—and listen to the radio until I hear that school's canceled, I get out the phone book and look up last names of kids I know from school who are sixteen and into skiing. I keep calling until I find someone who wants to be in line when the chairlift opens.

I spend eight hours skiing in the fresh inch of powder. By the end of the day, it seems like half the school has made it up here to Massanutten. We are all eating Ramen noodles on the wooden deck in front of the General Store.

"Ramen is so good," says Robert Frazier, the one who gave me a ride this morning.

"Only twenty-five cents!" I say.

The Ramen-is-so-good, only-twenty-five-cents exchange is a standard one all of us students have. It's like the way a Christian will say, "God is good," and the other Christian is supposed to say, "All the time."

"God is good."

"All the time, brother."

Like:

"Ramen is good."

"Only twenty-five cents, brother."

When I finish the Ramen, I carry my Styrofoam cup across the deck toward the trash can. As I walk I notice a group of guys standing in a half circle like they are huddled around a television. But it's not a television. It's a girl. And—*wow*—what a girl!

I stop walking and just stand there, holding the empty Styrofoam cup in my hand and staring. Then, suddenly, all the kids on the deck stop talking. All of them. All at once. Then a black hole forms inside the General Store and sucks up everyone on the deck like a giant vacuum, leaving just this girl and me, standing there, floating. There is a spotlight on her face, the beautiful face that is now . . . turning toward me! *Look away! Stop staring!* I look down at my foot. When I do, the black hole spits everyone back onto the deck—*zooooop*—and they all start talking again, as if they had not been temporarily pulled into another dimension but had in fact been there the whole time.

But I must (*must!*) look at her again, so I start to lift my eyes back toward hers. I see the ski and snowboard boots of the boys standing in the half circle around her, then I see in between them to her black pants, then her white coat, and then the high white collar of a fleece liner and the white headband underneath a ponytail, and there, framed by the fleece liner and headband, her face—yes no doubt the prettiest girl I have ever seen holy cow she is so hot—and she is . . . looking at me! Her eyes, locked on mine! We are in love! She is *the one*! We will be together forever!

"Lydia? Lydia?"

It's one of the boys in the half circle.

"What? Oh yeah, definitely," she says, returning her gaze, so perfect, to him.

I hate that guy. He's probably not even a good skier.

Remembering the reason I came over here in the first place, I throw my Styrofoam cup toward the hole in the top of the trash can, that little space between the rim of the can and the little four-legged roof above the opening. My cup bounces off the rim and starts to fall, tumble, spin toward the wooden floor of the deck in slow motion. *No . . . must not . . . fall!* I swing both hands around and smash the cup in between my gloves, breaking it into two pieces and creating a shockwave of sound loud enough to end several nearby conversations. I turn around, smile.

"Carry on, everyone."

Hopefully she was impressed by my catlike reflexes.

I walk back to Robert.

"Who *is* that?" I ask.

He does not bother to ask who I am talking about.

"Lydia Sease," he says.

"Wow man, she is hot!"

I want to say "dude" instead of the much lamer "man," as in "wow, *dude*," but we are not allowed to say "dude" in our family since Bart Simpson says it. This is a rule that Mom made when I was eight years old. I still follow it even though Matt doesn't anymore, so I guess I probably could get away with saying it, but . . .

"Yeah," Robert says. "She's hot."

"Sease? Is she related to Justin Sease?"

"Cousins."

"Wow, hot cousin."

"Yeah, hot cousin."

The next Saturday at Massanutten, Lydia's standing on the deck of the General Store again, but she's by herself, so I just walk right up to her and take off my glove and stick out my hand.

"Hi, Lydia Sease, I'm Josh Sundquist."

"Hi. Nice to meet you."

We talk a little—yeah, your cousin is in my geometry class—and find friends we have in common. She goes to Turner Ashby High, which is the archrival of my school, Harrisonburg High. *So you and I are kind of like Romeo and Juliet,* I think to myself, but decide not say it out loud.

"Are you going out to ski?" she asks.

"Yeah," I say.

"Wait for me just a second. I need to get my skis from my locker."

"Yeah, sure."

Is this really happening? Does she want us to ski together? I can't believe it!

"Are you with anyone?" I ask.

She tilts her head. "Huh?"

"Like, who are you skiing with?"

"Oh, I came with my brother. But he's at practice right now. You?"

Then I remember that I am with Robert Frazier and Graham Giovanetti and John Rose, but they're inside getting Ramen. They won't miss me, probably won't even notice I'm gone. But I can't really say, "No, I'm not skiing with anyone," because that would be a lie. I've never told a lie in my life.

"I came with some people," I say. "But I'm not skiing with them."

This is not a lie, because even though I was skiing with them this morning, I am not skiing with them *right now.*

"All right, I'll meet you at the lift?" Lydia Sease asks me.

"Which one?"

"Southern Comfort," she says.

"Sounds good."

I walk my clunky outrigger-and-ski-boot walk over to the lift, where my ski is propped against a railing. Is this really happening? How can I be so lucky? Lydia Sease! The hottest girl in Rockingham County, possibly in all of Virginia, is getting her skis from her locker to meet me at the lift so we can ski together! Well, actually . . . I guess technically I don't know for sure that she wants to *ski* with me, only that she is getting her skis from her locker and she going to *meet* me.

I see her skating over to me. She has very nice skis.

"Ready?" she asks.

"Yep," I say.

"Let's go."

She slides to the back of the lift line and motions for me to stand beside her. This is the first time I've ever been glad to wait in a long lift line.

Once we are riding the chair together, I realize I don't know what you're supposed to talk about with girls. I know you're supposed to impress them, right? But how? Should I brag about myself? About my grades, maybe? I'm not sure. *Note to self: Do some research about this topic.*

Then I think about how many important things have happened to me on this lift, the Southern Comfort lift. It's the first lift Mark Andrews took me to the day I learned to ski. It's the one I was sitting on with Lee when he told me about public school. And now it's the one I am sitting on with Lydia Sease, the most beautiful girl in Rockingham County, my future girlfriend. Maybe it will be the lift where I have my first kiss with Lydia Sease, too. Which reminds me—how do you do that? Where do you put your head? What do you do with your lips? The last girl I kissed was Keisha, almost ten years ago, at the homeschool potlucks, and I know I wasn't doing it right. *Need to do some research about kissing, too.*

Just then a skier below the Southern Comfort lift lets his legs separate, his skis sliding farther and farther in opposite directions until they catch on the front edge, throwing his body forward. He lands face first in the snow—or maybe chin first; it's hard to say from this angle—and both skis pop off and bounce like pole vaults without a pole vaulter attached. He lets go of his poles, and they fall in the snow, staying in about the same place, while he slides down the hill another fifteen feet.

I wait for a second to make sure the snow isn't turning red where his face landed . . . okay, good, we're safe. Now I can laugh. But before I can start, Lydia is already laughing. When Lydia Sease laughs, she leans against the back rest of the lift and tucks her chin forward a little bit, covering her mouth with her hand. We laugh together until we have gone far enough that we can't see the man or his poles or skis anymore, and then we stop laughing, at the same time, and our chair is quiet. She smiles at me.

Am supposed to kiss her? Now? Is this the moment? No . . . probably too soon. Maybe on our second lift ride.

"Why do you want to come to the library?" Mom asks.

She goes to the library every week to get picture books to read to Anna. I've never gone with her.

"To get some books," I say.

"What for?"

"To read."

Mom smirks and looks at me with her eyebrows raised. But I don't say anything else.

At the library, I use their computer to search for books, which is so much better than using the microscope to look at the little pieces of film with the book titles printed on them, like you used to have to do. I find my books, bring them to the front. The librarian at the counter looks up from the pile as she scans their bar codes. We make eye contact.

Please don't say anything, Librarian, please don't say anything.

"May I have your library card?"

She scans it and then I put all the books in my backpack so Mom won't see them during the drive home.

"Thanks. See you later," I say to the librarian.

Please, please don't say anything, Librarian.

"Enjoy your books," she says. But she says it like she's singing a song, the words rising.

Once I am at home in my room with the door shut, I lay out all the books on my desk. I slide them around until they are in a line, biggest to smallest, and then I squeeze the line together from the outside until the sides all push up against each other. Now I can choose one. I decide to start with the book on the far left, *Dating for Dummies,* by Dr. Joy Brown, because it is the longest.

Then I read the other books from the library, like *Men Are from Mars, Women Are from Venus,* by Dr. John Gray, and the sequel, *Mars and Venus on a Date.* I also read a couple of books from the Psychology section.

The main thing I learn from all this research is that girls don't care too much about how handsome a guy is. This surprises me since I myself mostly just want a girl who is really pretty. Girls, though, they want other stuff: Number one, a good listener. Number two, social status.

Dr. John Gray says in his book *Men Are from Mars, Women Are From Venus* that being a good listener means agreeing with everything the girl says, and never trying to help her solve her own problems. You should instead just show how you understand that the problem she is telling you about is a very serious one by repeating back to her what she's just said and then asking her how that makes her feel. For example, if she says, "My computer is broken." You should *not* say, "I will fix it for you," even though this is what you might want to say since her problem is very stupid and you could easily fix it. Instead, you should say, "I am so sorry to hear that *your computer is broken.* How does that make you feel?" And then, when she tells you how she feels, you should say the exact same thing as you did before, only now you put in the new words she's just used to describe her feelings. "I am so sorry to hear that you *are pretty annoyed about it, I guess*. How does that make you feel?" And so on.

And then there's . . . social status. According to the psychology books, social status comes from having large resources (which means being rich) and having eminence (which means being famous). Girls want boyfriends and husbands who have these things, even though they are very worldly things and are the exact opposite of the things that Christians are supposed to want. We Christians are supposed to give all our money to feed the poor and be humble and give all the glory to God and wash everyone's feet. So girls want pretty much the opposite of a Christian. Maybe that's why Jesus never got married. How can I get Lydia to like me *and* still be a Christian? I don't know. Would it be worth going to Hell if I could date her for a couple years? Maybe. But eternity is a really long time, so probably not. How about this: What if I could be a Christian *with status*? Maybe I can be both at the same time! I could use my wealth and fame and power to feed the poor and wash their feet, and also to get Lydia to like me!

But the problem is that I don't currently have any actual status. First of all, I am not rich. I have saved some money from doing chores at our house for my whole life, but those chores don't pay very much:

JOB	PAY	FREQUENCY
Vacuum	$0.10/room	Weekly
Sweep kitchen	$0.15	Daily
Shake out throw rugs	$0.10	Weekly
Dust house	$0.30	Weekly
Mop kitchen	$0.25	Weekly
Mop bathrooms	$0.10/room	Weekly
Wash, dry, fold clothes	$0.50/load	Twice per week
Clean bathrooms: Scrub tub, sink, toilet	$0.60/room	Weekly

So I have only a couple hundred dollars saved up. And even though Mom and Dad think I am famous, I'm not, because being on *Children's Miracle Network* and *The Brad Huddleston Morning Show* when you were ten years old does not make you famous. It just means you were on TV a couple of times and on the radio once. Being famous, really famous, means that people have heard of you and recognize you when you walk around the mall.

How can I do it? How can I become famous and rich? I got it! Of course! I will become a famous and rich *ski racer*! When I get on the Paralympic team, I will be on TV and in the newspapers all the time, and everyone will recognize me and know who I am. And then I will be so famous that companies like Nike will pay me to wear their logo when I ski race. That's how I will get rich. Then I will have more status than any other guy in Rockingham County, so Lydia will have to date me.

The only problem is that I still don't know how to *become* a ski racer. How do I try out for the Paralympics? Where do I learn how to race? How can I practice and get good? Mountain Cruisers can't help, because they don't teach you anything about how to race. Mark Andrews can't help, because four years ago he said he'd already taught me everything he knew. So how can I learn to race? Wait. How about this? There is a race at Massanutten, a public race called NASTAR, held every Sunday morning. You go over to this guy and give him ten dollars, and then you can ski through a race course and get a pin to put on your jacket. Maybe he can tell me how to become a racer.

But this would mean going to Massanutten on Sunday morning and missing church. Mom and Dad won't like that, and neither will Jesus. But I have to do it. I have to date Lydia.

And what a great idea this is! It's weird that I've never thought of asking the people at the NASTAR race about how I can become a ski racer. I've known about NASTAR for probably three years, but I've never thought of talking to the guy at the start house. Now it's only a matter of time . . . until I become a ski racer . . . until Lydia likes me. Yes, yes, yes. Awesome.

19

It's the craziest thing. I've been sitting around for three years wondering how to become a ski racer, and somehow I never knew that I could just skip church and go up to the guy at the start of the NASTAR course and find out that he was an assistant coach of the ski racing team, and that all I had to do to join the team was pay four hundred dollars. And that's what I did, last month. Mom and Dad said they'd pay half, so I got two hundred dollars out of my savings from doing chores around the house, and the next week I was at my first practice.

That night of ski practice changed everything. For the first time in my life, I knew I was in the right place, going in the right direction, at the right time. I knew this for sure after I met a certain kid on the team.

It was weird to meet a person in that situation, on the lift. It was weird because, like all of us racers, he was wearing a helmet with a big ski racing-style face guard over his mouth and mirrored goggles over his eyes, so even if I happened to have memorized his name and face in a yearbook—and I hadn't, since there's no yearbook for the ski team—I wouldn't have been able to recognize him. I had to introduce myself the normal way, where you don't know the person's name until he tells you it.

"Hi, I'm Josh Sundquist," I said to the face guard and goggles.

"I'm Zack Sease. Nice to meet you."

"Sease? Are you related to Justin Sease?"

"He's my cousin."

"Really? No way! He's in my geometry class," I said. "And wait . . . So are you related to Lydia Sease?"

"She's my sister."

"*Your sister?* No way!"

I realized I was almost yelling, and made a mental note to tone it down a little. I also made a mental note of how jealous I was, of how much I wished *I* was Lydia Sease's brother, so I could live in her house and see her every single day. That would be awesome.

"Yeah way, she's my sister," Zack said.

"Oh, that's nice," I said, trying to compensate for my previous reaction by speaking in a voice that sounded like I'd lost interest in the conversation.

But, inside, I was about to overheat with excitement. I couldn't believe it! Not only was there a ski team here, and not only was I on it now, but *Lydia Sease's little brother* was on the team, too! Of course he was. That's why she was at the General Store by herself that day. Her brother had gone up on the slopes for ski team practice.

It all makes sense now. It all fits together, perfectly, my life and my connections to Lydia Sease: I will become a great ski racer. I will have social status and a Paralympic uniform. And I will date Lydia. Thank you, dating and psychology books! Thank you for getting me on this team! To this race, to today, three weeks later! To this starting area at the top of a mountain, standing beside Zack Sease!

"Good luck, Josh," Zack Sease says.

"You, too."

You're going to need it, I think.

What Zack Sease doesn't realize is that I am going to win this race. I have been chosen to win. It has been predestined, foretold, and probably even carved onto the stone walls of caves by ancient peoples, in hieroglyphs of a one-legged stick figure defeating the two-legged skiers in his first race. It's too bad for Zack, since this means he will have to lose. Or I guess he could get second place. That would be fine.

Lydia. She will see me win and she will know right away, from this very day at this very race, that I am going to become famous and rich, that I will wear The Uniform. I might even let her wear it sometimes, ski around in it, so people will ask her where it came from, and they'll be so impressed with me when they find out I am dating such a hot girl.

The most important thing is not to fall. I've got to stay standing. Keep my weight forward. Arc the ski. Push into the front of the boot. Shoulders level with the hill. Bend my knee. Turn before I get to the gate, not after it. These are the rules for being a good ski racer, according to my coaches. I have them memorized, and I reviewed them in my mind probably two hundred times on the drive over to West Virginia last night. I got a ride with another family on the team—not the Seases, unfortunately—because today is Sunday and Mom and Dad didn't want to miss church. They didn't want me to miss it, either, but I convinced them of how important it was for me to get the chance to start training and racing if I was going to make the Paralympics. Just this once. I will always go to church after this Sunday, but just for this one race—

"Number forty-two," says a woman with a clipboard like the one Dr. Dunsmore always used to carry around.

"Yes," I say.

She motions me toward the starting gate. The starting gate is a platform of snow that's just big enough for two people—you and the timekeeper—to stand on at the top of the race course. At the end of the platform is a plastic stick about as wide as a pencil and as long as a ruler. According to the Official Rules of the United States Ski and Snowboard Association, which I have read three times, this stick should be attached to a pole so it is eighteen inches above the snow. When you enter the course, your ankle knocks it open, starting the timer.

I watch the racer in front of me and see how he lifts the tips of his poles over the stick—it's called a "wand" in the Official Rules, actually—and plants them on the downward slope of the starting ramp. Then the timekeeper counts down from five to zero and says, "Go, racer!" The racer now has a window of five seconds to begin the race. He takes a few loud breaths and then leans forward on his poles—for me, it will be outriggers—and kicks back his legs—for me, it will be leg—so his body is already accelerating down the eight-foot drop of the starting ramp when his ankles finally knock open the wand and start the timer.

As I slide into the starting gate, I notice the timekeeper hasn't closed the wand yet, so it is left pointing straight out towards what would normally be a valley, but today is just a blur of white. There is movement—snow is falling out of the fog and landing on the course—but my eyeballs are too pumped with adrenaline to watch the tumble of individual flakes. If you could see white noise with your eyes, this is what it would look like. Just a blur of static. Then, finally, the timekeeper bends over and pulls back the wand like a gate on a miniature fence.

"Ten seconds."

Ten? Oh my gosh wait not allowed to say euphemisms like gosh that's so little time I need to pull my goggles down get the goggles down hurry okay there. Now slide down put the outriggers over the wand on the starting ramp. Is Lydia here? I saw her parents but is *she* here?

"Five, four . . ."

Why is this thing not windproof? This is skiing, so of course it is going to be cold outside. Why don't they make race suits wind-proof?

". . . three, two . . ."

And why is this race suit so tight? I feel—

". . . one . . . Go, racer!"

Go! Go! Go! Kick back the ski so it opens the wand at the last possible second, yes! Now get ready for the first gate. A right turn. Brace yourself, brace yourself. It's a blue gate. No don't lean back, weight forward! Push against the front of the boot. It's going to hit my face—

I run into the slalom gate, a single plastic pole about six feet high and one inch wide. It bends at the bottom, at the part where the plastic turns into flexible rubber, where it is drilled into the snow. Ice, actually. All ice today. *Thwhap!* The gate bounces off me and smacks the ice. I was hoping to hit the gate with my leg, with my plastic shin guard or thigh guard, but I wasn't far enough inside the turn. I took it in my face, on the mouth guard.

When I used to watch the Olympics on TV and see slalom racing, I thought it was confusing. There were so many plastic poles everywhere, some red, some blue, and the racers ran right into them. Why not go around the outside? But now that I am a ski racer myself and I go to ski team practice twice a week, I know that it's not as confusing as it looks on TV. You just go around each gate, left right left right, as the colors alternate, red blue red blue. You run into the gates with your body because only your ski has to get around the outside of the gate. The rest of your body can be on the inside. And just like when we run the mile in gym and I run faster on my crutches than some of the girls do on two legs because I run on the inside lane, where it's shorter and faster, you can go through a ski course quicker by getting your ski closer to the gate and having your body just smack into it. The gate will then flex at the base, swing over and bounce off the snow like the inflatable punching bag I had when I was little. That thing just kept bouncing up again no matter how hard you punched it.

That's the way the first gate bounces after I hit it with my face. It smacks the snow, and by the time it bounces back, I've already skied over it. But I forgot to start my turn early. Now I'm late and I jam the turn and I am sliding. *Crrrrrrrr.* My ski skids over the ice, scraping like the volume was turned way up on the TV and then the signal went out. White noise. The kind you can hear. *Crrrrrrrr.* I tighten the muscles in my leg to brace against the ice, but this only pushes my ski farther down the hill—*it's so steep*—and I catch myself on my right outrigger.

Now I have almost stopped moving. I lost all my speed from scraping on the ice and—*this can't be happening!*—now the race is probably lost. No! The race cannot be lost. Lydia is watching, and I am going to win. I push off a few times with my outriggers, getting back into the track where the ice has been carved out by the forty-one racers before me, so it looks like a shallow bobsled run.

The gates are only about ten feet apart, and I wasted most of that space by sliding, so I have to jump, to literally jump and turn my ski to the left in the air so I can make the second turn. I am too far to the outside to hit the gate with my leg, but still close enough that my left elbow accidentally hooks around it, spinning my upper body. The gate bounces off my arm and slaps the front of my ski. I lose grip on the snow and spin left, turning until I'm facing straight up the hill. I stop moving and immediately feel myself start to slide backward, pulled down by gravity.

I jump, again pivoting in the air, and land with my ski pointing to the next gate. I cut across the hill and start the turn early . . . so I don't have to jam like I did on the first gate.

Oh no! Too early!

I try to slide out to the left to make it around the turn. My ski slides faster than I expected, and my leg extends fully.

Always keep your knee bent! Coach said never straighten your leg!

I push on my right outrigger to keep from falling, and I come back to upright. But I'm still too far inside the turn, heading straight toward the gate instead of around it. I try to slide more to the outside—*slide, slide!*—but the tip of my ski catches on the gate, gets stuck. And then—*Pop!* My ski binding snaps open, releasing my boot.

I fly through the air for several seconds—probably looking, in my skintight gray-blue race suit like some sort of snow dolphin, jumping out of the ice—and land with my arms out, jamming my wrists, and then continue forward in a flip. My head hits the ground next, and the space inside my helmet is like an echo chamber for the crunch of the ice against the outer plastic shell. As my flip continues, the hard-molded plastic heel of my boot swings over my body like an ax and chops a dent for itself in the ice. Momentum wants to carry me farther down the hill, but my foothold in the ice is secure, and it jerks me to a stop like a seatbelt when Dad is driving and he slams on the brakes. I take a deep breath. Exhale.

I fell. I fell! I fell I fell I fell! *Ahhhh!* How could this happen? How did I fall in my first race? I am a great ski racer, destined for national and even international glory, prophesied to win, and now I am lying on my back in the ice! And, oh—is she here? Did Lydia see me? Please let her be in the lodge drinking hot chocolate and surrounded by twenty boys or something. She cannot see this! And thank God Mom and Dad are at church, not here watching their son in this worst of all moments! I should be at church, too. Is this my punishment, God? You humiliate me because I skipped out on church this morning?

And then I look around and realize that everyone is looking at me. All the gatekeepers, standing every fifty feet or so down the course in their orange construction worker vests, watching and waiting for me to stand up and move on so they can send the next racer. I look up the hill. My ski is at least twenty feet above me, still propped against that blue plastic gate. How will I get up there? The hill is too steep! Too icy!

I wait. One of the gatekeepers will come help me. I look at the nearest one, up near the start of the course. He has his hands in his pockets. The wind blows. He shrugs his shoulders in a shiver.

I'll have to do this myself, I guess. I roll over onto my stomach, rotating my boot so that the toe side is in the hole that my heel pounded out when it hit the ice. Standing on this toehold, I swing my right outrigger overhead, pointy end first. It sticks into the side of the hill like an ice pick, and I pull myself up. Then I kick in another toehold and swing my outrigger another four feet up.

It's so cold. Everyone is looking at me, even all the way to the bottom, at the finish line, they are watching me. And thanks to my skintight race suit, I know they can see every right-angle of my zero-body-fat, zero-muscle body. That's what race suits do. They make you look naked.

After a few more steps of ice-picking, the gatekeeper above me side-slips down to my ski. (*Finally!*) He picks it up and carries it to me.

"You all right?"

I nod. I don't want to talk because I might cry, which absolutely cannot happen.

The gatekeeper sets down my ski beside me, knocking it into the hill until it stays in place. Then he squats down and puts his hands on the ice, pounding each knee once or twice to break through the crust so he can kneel in place. He puts the bony part of his right palm on the heel binding. Then he sets his left hand on top of his right and shifts his weight forward from his knees onto this stack of gloved hands. The binding opens with a *twack*.

"You ready?"

He holds the back of the ski in place while I step in front of him, planting my outriggers on the ice to hold myself up. I lift my boot, but as I try to stomp it into the binding, the smooth bases of my outriggers slip and throw me backward into the gatekeeper. He loses hold of my ski as I land on him, grabbing the ski with my left hand before it slides away.

"Sorry," I say. "Are you all right?"

The gatekeeper just nods.

He gets his knees back in their holes and grips my ski again with both hands. I step on the binding, but it doesn't shut. I bounce and try to force it closed with a stomp. It still won't close.

"Hold on. You've got snow on your boot. Here."

The gatekeeper guides my heel off the binding, and I balance on my outriggers and the toe of my boot, which is pressed against the front binding. My foot is numb from the cold, but I can feel the vibrations of something metal—a screwdriver?—as the gatekeeper scrapes chunks of snow off the heel of my boot.

"There."

I lean back and feel the heel binding clamp down with the same *twack* sound.

"Thanks."

I bend over to brush the snow off my leg and stomach.

"Hey, before you fell there," the gatekeeper says, "you were doing real good. Very impressive."

This makes me want to spit on the gatekeeper and watch my saliva freeze on his cheek, or maybe just smash his face in with my outrigger. I was not doing "real good," and we both know it. I lost all my speed—twice—got spun around, and then on the third of sixty turns, I wiped out. That's not good. That's terrible. And the only reason he said this is because I have one leg and he feels sorry for me.

I blow down the side of the course and ski past all the parents gathered at the bottom.

"Good job, Josh!" someone yells.

"Great skiing!"

One of the voices was female. I am too scared to look to see if it was Lydia.

I'm back in the gate for my second run, my second time through the course. According to The Official Rules, I am disqualified, but no one said anything when I came up and acted like I was supposed to have a second run. Everyone up at the top is just the same as that gatekeeper. They feel sorry for me. That's why they're letting me have a second try. In fact, the head referee even asked me if I wanted to ski first, before everyone else, for the second run.

"No," I said.

"You sure?"

"Yeah I'm sure."

"All right . . . if that's what you want. By the way, you're a very talented skier."

Yup, those insulting compliments just keep coming. Great skiing. You looked really strong on the first two turns. Very fast skiing young man. The only person who *didn't* tell me I skied well, the only one who respected me enough to look past my disability and acknowledge that five falls is a terrible race no matter how many legs you have, was Zack Sease. Zack and I sat together in the starting area before we lined up for the second run.

"Icy, huh?" was all he said. It was the best compliment anyone has ever given me.

Now I'm looking down the course, the front of my ski hanging over the starting ramp. I won't fall this time. I will stay standing, stay up and finish the race, and I may not win, but I can still have the fastest time for this second run. I will make that gatekeeper see how I actually *am* really good, that the first run was just unlucky.

". . . four, three . . ."

I will win.

". . . two, one . . ."

Knee bent, shoulders level, weight forward, turn early—

". . . Go, racer!"

I plow through the first gate, and it slaps down on the snow. I am fast, smooth, confident. Shoulders level. Weight forward. I turn early for the second gate, at exactly the right place. But then I start to hear that scraping sound on the snow, and my leg muscles freeze automatically in response. This makes the scraping sound turn up twice as loud. *Crrrrrrrrrrr.*

I hit the third turn—*that third gate*!—and it's so icy you could almost figure-skate on it, and my ski slides out and I am flying again, sideways down the hill. The ice jumps out of the side of the mountain and pounds into my right hip. As I lie there on the snow, the thought hits me. *I lost. It's over.* I feel cold all over. *I am not a great ski racer.*

I look at my boot. My ski is still on. I remember: A racer is permitted to return to standing position and continue the race if his or her skis do not release from his or her boots. *But why? Why does it matter anymore?* I let my body relax against the mountain, and I feel myself slide about a foot down the ice, then stop, then slide another foot. *I can't believe I fell. Twice.*

"Do you need medical attention?" someone yells. A gatekeeper.

"No."

"All right, then please clear the course."

I look up past three gates to the top, where the next racer is standing in his skintight race suit, poles planted on the steep part of the starting ramp so he can get the fastest possible start. He is ready. He is waiting for me to move. Then I look in the other direction, down the hill, and see mostly fog. It's warm enough now that what was snow this morning has turned into frozen rain. I've never been sure of the difference between snow and frozen rain. That is, until this race, when I know without a doubt that the cold, icy piles of wetness that are disappearing into my race suit can only be described as drops of frozen rain, not snowflakes. One hits my goggles. It looks like someone sucked a sip of Slurpee in a straw and blew it out on my lens. I wipe off the goggles with my glove, and now there's just a wide smear.

I look down through the Slurpee-covered goggles and freezing rain and I can see a few patches of red far down the course. All the patches seem to go along in the same direction, so I know it's a line. *The* line, actually. The finish line.

I've been sitting here long enough now that the ice has melted under my body and is soaking through the back of my race suit and long johns and underwear. This is probably for the best, though, since during the time I've been lying here, the frozen rain has already soaked through the entire front side of my body. I wouldn't want uneven water weight throwing me off balance when I bounce back up.

I push my hands against the snow and stand up on my ski. I wrap my cold, water-logged gloves around the handles of my outriggers. And then I push off toward the next gate. I take it on the left shoulder. *Thwap!* It buzzes through the freezing rain and slaps the snow. I take the next gate on my right shoulder, and the one after that on my leg. Each time I hit a gate, the ice frozen to its plastic shatters like glass confetti.

Then I fall again. But my ski stays on, and I haven't even stopped moving before I get back up. I go through more gates and fall, get up and fall, three more ice-covered gates, get up and fall. On the fifth time I fall—so close now I can make out faces around the finish area, faces like Lydia's mom—my cheek gets cut on the ice, somehow, even though I have a face guard on my helmet. The chemicals in the fake snow melt into the blood in my cheek. It stings. I stand up again, go through two more gates, and then I watch as a red line slides underneath my ski and disappears below the window of my goggles.

A few people clap. It's the sort of muffled clap you get when people are wearing gloves, like the sound when you shake out a rug. I look around.

"Good race," someone says.

"Thank you," I say, because it *was* a good race. It wasn't fast—the scoreboard referee writes my time on the board as two minutes and thirty-six seconds, exactly two minutes slower than the leading time—but it was a good race. Really good. I see Lydia's mom. She smiles at me. I look around. No Lydia. It doesn't matter. After this race I am sure I will be able to make the Paralympic team, sure I can keep training and trying and getting back up until I actually get that uniform, so I'm also sure Lydia will eventually date me, or even if she doesn't, she will wish she had, eventually.

20

I call Lydia on my sixteenth birthday, the day I am allowed to finally start dating girls. It's easy to find her number because there are only two Seases in the phone book. The one that has an address in the city, in Harrisonburg, must be Justin Sease's family, since he goes to school with me at Harrisonburg High School. So Lydia's family is the other one.

I once read where a psychologist said the best way to deal with grief after a family member dies is to go in your room and cry for thirty minutes, exactly. The next day you cry for twenty-nine minutes, the next, twenty-eight, and so on, until you get down to zero minutes after one month. Then you are done with your grief. I decide that I will use a similar system, though the numbers will increase rather than decrease, to build up the courage to call Lydia. I pick up the phone, listen for the dial tone, and then dial the first number: eight. Then I hang up. Then I pick it up again and dial the first and the second: eight-two. Then I hang up. I breathe in through my nose. Out through my mouth. One more number and I'll be almost halfway there. I work my way up to all seven digits, but then I hang up as the phone starts to ring. I almost made a big mistake—I almost forgot to *practice my opening line*!

"Hi, Lydia, this is Josh Sundquist."

"Hi, Lydia, this is *Josh Sundquist.*"

"Hi, Lydia, this *is* Josh Sundquist."

"Hi, Lydia, *this* is Josh Sundquist."

"Hi, *Lydia,* this is Josh Sundquist.

"*Hi,* Lydia, this is Josh Sundquist."

I like the first one best. It sounds the most natural.

"Hello?"

It's Zack, her brother from the ski team. Hearing his voice reminds me of our ski season together, the one where I finished last in every single race. This year, though, it's going to be different. I'm going to enter some disabled races, and I'm going to win them.

"Is Lydia there?" I ask.

I don't tell him my name because I don't want him to find out that I am calling his sister. That might be weird.

"Sure. Who is this?"

Cover blown.

"Josh Sundquist," I say.

"Oh, what's up, Josh? Hold on a minute I'll get her. *Lydia! Lydia! Phooooone!*"

I turn the ear part away from my head while he yells.

"Hello?"

Like a lot of people who live near but outside the city limits of Harrisonburg, she has a southern accent. So she says it, "Hail-lo?"

It only makes her hotter.

"Hi, Lydia!"

"Hi," she says. "Who is this?"

Whoops, forgot.

"This is Josh Sundquist," I say.

But wait? What if she doesn't remember me? I was assuming she would, but maybe not—

I jump off script, start putting words together in combinations I haven't practiced. This is risky, but it must be done. We can't have a conversation if she doesn't remember who I am.

"Remember me? From skiing? I'm on your brother's ski team?"

If she doesn't say yes, then I will have to say "the guy with one leg?" which always makes people remember me, but not for a reason I want them to. So that's only a last resort.

"Yeah, of course." Her accent makes all her words take longer to get out. She says it, "Yee-aye-uh, uh-cowz."

Good. She remembers. It's been, like, five months—a long time—so I wasn't sure.

"Great," I say. "How are you?"

"Good, you?"

"Awesome."

I used to just say "good" when people asked how I was doing. But that was before I decided to become a motivational speaker.

I've always sort of wanted to become a motivational speaker, which is weird, I know. But that's what I wanted. I saw speakers at church conferences and stuff, and I thought, *yeah,* I'd like to do that. But how do you become a motivational speaker? I had no idea. It seemed like you had to be famous, like super world famous, or have a really dramatic life story that you could talk about, like being a prisoner of war in Vietnam for twenty years, or maybe being in the *Guinness Book of World Records* for climbing Mount Everest blindfolded. I haven't done anything like that.

Then a speaker came and talked at Harrisonburg High School. His presentation was about how you shouldn't do drugs. I noticed that he didn't talk about himself much, because he's not famous and he doesn't have a dramatic life story. And that made me wonder: If *he* can become a motivational speaker, then why can't I?

But . . . I didn't know how. I didn't know whom I'd give speeches to, or what I'd talk about, or how I would even get started. I was thinking about all this during his speech. Then he said something that interrupted my thoughts.

"A leader has to have guts," the speaker said.

Guts. I grabbed a pen from my pocket and wrote this down. I didn't have any paper, so I wrote it in large letters on my forearm.

That afternoon I went to a computer at the school library and did a search for "motivational speaker." I went to all the motivational speakers' websites and wrote them emails like "I am Josh I am fifteen years old I want to be a motivational speaker blah-blah-blah."

And they wrote back, gave me advice, and sent me stuff, too, like books and CDs and videos. I have them all pretty much memorized.

And that's why I don't just say "good" anymore when someone like Lydia asks me how I'm doing, because one of the speakers, an old guy named Zig Ziglar, says you should always say really enthusiastic things when people ask how you are. He himself says, "Better than good and getting better," but that seems a little over the top to me. So I usually go with "awesome."

And that's what I say to Lydia when she asks how I am.

"Awesome," I say.

Then no one says anything for two or three seconds.

"Anyways . . ." I say, but she still doesn't say anything, even though it is clearly her turn to talk, since I've just said "anyways." So I say, "How is your summer going?"

"Good. You?"

"Yeah, awesome. How's Zack?"

"He's real good."

"Okay. Yeah, so it's, like, really hot outside."

Now you are delaying. Get to the point.

"Yup."

"Can't go skiing in this weather!"

That is the stupidest thing you've ever said. Just ask her.

"That's true."

"I think one time you said you like to read, right?"

On February 8, in front of the General Store, to be exact.

"Yeah, sure."

"So do you know the Green Valley Book Fair?"

"I love the Green Valley Book Fair!"

She sounds very happy now, like how I had hoped she would sound when I said, "This is Josh Sundquist."

"I was thinking about going there tomorrow"—*this is it, say it, say it, say it*—"You want to"—*come on, you practiced this line a hundred times*—"come along?"

I am glad about the phone being between us, because it muffles the sound of my heart, which is so loud . . . *maybe she can still hear it . . .*

I am holding my breath. Literally.

"Sure, that would be fun."

"Oh, awesome!" I say. *Try not to sound so surprised, you idiot.* "Well I can pick you up at two . . . in the afternoon."

"Sure. Do you need my address?"

"No. I know where you live."

"You do?"

"Yeah"—*your address is in the phone book. Hello? Where do you think I got your number?* "I'll be there at two."

At Lydia's house, I park at the top of the driveway in front of the garage. Then I realize I've made a mistake. I turn the car around and park it again. Then I lock it, even though I don't expect to actually go inside.

I knock on the door. Her mom, who saw me fall five times in my first ski race, answers.

"Hi, Josh."

"Hi, Mrs. Sease. How are you today?"

"Fine, thanks. How are you?"

"I'm doing awesome. This is a very nice home you have here."

"Oh, thank you. Lydia's excited about going with you. She loves the book fair. Hold on—*Lydiaaaa*?"

Lydia slides into view down the front hall. She is wearing shorts and a T-shirt. I am, too, but my shorts end just below my knees. Lydia's are cut off exactly one joint higher.

When I first started going to public school, I noticed that I was always staring at girls' bodies—their long tan legs dropping out of tight denim skirts, their arms with little white hairs on them, their smooth shoulders, and the line between their nipples—cleavage, it's called—which you can see when they wear low-cut tank tops. They were so different from the homeschool girls I grew up with, the ones who always wore floor-length cotton dresses to our monthly potlucks on the playground. So for those first few weeks of school, I was always staring. I thought I would eventually get over it, just adjust to all the skin everywhere and be able to maintain eye contact. But I never did. I still stare. I know that I shouldn't, because it's a sin, and it is the first stage in getting addicted to pornography, and after you get addicted to pornography, you are much more likely to have sex before marriage or commit adultery or rape, but I still do it.

"Hi," Lydia says. She smiles. I watch her slip her toes into a pair of flip-flops.

I have been trying to get up the courage to call her "Lid," because that is the nickname listed on her Instant Messenger profile. I think if I call her Lid, like her best friends apparently do, that would be a subconscious signal to her that I, too, am a close friend. It's like Tony Robbins says about the power of neurolinguistic programming. We all have subconscious associations with certain words, and they produce an emotional response in our body.

But I am too scared. What if Lid was her *old* nickname, and she just hasn't updated her profile? Or what if that is a decoy nickname, set up to trick people into using it so she can figure out who her real friends are and who is just researching her on her AOL profile?

So I say, "Hi, Lydia."

Lydia kisses her mom.

"Bye, mom."

"Bye, Mrs. Sease," I say. "Nice to see you. Have a wonderful afternoon."

"You, too, Josh. Have fun."

Adults always say that I am well spoken. If this is true, it must be true only around adults. Not their daughters.

"You look"—I pause to scan Lydia's shirt, shorts, and flip-flops so she will know this is a sincere and thoughtful compliment based on a thorough visual inspection, not just flattery—"nice."

"Oh," she says. "Thanks."

We arrive at the passenger door first, due to my last-minute parking direction change. And since it is locked and I have to insert the key and unlock it anyway, it is a very natural thing that I would also hold the door for her. Perfectly planned, perfectly executed. Very smooth.

Lydia and I walk down the long rows of tables at the Green Valley Book Fair, a warehouse-type building in the middle of a cornfield just outside the city. The Green Valley Book Fair is like a thrift store for books, except that unlike a thrift store, where everything's used, so you have to watch out for stains in the underwear they sell, the books here are all brand new. No skid marks. I wanted to bring Lydia to the book fair because I always walk out with several crates of books, a purchase that might be only twenty-five dollars in price, but that definitely makes me look rich by its sheer weight and volume.

"I love books," she says, sorting through a box of paperbacks. "But I just never have time to read."

I open my mouth to tell her about how she should just prioritize her schedule using *The Seven Habits of Highly Effective People* method, which involves Roles and Goals and something called Quadrant II. But then I remember *Women Are from Mars, Men Are from Venus.* Never try to solve a girl's problems. Just listen and repeat.

"So you never have time to read," I say. "How does that make you feel?"

"Busy, I guess," she says, glancing up at me from the box.

We go downstairs to my favorite section, Self-Help. I sort through the piles of books on the table. Anything under two dollars automatically goes in my shopping basket. Over two dollars and I buy it only if it's an author I recognize, like Tony Robbins (though he puts his full name, Anthony, on his book covers), Steven Covey, the bald Mormon who wrote the *The Seven Habits of Highly Effective People*, Zig Ziglar (actually born Hilary Hinton Ziglar), Mark Victor Hansen and Jack Canfield of *Chicken Soup for the Soul*, Deepak Chopra, and some dead authors, too, like Dale Carnegie, Norman Vincent Peale, and Napoleon Hill. If they made trading cards of self-help gurus, I'd have the rookie edition for all these guys.

"Lydia," I say. "What are your goals in life?"

I ask her this because talking about your goals and dreams in life puts you in what Tony Robbins calls a Peak Emotional State. Anything you associate with a Peak Emotional State gains importance in your mind. If I can get Lydia in a Peak Emotional State while she is on this date—*this is a date, right? I think so*—then she will associate those strong positive feelings with me, and she'll want to be my girlfriend.

"I don't know," Lydia says. "I've never really thought about it."

So much for that plan.

"What about you?" she asks.

"I want to ski in the Paralympics," I say. "And I want to become a motivational speaker and talk to ten thousand middle school students this year."

There's this other goal I have, actually, the most important one: to date Lydia Sease. I even wrote it down, because writing a goal down increases the likelihood of accomplishing it by 400 percent. But I don't think we need to discuss that goal just yet.

"What will you talk to the middle-schoolers about?" she asks.

"Setting goals."

"Oh. That sounds . . . nice."

"Hey I just thought of something!" I say, getting an idea that instantly puts me in a Peak Emotional State. "My first speech this fall is going to be at Pence Middle!"

"Cool! So Zack will be able to see you?"

"Yeah, I think so. I am going to speak to the eighth grade first, and then to the seventh grade later that morning. What grade's he going to be this year?"

"Eighth."

"Perfect, that will be great."

And this means—can I ask? Can I do it?

"You should come watch," I say.

I say it this way—as a statement, not a question—because if you ask a girl a question, she can say no. Much better to phrase it as an opinion.

"When is it?"

"Two months. October."

"Just remind me when it gets closer."

"Definitely."

If Lydia sees me give that speech in front of hundreds of middle-school students, she'll think I am famous. Then she'll want to be my girlfriend. It's all paying off, all that work this summer, calling the principals of the fifty nearest middle schools, telling their secretaries that I was a fifteen-year-old, almost sixteen-year-old, motivational speaker and then being told that, no, the principal was not available. He or she was in a meeting. All fifty, in meetings. Then going back through the list and calling all of the principals again, leaving messages, and still no returned calls. And calling all fifty a third time, speaking to a total of three principals. The first hung up during my description of our speech. The other two were interested, and they scheduled me on back-to-back days in October. And now it's all worth it because Lydia will be there, and she'll date me, and then I will have reached that other goal.

21

The morning of my first speech, after I spend most of the night awake and staring at the ceiling—*What if the microphone doesn't work? What if the video projector breaks? What if the kids don't pay attention?*—I am backstage. I go through the psych-up routine I learned at a Tony Robbins seminar, the one where I walked on hot coals.

"Yes! Yes! Yes!" I chant, clapping to the beat of the words. Then I karate-chop the air while pushing a breath out through my teeth. The key is the teeth part. It has to be loud enough to get you into a Peak Emotional State. I stop my breathing and karate-chopping and listen. I can hear the chatter of four hundred eighth-graders on the other side of the curtain.

Will they like me?

"You ready?"

It's the principal, or, actually, just his head, floating without a body in the center of the curtain.

"Yep," I say.

The head disappears.

I pull my microphone from where it's hooked onto my belt. It's a headset, of course. Same as Tony wears. I put it over my ears so the black foam part sticks right in front of my mouth, close enough that I could lick it. The principal is onstage, reading my introduction.

"Today's assembly is about," he says, then pauses. I smile. He continues to read from the introduction I gave him. "It's about the health benefits of lima beans and other non-legume plant species."

I wait for the wave of laughter to roll through the curtain. Instead, there are just murmurs. Don't they get it? Weren't they listening? It says "*non*-legume plant species," even though everyone knows lima beans are *totally a legume. Ha!* It's hilarious! Or at least . . . it was last night, when I wrote it. Guess you had to be there.

"Please provide him your full attention," the principal says.

I walk to the front of the stage. I'm wearing khaki shorts and a black T-shirt. The kids can see that I have one leg, because last year, after hair appeared on my real leg but not on the shiny, bald rubber skin of my fake leg, I removed the fake skin altogether, exposing the poles and joints inside my artificial leg.

There is a spotlight in my eyes, so all I can see are the dark outlines of four hundred heads, like shadows. *Which one is Lydia?* That reminds me of my plan. *She's going to be so surprised.* A few of the other shadows, probably the ones in the back, are the reporters I sent press releases to at *The Washington Post, USA TODAY,* and all four major TV networks. Last month I read a book on writing press releases, and I followed its instructions exactly. My press release was fascinating. Once the reporters make me famous, I won't have to call lists of principals anymore. They'll start calling me. Then I'll go on a nationwide tour to create positive change, speaking onstage in middle schools and on milk crates on street corners.

"How many of you want to change your life today?" I ask. No one raises their hand. "Sorry, I meant raise your hand. Raise your hand if you want to change your life today!"

I see only about ten hands. But I stick to the script.

"Wow!" I say. "That's great! Because I am all about positive change, and today I am going to show you how you can make positive change in your life."

Then I ask another question.

"How many of you have ever run in a race?"

Lots of hands. Good.

"How many of your races had a finish line at the end?"

Same hands.

"How many of your races *didn't* have a finish line at the end?"

A few hands go up. The students laugh.

That wasn't supposed to be a joke.

"I'm here today to tell you that a life without goals is like . . . a race without a finish line."

I pause to let these words sink in and start creating positive change.

"What is my goal, you might ask? I am a ski racer. I joined a ski team this past year. And here is my goal"—pause, hold it—"I want to be . . . the best . . . one-legged skier . . . in the world!"

I wait for them to applaud. That's in the script. They are supposed to applaud when they hear about my goal, because it is just *that* inspiring to see a guy with one leg who wants to be a ski racer. I bite my lower lip, waiting. Finally the applause begins, and I smile, just like I practiced.

I say some other stuff and then tell the students I have a video for them.

A few cheers.

"Could we get this spotlight off? So we can see the screen?" I ask. "There. Thanks. So this video is interviews I did with teenagers where I asked them a very important question, which was, 'What would you do if you only had twenty-four hours to live?'"

I hop off the stage and press Play, and Robert Gu's face appears on the projection screen. You can see behind him students dressed in Harrisonburg High blue and white and, above him, the humidity glowing over the football stadium on a Friday night last month where I did the interviews. And you can see his mouth moving. But you can't hear him. There's no sound. *What's going on?* Now Robert Gu's interview is over. Kent Barnes is on the screen. *Must have the cords wrong!* I switch one of the plugs, and then the screen turns blue, and reads, "No input detected." *Hurry, fix it, this is a disaster!* I switch a few more cords and bring the image back, but still no sound.

I start talking.

"Okay, well this guy is saying he would . . . eat a lot of ice cream, I think that's what he said, yeah"—the screen switches to Jon Small—"And here this guy is saying that if he only had twenty-four hours to live, he'd go sky-diving over and over."

And then the video is finished and the screen goes black. The spotlight turns back on. There's some clapping as I climb on the stage from the ground level. I put my hands on the platform, straightening my elbows and swinging my foot up, the way you climb out of a swimming pool when there's no ladder. That's the fast way to get onstage, the way you get up there when you are in a hurry to get it all over with. *But don't forget the part about Lydia.*

The spotlight comes back on.

"I wanted to show you that . . . video because it's such an important question to ask yourself," I say. "Because *you* might only have twenty four-hours to live. Have you thought about that? You could get hit by a car this afternoon and die, just like that! Or your house could burn down tonight while you are sleeping!"

I share a few more death-within-twenty-four-hours scenarios and read some statistics about drunk drivers, about how many of them are really out there and how they are killing unsuspecting middle-schoolers every day. I talk loudly, swinging my arms. Sweat drips off my forehead. This is so important! Are they getting it? They need to stop thinking they'll live forever! They need to know that they could die anytime, that being young doesn't make you immortal! They need to know that they could have a rare form of bone cancer in their left leg, or that there could be spots on their lungs, or that they could have an incurable cantaloupe-size tumor in their stomach, right now, this very minute they could. They need to know that just by living they are already dying.

"Earlier I told you how you need to have goals in life," I say, getting near to the part that is making me so nervous. "The reason the twenty-four-hours-to-live question is so important is because it tells you what those goals should be. See, whatever things you'd do if you only had twenty-four hours to live—those should be your goals. And whatever you'd *wish* you could do but wouldn't have time for with only one day left in your life, those things should be your goals, too."

This is it. I walk to the corner of the stage and reach my hand in between the American flag and the curtain. I can feel it there, sitting on the chair. I pick it up, hold it behind my back. *Here we go.*

"I'll tell you what I would do, if I only had twenty-four hours to live," I say. *Where is she? I need to figure out where she's sitting.* "I'd go find the girl I have liked for so long and tell her how much I like her. I'd tell her how she's beautiful and how I think about her all the time and how meeting her was one of the best things that has ever happened to me. Then I'd give her flowers and ask if she would be my girlfriend."

That's the end of what I had planned. I'm not sure what was supposed to happen next. I guess I was thinking, by this time, that Lydia would run down the aisle to the stage, and I would pull the flowers from behind my back and give them to her and we'd kiss and everyone would applaud. They'd be inspired to go out and pursue their dreams, just like I did. That was going to be my dramatic conclusion. But Lydia isn't running down the aisle. Maybe she just doesn't realize I am talking about her? I slip the bouquet back behind the flag and leave it on the chair. I walk to the front of the stage and bend down below the beam of the spotlight, shielding my eyes so the shadows turn into faces. There's feedback. *Skerrrrrrrrrrrrrreeeee!* I'm too close to the monitor. I sidestep, and the feedback stops and the room is quiet. I scan the rows of faces, the rows of eighth-graders. They are seated in clumps, with one adult for each clump. I sort through them quickly. *No, not in that one.*

No . . . no . . . no . . . no. I work my way to the back of the room, where the principal and a few others are standing along the wall. *Is that Mom?* But no Lydia.

I walk back to center stage. This wasn't in the script. I'll have to make it up.

"So that's what I want to leave you with this morning," I say. "Remember that you could die anytime. So you need to write goals for your life. Go after . . . go after your dreams."

I sit down on the front of the stage, my real foot and my fake foot hanging off the edge. There are a few claps, and then some murmurs, and the students are shuffling out of the room. Then the principal is standing in front of me.

"Unfortunately, we are not going to be able to do that second assembly today," he says.

"What?" I say. "Why not?"

"Scheduling difficulties."

"I don't understand. We scheduled this three months ago!" I say, karate-chopping the air with both my hands spread far apart to represent three months, that being such a long time.

"Some things have changed."

"What kinds of things?"

"Just some things."

"What things?"

"We—look—if you want to know, I am—there is concern that some of your content may not be appropriate for the seventh-graders," he says. And before I can argue, he turns and disappears into the stream of students moving toward the back doors of the auditorium, taking my nationwide tours along with him.

I lean forward and wrap my arms around my legs. I sit like that for a long time and it's very quiet because I stop hearing and seeing what's going on around me. I failed. I worked so hard for so long and I failed. I got turned down by forty-eight principals and then had my second speech canceled. I tell these students to live their dreams, to achieve their goals, but I can't seem to achieve mine no matter how hard I try.

And Lydia. Where did I go wrong? I followed all the rules. I did everything John Gray told me to do, like listening to her and trying not to solve her problems, and I did neurolinguistic programming, to try to get her in a Peak Emotional State. But the rules didn't work. She didn't come today.

She doesn't like me.

The thought stabs me like thousands of needles, the same way my phantom limb pain used to, except these needles are all over my body, every square inch. She doesn't like me! It's so obvious. How did I miss it? We rode the lift together, laughed together. But only once. She went on a date with me. But only once. All the other times—how many has it been now? Ten, I think—when we set up a time to meet, she didn't show up. I was tenacious! I was persistent! I didn't give up, because I never, never, never give up! But it didn't matter, because she just doesn't like me.

I look around and realize the room is empty except for Mom. She is sitting in the second-to-last row. She came to watch today. Of course she did. What has she ever missed of mine in my entire life? Nothing. I spend all my time thinking about Lydia, about ski racing, about Tony Robbins, and I always forget about Mom.

It's like when she was on chemo. When I had cancer, the world revolved around helping me get well again. The family gave up so much for me that year. Mom and Dad spent all their time meeting with doctors, dealing with insurance companies, living with me in the hospital. Matt and Luke went from house to house, staying with different families from the church every day. And then, when Mom had cancer, it was the exact opposite: It was as if Mom gave everything she could so that the rest of us wouldn't have to give up *any-thing*. She put a scarf on her head and drove us to school, just like she always had. She put gloves on her hands and went grocery shopping, just like she always had. Sure, I didn't get to ski much that year, but when it comes down to it, I can't believe how little effect Mom's cancer had on my life. When I think back on my own battle with cancer, I can watch hours of memories in full video and surround sound. The hospital stays. The surgeries. How it affected Matt. But when I think back on Mom's cancer, it's like I have only a few snapshots, still frames of certain moments. Mom feeding Anna from a bottle. The Marshes decorating our house. Finding out it was incurable. But no video.

I look at Mom, in the back of the auditorium, waiting until I am ready to talk. She knows about Lydia; she helped me pick out the flowers yesterday. And maybe she's figured out that my second assembly was canceled, too.

"Hey, Mom?" I say, as a question.

I hear an echo of the words. My microphone is still on. I guess she heard me talking to the principal. I guess everyone did.

Mom looks up at me. I walk to the back corner of the stage, to the American flag.

"You want some—some flowers?"

I hold up the bouquet and bite my lower lip so I don't cry.

Mom comes down the aisle. I turn off the mic and set it on the stage. I hop down to the ground level and hand her the flowers. She hugs me.

"I'm sorry sweetheart," she says.

Then there's a third person in the auditorium, a student. She follows the downward slope of the room to the stage, walking slowly by each row of seats. She keeps her eyes on the ground a few feet in front of her, never looking up to reveal her face. She wears jeans and an oversized T-shirt. *What is she doing? Doesn't she know the other assembly was canceled?* She stops in front of me, holding something out in her hand. I take it. It's a little card, like a business card.

"Thanks to you I don't need this anymore," she says, speaking for the first time, but still looking at the floor.

And before I can say anything, she floats back up the aisle. I look down at the card. It's reads, "Suicide hotline. 24/7 free and confidential. 1-800-273-TALK."

I want to call out to her, chase her down and talk to her. But what could I say that would capture how I feel? Thanks? I appreciate it? Now it all makes sense, at least a little bit, thanks to you—all those hundreds of calls I made to the principals and all the hours I spent practicing, and even now that I made a fool of myself on stage this morning, it was all worth it thanks to you? Is that what I would say?

But she's gone, out the back door of the auditorium.

"Hey Mom," I say. "Come check this out. I'm, like, changing the world."

That afternoon I take my microphone and sound equipment to Hilyard Middle School to set up for my second school tomorrow morning. After I carry everything in, I realize I've left my microphone at Pence. *One thing after another.*

I drive forty minutes back to Pence Middle School. I park. As I climb out, I see a white Jeep in the line of minivans and station wagons that are waiting to pick up students. The Jeep has a pink Roxy sticker on the back.

I turn around. Too late. Lydia is already running across the parking lot.

"Joooooooooooooooshh!" she yells.

I stand still, watching her run.

"Josh!" she says, throwing her arms around my neck.

"Hi Lydia."

I don't smile.

"I overslept this morning and totally missed your speech. How'd it go?"

"Um, okay."

"Was Zack there?"

"I guess."

"Yeah. I'm here to pick him up."

"I figured."

I don't say anything. This is her cue to walk away, to walk out of my life, please, and don't ever talk to me again, but she doesn't take it.

"You know we haven't hung out in *forever*," she says. "We need to get together."

"Whatever you say."

"Hey are you going to do any more of these speech things? I'd still like to see it."

I can't help it. I have to tell her.

"Tomorrow actually," I say. "At Hilyard. On the other side of the valley."

"Oh that's perfect! What time?"

I give her the details. She will be there. She promises.

Maybe just this once, she'll be there. Maybe that's why I left the microphone here . . . it was all *meant to be* . . .

I am hungry. I go home to eat. After I get a sandwich, I try to slip out the front door.

"Going somewhere?" Mom yells from the kitchen.

There's no use trying to hide it.

"The floral shop."

There's a pause.

"She said she's coming tomorrow?"

"Yeah."

Another pause. I know Mom thinks the flowers will cost me too much, and not just in terms of money. But if there's a chance Lydia will be there, I have to try, because that's what I would do if I had only twenty-four hours to live.

The next morning, the sound on the video projector works correctly so the students can hear the interviews. And I drop out all the parts of my speech that the students didn't pay attention to yesterday. I still talk about how I'd give flowers to the girl I like if I had only twenty-four hours to live, but I don't expect Lydia to come running down the aisle. I don't even expect that she's in the room.

After the assembly is over, I get some applause and cheers. There's even a little line of students who want to talk to me. And then Lydia is the next person in line.

"Hi," she says.

"You came!" I say.

"Of course I came!"

"I'm glad you did."

"It was great."

"Thanks."

I smile.

"Hold on," I say. "I have something for you."

I hobble backstage as fast as I can on my fake leg.

This is it! She's here! She saw me speak! She will think I have social status! I am going to give her the flowers and she'll know that the speech was about her, that I like her. In fact—that's it! That's the problem! *She doesn't know I like her.* I've never told her. Once she knows, she'll tell me how she likes me, too!

I hand her the flowers.

"I—uh," I stutter. I want to say everything I planned, about how much I like her, how she's beautiful and awesome and a bunch of other adjectives, but I freeze. "I wanted you to have these" is all I say.

"Thanks," she says.

I nod. *Is she making the connection to my speech? Does she understand what the flowers mean?*

"Hey, what are you doing tonight?" she asks.

"No plans."

"Let's hang out!"

"Yeah, that'd be great."

"I'll call you," she says.

"Perfect," I say.

I go home as happy as I've ever been. Tony Robbins was wrong. Happiness is not a choice. Happiness is when your second day as a motivational speaker goes well and you have plans to hang out with the girl who knows you like her.

I'm not sure when Lydia will call, and I don't want to miss her, so I get a book and go to Mom and Dad's room at 4:14 p.m., right after I get home. I read until dinner, take a short break, and then go back and wait by the phone. She'll call anytime now. It's seven o'clock. Eight o'clock. Nine. Does the phone work? I pick it up, listen to the dial tone. At ten o'clock Mom and Dad want to go to bed, so I leave their room and go to mine.

I think about Lydia, about the conversations we've had over the last several months. The truth is she never really seemed to be listening to anything I said. In fact, it's almost like how it was with Nana in her final months, when the Alzheimer's had completely taken over. Mom made a rule that whenever we visited her, Matt and I had to talk to her for at least five minutes a day. I would always wait until no one else was in the room. Then I would stand beside Nana's bed, look at her lying there in her floral print dress, her eyes focused beyond the ceiling, her body so thin that the only shape rising above the mattress was her head and her diaper. I'd start talking about the stuff I couldn't tell anyone else—how I was tired of homeschooling, how much I wanted to go to public school, how I hated Mom and Dad—and sometimes her gaze would shift toward me and we'd make eye contact, and I'd wonder if maybe she could understand after all. Then one day she let out a long, loud laugh at a completely wrong time, when I was mid-sentence, saying something serious. It startled me. I hadn't heard anything from her—speaking, laughing, anything—for months. But after that day I knew she wasn't really listening.

And Lydia is the same way. She doesn't pay attention. She's never really listening. She doesn't like me. I've just never been willing to admit it to myself. And now I've wasted my Friday night, just as I have so many other nights that she hasn't called back, buying into a lie that I told myself over and over. I stare out the window of my bedroom, looking at Southampton Drive. It's empty and quiet. I can see my reflection, and the image is transparent in the glass. I can see right through myself. I get out a sheet of paper and write a resolution.

"Never let yourself look like a fool. Never let them see you fail."

I sign it and date it.

22

Two weeks after I gave that first speech, a brochure comes for me in the mail with a photo of a one-legged ski racer wearing a red, white, and blue race suit, snow shooting up behind his ski like water behind a motor boat. In one quick motion, my left pointer finger goes inside the mailer just below the white tab sticker that keeps it closed and I jerk down with a snap of my other wrist, tearing the sticker so I can unfold the brochure on my desk. Inside is a schedule. Dates, times, places. It reads, "U.S. Disabled Ski Racing Tour '00– '01 Season."

This is it! The answer I've been waiting for! This is how you get to the Paralympics!

I dial one of the for-more-information numbers listed in the brochure, using the phone in Mom and Dad's room.

"Comp Center! This is Paul!" says the voice that answers. It's a deep, scratchy voice that seems to be shouting. If bears could talk, this is most likely how they'd sound on the telephone.

"Is this Paul DiBello?" I ask.

"Yeah."

"At the National Sport Center for the Disabled?"

"Yeah, what do you want?"

"I want to be a ski racer."

"Who is this?"

"My name is Josh Sundquist."

"Okay, Josh," says the voice. "Are you a gimp?"

"What?"

"A gimp. Are you disabled?"

"I lost my left leg when I was nine years—"

"And you say you want to ski race?"

"Yes," I say. "I got this brochure, and I saw you have a disabled ski race in February. I want to sign up for it."

"Huh," he grunts. "You ever raced before?"

"Yes, on the Massanutten Junior Ski Racing Team."

"Never heard of it. You raced any disabled races?"

"No, just normal ones," I say.

"How old are you?"

"Sixteen."

"All right, Josh, here's what you do: You go to your parents, tell them all you want for Christmas this year is a plane ticket to Learn to Ski Race Camp," says Paul DiBello, the grizzly voiced race director. "Then you come out here over Christmas vacation. We teach you how to compete. Then, when you come back in February for the race, you don't show up with your dick in your hands."

At first I take this literally—*why would I be holding . . . ?*—and then figure it must be some sort of metaphor.

"Okay, yeah, wouldn't want to show up . . . doing that," I say.

It's December 25. In our family, we get three presents from Mom and Dad for Christmas. Mom and Dad chose this number, three, because that's how many gifts Jesus got on Christmas (count 'em: gold, frankincense, and myrrh), so if it's enough for Jesus, it's enough for us. This year, my plane ticket counted as two items, since it was more than thirty-five dollars, the normal limit. As for the Zig Ziglar tapes, I thank Mom and Dad, but to be honest, I would've been a lot more excited about getting them, say, last summer, before . . . before . . . that whole motivational speaker thing kind of . . . *fell apart*. Before all the rules in my self-help books let me down.

I hug Luke and thank him for the five miniature Reese's Peanut Butter Cups. And I thank Matt for giving me the exact same present he gives each of us every year: a five-dollar bill, in an envelope, which is so uncreative that it has turned into an annual joke. And I hug Anna, kiss her on top of the head. She's three now, too young to give presents. But she still receives them. This year I gave her a pair of pink gloves that Mom picked out for me.

That's how Christmas works around here. For some reason, in our family, no one really gets excited about buying presents for one another. Except for that Christmas the Marshes decorated our house—two years ago, when Mom was on chemo—we just don't have that atmosphere of Yuletide magic that you see in Christmas movies. So to make sure everyone still exchanges gifts, Mom buys stuff from the sale rack and wraps them for us. After Christmas, she reads you a list of what you owe her for the gifts she bought on your behalf. No one price tag ever reaches double digits. "Five dollars for Anna's gloves, two dollars for Dad's chocolate bar, six dollars for Matt's CD, because you split the cost with Luke . . ."

After the gifts, I hug Mom once more. Her eyes glisten.

"Be careful," she says.

"I will."

"We're really going to miss you."

She wants me to say, "I'll miss you, too," but I am not sure if this is true. It's not that I don't love Mom, because of course I do. It's just that I am so excited about going to Colorado that I'm not sure I will think about home much. I guess I could lie, say I will miss you, too. That would make her feel good. But lying is wrong, even if it's just a little lie to make your parents feel warm and fuzzy. So I don't say it. I say, "Thanks."

Mom smiles. It's sort of a sad smile, because she noticed what I said, or actually, what I didn't say.

Then Mom says, "Have a happy New Year out there. I hope you make some friends you can celebrate with."

"I will."

"I don't want you to be all alone for New Year's."

"I won't, Mom. Don't worry."

"But don't stay up too late, either . . ."

"Bye, Mom."

"I love you, Joshua."

"I love you, too."

Dad and I get in the minivan for the drive to Dulles Airport, up near Washington, D.C. Mom, Luke, Anna, and Matt stand on the front porch as we drive down the block. Mom, Luke, and Anna wave. Matt holds up two fingers. Peace.

Yes, Matt, peace.

On the plane, the first thing I do is eat all five Reese's Peanut Butter Cups. If I were at home, this much candy would have taken five weeks to eat, since I still follow the Candy Day rules. But I'm not at home anymore. I'm on a plane, and soon I'll be in Winter Park, Colorado, where I will become a Paralympic ski racer. So I can eat as much candy as I want.

I look around at the other passengers, and I feel sorry for them. They all wish they were at home with their families, eating fruitcake and drinking eggnog. I can see it in their faces. But not me. There's no place I'd rather be than on this plane, up in the clouds.

The next morning I walk into the office of Paul DiBello, grizzly voiced race director, at exactly seven o'clock. Paul is already there, bent over a calculator on his desk. The top of his head is completely bald. Not shiny bald like mine was when I had chemo, though. It's dark and rough. He looks up. I notice that half his nose is missing—not one of his nostrils, but the entire front half, as if his face were permanently pressed up against a window.

Having a disfigured nose would be annoying, I think to myself, because it would be impossible to tell if someone was staring at it or just making sloppy eye contact. Not like if you are missing a leg—that kind of staring is totally obvious.

"Josh," Paul says, as a statement, not a question.

"Nice to meet you, Paul."

I put out my hand. He reaches up to shake it. His fingers are unnaturally short, cut off at different lengths, so his hand has the staggered shape of a downtown skyline.

"Sit down," he says.

I obey.

"We pulled that one over on your parents, huh?" he says.

"What?"

"We got you out here! On Christmas! Got them to pay for it!" Paul DiBello leans back in his chair, pleased with himself.

"Actually I paid for most of it with my savings."

This surprises him. But only for an instant, the sort of facial twitch you would miss if you blinked. Then it's back to pleased-with-self.

"We did get your parents to let you leave on Christmas Day, though," he says.

"Yeah," I say. "That's true."

I notice a pair of ski boots in the corner of Paul's office, behind his chair. Growing out of each boot like a potted plant is an artificial leg. Both legs are a dark flesh color, the same shade as the top of Paul's bald-but-not-shiny head. Ski legs. Paul DiBello is a double amputee.

"You ready to work hard out there?" he asks, motioning toward the ski slopes outside this building.

"Yeah!" I say. I want him to hear in my voice that I am enthusiastic, that I am not afraid of hard work, that I finished my first ski race even though I fell five times.

Hear me, Paul DiBello! I am a prodigy! I am destined for the Paralympics! Never again will I let them see me fail!

"Good. I hope you left your panties back in—where are you from?"

"Virginia."

"Virginia," he repeats. He snorts as he says it, as if being from Virginia means I am probably wearing panties right this very minute.

Just then a guy a few years older than me appears in the doorway to Paul's office. He wears a hat with "NY" on it. He has this hat turned around sideways, but not all the way—if his head were a clock, with his face being twelve and his ears being three and nine, the "NY" would be at two. The hat is tilted back, also, sitting on the crown of his head, exposing a hologram sticker underneath the flat bill.

"Look who it is," says Paul.

Sideways NY Hat takes another step inside the doorway. He's wearing big, light brown Timberland boots. Actually, boot. Just one boot. And crutches.

"What up, Paul?" he says.

"What is it today, Ralph?" asks Paul, as if Sideways NY Hat— Ralph, I take it—interrupts Paul's 7:00 a.m. appointment each morning with some new and annoying problem.

"Ain't you happy to see me, Paul?"

"Fucking ecstatic. What is it?"

"Peoples been talking about them meal discount passes you giving out. Fifty percent off or some shit?" Ralph says. Ralph talks with an unusual accent.

Peoples been talkin bout dem meal discow passes you been gibbin out. Fiddy puhcent off a sum shit?

"Yeah?" says Paul, as if to say, "And you think I'm going to just *give* you one?"

"You goan hook me up?"

Paul doesn't speak for at least five seconds, like he is hoping to wait long enough so Ralph will forget about the discount pass and leave. Ralph doesn't move. He stands there, staring at Paul.

During this showdown of eyeballs, I wonder how Ralph squeezed through that doorframe. Underneath an oversize ski jacket and baggy snow pants, I can see that his thigh is easily as wide as my twenty-seven-inch waist, and his upper arms are probably bigger around than my head. His neck flairs up out of his ski jacket like a football player's, and his fingers are almost long enough to wrap around the entire crutch grip and touch his wrists.

All that bulk continues to stand there, just inside the doorway.

"Yeah," Paul DiBello says. "I'll give you a fucking pass."

Ralph laughs, like this was all a big joke.

"HIH-ha-ha-ha!"

The first part of his laugh, the "HIH," sounds a bit like a hiccup, and the "ha-ha-ha," a little quieter, like a softer echo of the initial burst. *HIH-ha-ha-ha.*

If I were standing outside right now, in the snow, I would still hear this laugh.

"Thanks, Paul! My man!"

Paul signs a blue slip of paper and hands it to Ralph.

"Now get the fuck out," Paul says.

"Wait, who this?" Ralph says, nodding at me.

. . . who dis?

"New racer. Josh Sundquist, meet Ralph Green."

"Oh what up, man? Welcome to Winter Park."

Ralph uses underarm crutches, not the forearm kind I do. This allows him to keep his crutch in place underneath his shoulder while he swings his arm out wide—like he's throwing a discus—to shake my hand. I intercept his swinging hand in mine and try to keep up as our handshake slides into interlocked thumbs and then down until our hands are bent like hooks, holding on to one another like a yin-yang. It's the standard handshake of young males, but Ralph does it much faster than Matt and I do.

"You tell Josh my favorite story?" Ralph asks Paul.

"Which is . . . ?"

"About the blind chick?"

Ralph laughs as he remembers his Favorite Story About the Blind Chick. Even Paul smiles a little bit, revealing a surprisingly full set of teeth.

"We're having a meeting here, Ralph," says Paul.

"You got to tell him!"

Paul thinks again about the blind chick and chuckles.

"All right," Paul DiBello says. "There was this girl on the disabled ski team here. She came to train with us."

"Like four year ago," says Ralph.

. . . foe yeah ago.

"Who's telling the fucking story?" Paul barks.

Ralph nods for Paul to continue, while *that word* echoes in my mind. People swear a lot at public school, but two minutes with Ralph and Paul are like an entire month of school. The swear words flow out of their mouths without significance or meaning, part of their normal vocabulary. This makes it hard for me to keep up with the things they are saying, especially Ralph. In addition to his accent being hard to understand, when he swears, that's the only word I hear.

"So she says she's blind," Paul is saying. "And you know how factors work, right?"

"No," I say.

"Damn rookie," Paul says to Ralph. Then to me, "Factors are like a handicap in golf. Every disabled skier has a factor based on their disability. That way you and Ralph can race against a guy without an arm, or a guy in a wheelchair—"

"Or a blind mother fucker!" Ralph interrupts.

. . . bline motha fucka!

"Do you want me to tell the story or not?" Paul snaps.

"Shit," says Ralph. That's all he says. The whole sentence. Just "shit," with extended vowels, like "*sheeeeiiiiiiiiiit.*"

Paul continues the story.

"So she says she's blind, and that gives her a big factor, knocks probably a minute off her races," Paul says. "And she starts cleaning up. Winning medals at every race. Coaches have never seen a blind person ski so fast."

I see where this is going.

"But turns out she wasn't blind," says Paul. "Best part was she had told everyone she was a black belt in karate, and challenged guys on the team to fight her. But she said they had to wear blindfolds to make it fair."

Ralph is laughing at this part, his head thrown back so the sound echoes off the ceiling. Paul continues talking.

"So we've got disabled guys—amputees, wheelies—with blindfolds on, fighting against this girl with normal vision. She just"—now Paul starts to laugh as he tells it—"she just kicked their *asses!*"

I laugh, too. It's the hardest I've ever laughed at 7:06 in the morning.

"So what'd you do?" I asked.

"We fucking took her down, charged her with fraud," says Paul, as if I this were so obvious I shouldn't have had to ask. "Someone saw her shopping by herself at Safeway, so we figured it out. Then we set a trap for her. Had the cops waiting at the bottom of the race course. She skied down behind her guide, and when she saw the cops, she took her skis off and started running for the parking lot. So I tackled her."

"Wow," I say, imagining Paul running after her on his two below-knee artificial legs, the cops struggling to keep up. That must've been a sight.

"That's why now when you want to race disabled world cup, you have to have a doctor examine you and approve your disability," Paul says. "And the blind skiers have to put cardboard in their goggles. Just in case."

An hour and a half later, after the resort opens for skiing, I'm sitting on a lift chair beside Ralph.

"So where are you from?" I ask.

"Brooklyn," he says. "You?"

"Virginia."

"Awe'ite, awe'ite," he says. Must be his version of "all right."

I like sitting beside another amputee. It's kind of a relief, like a chance to have a get-to-know-you conversation that doesn't involve questions like "Do you have to buy pairs of shoes?" and "What did they do with your leg after they cut it off?" A normal conversation about normal things just like normal people have.

The problem is I am not really sure what else we can talk about. Tony Robbins says that you should always try to talk about things you have in common. But I don't think Ralph and I have much of anything in common—except, of course, for being amputees. Otherwise we are pretty much different in every way. What should I do, Tony Robbins? What are the rules here?

I'll have to make them up as I go along.

"So that was a pretty crazy story," I say. "About the blind girl."

Ralph laughs.

"Yeah . . . blind girl," he says.

There's a pause.

"A couple years ago, this chick and me always be having sex blindfolded," Ralph says.

What? Where did *that* come from! What was the connection to the blind girl? Oh, right. Blindfolded. Like blind. Got it.

Normal conversational rules would say that it's now time for my follow-up question to his anecdote. But how do you follow that?

What would be an appropriate follow-up question for "This chick and me always be having sex blindfolded"?

Hmmmmm.

"Well . . . where did you get the blindfold?" I ask.

"I wear her panties," Ralph says, chuckling to himself. "We was crazy."

Who is this guy? And what's the deal with this place and panty references?

"Ever try that shit?" he asks.

"Me? No, never tried that," I say, emphasizing *that*, as if I have tried a great many things in my day, just not that thing in particular, not yet at least.

"You a hip disartic?"

"Yeah," I say.

Hip disarticulation. The level of my amputation. An amputee discussion. I was hoping to talk about something else, but at least it's no longer about sex. I can't think of a topic that I know less about than sex.

"You, too?" I ask.

"Hell yeah son. You know chicks be wanting a hip disartic!" he says.

"What do you mean?" I ask. This has not been my experience, exactly. At least, not with one particular chick I can think of.

"You missing that one leg and you get your junk all up that pussy! Shorty be wanting more of that!" he says. "HIH-ha-ha-ha!"

Ya missin' dat one leg an ya git yo junk all up dat pussy! Shawdy be wantin' moe ah dat!

What are all these words? They don't seem to be swear words, just words I don't know. All right, pick out the key phrases, see if you can piece it together. *Missing a leg*, right, got that. *Junk?* I think that can be a euphemism for the male reproductive organ. But . . . I'm not sure about *pussy*. And *shawdy?* No idea. Sounds kind of like "shorty" . . .

"I don't understand," I finally say.

"She think yo junk long!"

Oh, I see. When you have sex. Girls think you have a longer erection. Got it. But why would this be important? Why would a girl *want* that? Seems like that might be kind of painful for her.

Time to change the subject!

"So you ski race?" I ask.

"What you think, man?"

Wha'chu thank?

"Yeah, I guess you do, huh? So do you live out here?" I ask.

"Yeah, man. Just move in November."

"What brought you here?"

"Shit," he says, sounding surprised that I would ask such an obvious question. "Trying to make the Paralympic team."

I sit up straight in the lift. All my nerves awaken to full attention. Ralph is . . . my competition! He wants the same thing I do! He's pursuing the same goal! . . . but of course he is. Why else would he be training here?

"You in high school?" he asks me, breaking the silence.

"Yeah," I say.

He nods.

"I come out here back when I be yo age. For a season. Then I go back home for a couple years, now I back. I wish I stay, though. I wish I stay."

"How come?"

"To train, son! Can't nobody get on the Paralympic team if they ain't training here!"

"Why not?"

"This the best training around, son. For real. You ain't never goan get on the team if you ain't living here, training here."

Livin' here? *Trainin'* here? But I live in Virginia! I go to Harrisonburg High School! I live with my mom and dad and two brothers and a baby sister! How can I move out to Colorado? How can I just up and leave everything, come live here, where I don't know anyone? How would I finish school? Where would I live? What would I eat? How would I pay for it?

No, Ralph Green, you are wrong. I am a prodigy. You haven't seen me ski yet. I am the best one-legged skier in the world. I will race in a few races each year, train once a week at Massanutten, and that will be enough to get me on the Paralympic ski team. *I* don't need to live here to make the team.

We get to the top of the mountain.

"Follow me," Ralph says. "I goan show you where we be training at today."

I follow Ralph down a long, flat trail. It's a beginner slope, packed with novice skiers, skiers who are falling, skiers who are standing still and talking to one another. Ralph weaves in between them on his one ski, and I follow closely in his track. I watch heads turn as Ralph slips through the mass of skiers. People watch him, they nudge their friends and point at him, they nod at one another. It's a *one-legged skier*! Look at him go!

But all this happens in Ralph's wake. He can't see it.

Ralph leads me to the top of a trail that is closed off with an orange rope stretched between two trees. On the other side of the divide is the greatest disabled skiing show on earth, a circus of eye-popping physical defects mixed with athletic builds. There are a few one-legged skiers—three trackers—like Ralph and me. There is a girl with one arm who is (*wow*) so hot, standing there in her skin-tight race suit. There's a skier with a bright orange vest that reads, "Blind Skier," and another whose vest reads, "Guide." And several of the athletes are sitting in fiberglass seats molded around their legs and lower back like a giant hard-shelled shoe. Under their chairs are fat springs and hinges, all attached to a single ski. They stay balanced with a pair of foot-tall outriggers.

A young guy, probably twenty or so, scoots his sit-ski over to a radio hanging from the orange rope.

He presses it, says something.

A crackling voice comes back: "Clear."

"Hup hup," someone says as the sit-skier points his ski down the hill and pushes off with his outriggers.

With his back turned to me, I can see the coat he is wearing, which covers his upper body and slides over the fiberglass at the top of his seat, too, like the skirt on a kayak. But this coat—it's no neoprene kayak skirt. No. This is a dark blue ski parka embroidered with raised white and silver threads stitched to form an eagle on his back, an eagle whose wings stretch nearly shoulder to shining shoulder. Underneath the feathers of the wings are more threads, more stitches that form three letters. I lean around the one-armed girl to get a better look as that jacket turns under the first gate of the training course.

Later that morning the Winter Park Disabled Ski Team assembles in a locker room in the basement of the ski lodge. There are about twenty of us. We walk in, crutch in, limp in, wheel in, and are led in—carefully holding on to the elbow of an orange-vest-wearing guide—to huddle around a TV.

"I'm going to show each of you your first training run," says one of the coaches on staff here, a young guy with a goatee and a bright red face—a product of windburn or sunburn, or maybe both, from being on the slopes every day. "I want you to name something that you think you could improve on."

I knew the coach was filming this morning. When I came down that training course, I went as fast as I possibly could, faster than I've ever gone before, as if there were rockets glued to the back of my ski. I can't wait to see the video. The team will be speechless, shocked by my speed. They will know they are in the Presence of Greatness.

The coach presses Play on a handheld camcorder strung to the TV. We watch a few athletes. Finally it gets to me.

"All right, here's the rooksta," Coach says. "Where are you?"

I raise my hand.

"Ready? Here goes."

He presses Play and I see my coat, my ski pants, my helmet come onto the screen. Yes! There I am! I'm ready, Video Josh! I'm ready to see you turn into a blur as you fly by the camera!

But the blur never comes. Instead, I see myself inch down the mountain. Sometimes it looks like I have just stopped completely. What's going on? What's wrong? Then I realize: The coach is playing it in slow motion! Of course! Good one, coach! A joke on the new guy! Ha!

I look at Coach, waiting for his red face to break into a laugh. But he is serious, studying the video. This is not a joke.

I'm just *that* slow.

"Pretty stiff-looking," someone says.

And it's true. I am skiing . . . stiffly, as if I'm afraid of falling. Which I was.

"Look at me," the coach says in a voice like a little girl's. "I'm Stick Man!"

Everyone laughs. All twenty of them, these disabled jerks, they laugh at me. I hate you, Coach! How could you mock me like that, get a laugh at my expense on my first day? Someday I will be the best one-legged skier in the world and you will try to tell everyone that you helped get me there with your coaching. But I will tell them that all you did was make fun of me, which didn't help me at all. It just made me angry, made me want to prove you wrong. It was the opposite of helping me.

"What do you think you could improve?" the jerk-of-a-coach asks.

I consider ignoring him. *Why should I answer you, Coach, you who make fun of me?* But I decide to answer the question—for my benefit, not his.

"My knee needs to be bent," I say. "And my weight forward. I need to start the turn earlier. My shoulders should be more level."

"You're pretty hard on yourself," he says.

Hard on myself? You're the one who's mocking me!

"Actually," Coach continues. "Your technique isn't all that bad. You just aren't aggressive enough. You need to take more risks, push yourself."

Whatever, jerk.

I look back at the screen, watch Stick Man Josh make the last two turns. And then it hits me. *I am not even close.* My skiing isn't good enough to make the Paralympic team. *Ralph was right.* I have so much training to do, so many miles of practice left to go. *I will have to move out here after all.*

Ralph himself appears next on the TV, blowing down through the course. When he goes by the video camera, I watch carefully, and sure enough—*how does he go so fast?*—there is the fraction of a second, when he is closest to the camera, when his body turns into this colorful blur, racing past. I study Video Ralph as he leans into each turn. Sometimes his knee is bent at ninety degrees. Other times it snaps straight out. Sometimes his weight is forward, sometimes way back, sometimes too far right or left. At random times, his right arm swings up and around in the air like the way it did when he shook my hand this morning. It's like he's in a boxing match with the race course. And then, on the last turn, he crashes, spraying up snow, tumbling.

"You see this, rooksta?" the coach asks, pausing the tape and turning back to me. "Ralph and you are opposites. You need to loosen up, let your body relax. Forget about technique, just go fast. Ralph, though, he's out of control"—Coach is still looking at me, but you can hear in his voice that this part is meant for Ralph to hear—"Ralph has got to focus on his balance and his technique."

"Shit," Ralph says, in a tone that says, "I ain't gotta focus on nuttin'."

"Ralph, who would you rather ski like? Hermann Maier or Bode Miller?" Coach asks.

Anyone in this locker room, anyone who reads *Ski Racing* magazine cover to cover each month like I do, understands the question. Hermann Maier is a technically perfect skier, sometimes boring to watch, but perfect, and perfectly aggressive, too. Most important, he's a world champion, a consistent podium finisher for the Austrian national team. Bode Miller, on the other hand, is a young upstart, a cocky, brash skier who recently made the U.S. national team. Some people think he has the potential to be a world champion in a few years, but right now he just falls too much. He's always out of control.

Coach wants Ralph to ski like Herman Maier, to choose a career of consistent world championships. That's the right answer. But I think Ralph will pick Bode Miller, because that's his skiing style: Wild, fast, cocky.

But Ralph chooses neither.

"I wanna ski like Ralph Green," he says.

All twenty of us are silent. Somehow it was exactly the right thing to say, so much the way we all know we should think and ski. And in the silence I wish *I* was the kind of person who could think of answers like that, who could think of them and then have the courage to say them out loud. Because that's not who I am at all. I would've said whatever I thought the coach wanted me to say. I would've followed the rules.

A week later I am back in Paul DiBello's office for another 7:00 a.m. meeting.

"How do you like race camp?" he asks.

"It's awesome."

"You think disabled racing is something you want to get into?"

"Yeah, definitely."

"People have been saying good stuff about you."

"Oh yeah?"

"Yeah. The coaches say that you have a lot of raw talent."

Talent! That's right! I am a prodigy after all! The coaches have recognized it, identified it!

"Do you want to be on the U.S. team?" he asks.

Last night I was thinking about the conversation Paul and I would have this morning, imagining what would be said. That's when I realized he'd probably ask something like this. That's also when I decided to use a euphemism in response. So Paul DiBello will know I am really serious.

"Heck yeah."

I have never said that word out loud before. *Heck.* Saying it, and thinking about it now—*heck yeah, heck yeah*—makes me feel strong and independent and dangerous. I guess that's why people swear. It's addicting. Like drugs.

"It's going to take you five years of training," he says.

"Okay."

As long as it takes.

"It's going to take a lot of work," he continues. "You're going to have to be an animal out there. You have to train like crazy and go in the gym to get big."

That's true. The other day I found out Ralph weighs 200 pounds. And most of the other skiers out here are pretty muscular, too. Me? I weigh 116. When I take off my shirt, you can count all my ribs. My elbows are the widest part of my arms.

But I will do what it takes. I will figure out how to get big, strong, so that when I walk through that doorway there I'll barely fit, and maybe one day I'll even get stuck.

"Okay."

"You'll need money."

"Okay."

Paul sets his palms down on his desk, mangled fingers spread out, and stares at me.

He continues, "You'll need a *lot* of it. Probably ten thousand dollars per season."

"Okay."

Paul looks me over as if he's watching for clues that I'm guilty of a certain crime. He's the sweaty, angry cop, top collar unbuttoned, tie loosened. I am sitting at the lonely table underneath the naked light bulb.

"Where are you going to come up with that kind of money?"

"Like, I'll get a sponsor or something, I don't know. I'll find it."

He nods, unconvinced, but ready to move on to his next test.

"Sundquist . . . you would also have to move out here."

So I've heard.

I nod.

"It would mean leaving high school your senior year."

"I know."

"I bet you have a lot of friends back in Virginia."

Today, when Paul says the word "Virginia," as in, "I bet you have a lot of friends back in *Virginia*," he doesn't say it like it's a joke, like he did last week. He says it like Virginia is an oasis, a Heaven on earth, a Promised Land of milk and honey that I could not possibly want to leave. He says it and then he waits, staring me down from behind his desk, like he might be able to wait long enough so that I will give up on my dream of a Paralympic uniform and leave his office, walk out that door, and go back home to beautiful, wonderful Virginia. But I just sit still, all my bulk (or lack of it) not moving from the chair.

Then the perfect words come to me, words to end the conversation, words to show Paul DiBello that I am serious about all this, that he cannot intimidate me into walking out, into making a confession of weakness, into accepting a plea bargain that would give up my greatness.

"Look, there are some things that are important," I say. "And then there are goals."

Take that, Paul DiBello.

He nods.

"Good," he says. "Very good. Now get the fuck out. I'm trying to work here."

23

In February, after Learn to Race Camp at Christmas, after coming back home and going to school for a month, after thinking about Winter Park each and every day, I go back out to Colorado for that race I originally called Paul about. I do poorly in the race, though. I don't fall, but I don't ski fast, either. In March, I go to Nationals in Montana. Same deal. The only good news about my pile of losses: evidence. See those losses, Mom and Dad? What do they tell us? That I am a terrible ski racer. That if I want to make the Paralympics, I need to start training full time. That I need to move to Colorado in December.

How will you finish high school?

I don't know.

Where will you live?

I don't know yet.

How will you pay for it all?

Don't know.

The questions are endless, spewing out of their mouths in between bites of food each night at the dinner table. I can't answer them all, because I don't know how, exactly, it will all happen. No, Mom and Dad, I don't know the *how*. But I do know the *what* and the *why*.

The *what*: A gold medal in the 2006 Paralympics in Turino.

The *why*: Because of that morning when I met Paul DiBello and

Ralph Green in Winter Park the day after Christmas. That morning when I went out and trained with the team and saw the video and understood how many improvements were left to make in my skiing, that morning I saw a place to train, a team and coaches who could help me make the Paralympics. Finally there was a clear path leading straight to my dream. When I got home to Harrisonburg after Learn to Race Camp, the first thing I did was rearrange the furniture in my bedroom. I was a new person. I couldn't live in my old space.

And that's why no matter how many unanswerable *how* questions Mom and Dad can think of, they know, and I know, that I will move to Colorado this year, my senior year of high school, because my *what* and *why* are so much bigger than their *how*. The boy who left the house on Christmas Day, you might have been able to persuade him to stay in Harrisonburg, to make his parents happy, to graduate from Harrisonburg High School. But the young man who came back one week later—the one who eats five Reese's cups in one sitting and who uses euphemisms to express himself and won't quit until he makes the Paralympic team—you can't change his mind . . . about *nothin'*.

But the how questions are still big ones. *How* will I gain weight? *How* will I pay for it? *How* will I finish high school?

I decide to attack the weight issue first. I need to build muscle. Get bigger. I start where I always start, with books. Books about fitness, books about muscle gain, books about weight lifting. I need to join a gym. I visit the closest one, the RMH Wellness Center.

"I'd like to join here," I say.

"Can I get an ID?" the girl in the Membership Office asks.

I hand her my license.

"You're sixteen?"

"Yeah."

She doesn't look happy.

"Almost seventeen," I say.

Still not happy.

"Next month," I add. "That's when I turn seventeen."

"Are your parents members?"

"No."

"You can't join until you're eighteen if you're not on your parents' account."

Eighteen? Really?

"Can I speak to a manager?"

The manager tells me the same thing, and no, there's no exceptions, and no, there's no one higher up I can speak to about this. I try other gyms. They all tell me the same thing. One gym manager suggests working out at home with large books, using them like dumbbells. *I wish I had a large book to slap you with*, I think.

How can I work out?

Then I remember. Back when I was reading two or three self-help books each week, thinking they'd help me become a great motivational speaker and a boyfriend to Lydia Sease, I learned a strategy that might help: If you have a problem, you put it on a sheet of paper as a question. Then, every night before you go to bed, you write down twenty possible solutions.

So I get a legal pad, title it.

"How can I work out?"

For three days, I write twenty answers each night before bed. Then I scan a few of the ideas on my list:

23. Get fake ID and use to join RMH Wellness Center.
34. Break into RMH Wellness Center after closing each night and work out then.
48. Get rid of bed, desk, dresser. Buy home gym and set up in bedroom.

One idea, number fifty-two, might actually work. The RMH in the RMH Wellness Center stands for Rockingham Memorial Hospital. In other words, this is a hospital-owned facility. So I think of an idea. I tell it to Mom. I ask her to help. I can tell she doesn't like my idea because she doesn't want me to move away to Colorado. But she says she will help anyway, I guess because she knows that skiing makes me happy, and ever since she had cancer, it seems like Mom wants all of us to be happy. So she calls Dr. Kimberly Dunsmore, my doctor from UVA who treated me for cancer, who always carries a clipboard, who cried on the phone when she thought I had relapsed. The next day Dr. Dunsmore faxes a prescription saying that due to my disability I need a place to strengthen my leg muscles in order to avoid contracting arthritis later in life, and that afternoon I become a member of the RMH Wellness Center.

Once I start working out and gaining weight, I decide it's time to find the money. I use the twenty-ideas-each-night brainstorming technique—Question: How can I get $10,000?—until I have plenty of ideas. Then I try a few of them. I apply for grants. Nope. I call Nike. They don't want to sponsor me. Same with all the other big companies I can think of. My senator does not want to give me the money (either personally or, as I had sort of hoped, via a pork-barrel amendment). And I am not old enough to gamble in Vegas.

Then one afternoon I get the mail from the mailbox and I notice an envelope addressed to Mom and Dad. Printed on the outside of the envelope is a picture of a tiny African boy, his ribs visible, his stomach sticking out, his head too big. There is what appears to be a fly crawling on his eyeball. What is this? Inside the envelope are three things. First, there's a letter about this boy, Abasi. The letter asks you, Mr. and Mrs. Paul Sundquist, to consider helping Abasi by making a donation. The second item in the envelope is a slip of paper about the size of a check:

❑ Yes! I want to help Abasi by making a donation of

____$1000 ____$500 ____$250 ____$100 ____$50 ____Other

Name   _____

Address _____

        _____

And the final item is another envelope, this one stamped and addressed (though the discerning donor might notice that it is not addressed to Abasi himself, but rather to a relief organization in North Carolina).

Thank you, Abasi! You have given me the answer!

Last week after I read everything in the Abasi letter, I put the papers back in the envelope and glued it shut so Mom and Dad wouldn't know I'd opened their mail. That's a felony. And this, I realize today, is the difference between Matt and me. I do my best to shut envelopes to maintain my image as a law-abiding citizen. Matt, on the other hand, comes home in squad cars.

This is what happened, as Matt explains it: He and his friends were throwing water balloons at people walking down the sidewalk. Actually, oh wait, Josh, you're going to love this part, they were wearing jogging suits and headbands, and they would jog in formation until they surrounded someone walking on the sidewalk, and then they would unleash the water balloons hidden in their jackets. People were getting, like, soaked. It was freaking hilarious. Anyway, so this cop showed up out of nowhere, right, just jumped over the bushes, and Matt was the first one he could grab.

Matt ended up in the back of the squad car. He got a lecture through the glass about how he'll never go to college, never get a job, all that, because this is going straight on his permanent record. Permanent! Record! Meanwhile, Matt was calling his friends on Mom and Dad's cell phone, which he uses more than they do. Guess where I am? In the back of his car! Yeah, right now. He's taking me home. I know, right? It's hilarious!

Matt was not worried at all, like zero percent worried, because, first of all, this was a university cop, and everyone knows they can't really do anything to you, and second, the cop never actually *saw* any of them launching the water balloons, since they were so well hidden in those bushes.

When they pulled up to the house, Matt saw Wayne Berman standing outside watering his lawn. Wayne looked high, as usual, so Matt thought of an idea. That's my Dad, Matt told the cop. So the cop started walking toward Wayne, and Wayne dropped the hose on the ground and started to walk away. Excuse me, the cop says, we've got a problem with your son. And Wayne's flipping out, What? I don't have—wait—no, I definitely don't have a son! And Matt's like, Just joking, officer, this is my house over here.

Needless to say, Mom and Dad believed everything the cop said about Matt not being able to go to college anymore and his permanent record being ruined or whatever. So they gave Matt a list of punishments that included memorizing twenty Bible verses and writing an essay on why he shouldn't have been launching water balloons. And he can't use the cell phone again until he recites all the verses.

While Matt worries about his Bible verses, I worry about why I've stopped gaining weight. Whenever I hop on the scale it balances at the same point, at 120 pounds. So I meet with a nutritionist. I tell her my daily diet: Oatmeal or Tasteeos (you will love them if you like Cheerios, trademark General Mills) for breakfast. Mom and Dad still pay for school lunch twice a week, so on the other days I usually skip or buy a carton of milk for thirty cents. For dinner, we usually have salad with lentils, three-bean soup, or spaghetti. I also drink several whey protein shakes every day, like all the health books said to do if you want to build muscle.

"That's it?"

"Yes, that's it."

She says we should probably look at my caloric needs. She asks my height, weight, activity level. Then she looks at some charts.

"Looks like you need about four thousand, three hundred calories if you want to gain weight," the nutritionist says.

"Every day?" I ask.

"Uh-huh."

"That's a lot."

"Uh-huh," she says. "But your metabolism is high, and you're not taking in enough calories right now, so your body is burning your protein as energy instead of using it to build more muscle."

"All right," I say. "I'll eat more."

"A lot more."

"Okay."

I know exactly where I can get those extra calories. I drive directly from her office to GNC, where I buy Pro Performance Weight Gainer 2200 Gold. Normally when something has a four-digit number like 2200 in its name, the number is there to make it sound high-tech or futuristic. But in this case, the 2200 is just the number of calories per serving: 2,200. More calories in each serving than the total that the average human being is supposed to consume in an entire day. That one serving contains 74 grams of a proprietary protein blend as well as 437 grams of carbohydrates. *Four hundred and thirty-seven!* I calculate this to be around the same number of carbohydrates in an entire loaf of white bread. The instructions on the outside of the bottle suggest mixing the powder with cold water in a blender. Apparently each serving contains so much nutrition that you need the spinning metal blades of an electric appliance just to make it dissolve.

The shakes start working immediately. I am gaining about two pounds a week. And I am starting to get the self-addressed stamped envelopes back, too. But the first things we received, actually, were angry emails and phone calls. They came to Mom and Dad, mostly from the relatives and distant friends whose names I had copied to my mailing list from Mom's address book in the kitchen.

Can't he just get a job like the rest of us?

Why does he think he deserves my money?

I've got kids of my own. I pay for their sports training. Maybe you should pay for your son's training?

I was surprised. Why were they so mad? Do they call and yell at *Abasi's* parents after receiving fund-raising letters about *him*? I told Mom and Dad I was sorry, but I don't think they minded the calls that much, because the truth is they couldn't pay for my training even if they wanted to. It costs ten thousand dollars per year, for crying out loud. Mom and Dad can't afford that, what with having to buy me a new artificial leg every year (which costs twenty thousand dollars . . . usually insurance pays most of it, but the exact amount of coverage seems to depend on the agent's mood on the particular day Dad submits the claim) and saving for college for four kids. Mom and Dad still made a donation, though, in the amount of five hundred dollars. That's an enormous amount for them. So I know they support the dream now.

And I can't get a job to *earn* the money, because I'm in school full time, and I will be training full time after I move. So Mom and Dad know, and I know, that the other $9,500 is going to have to come in self-addressed, stamped envelopes returned from people on that list.

Most of the list was random rich people who live in Harrisonburg. I got their names from a friend who's a fund-raiser for a charity around here. She also gave me a directory of every business registered in Harrisonburg that had ever made a donation to a nonprofit. So all together—the random rich people, the business directory, the relatives and distant friends of Mom and Dad—there were about six hundred names on my list.

And now those self-addressed, stamped envelopes are arriving in our mailbox every day. Inside each envelope is a slip of paper the size of a check where people have put an x beside "Yes, Josh! I want to join your team and help you make the Paralympics in 2006!" The Gold Medal members put an X beside $1,000; Silver, $500; Bronze, $250. They could also check $100, $50, or "Other," but there's no medal for these categories.

Each envelope also comes with a check. Sometimes I recognize the names on the checks; sometimes I don't. I get a check from the Marshes, the family of Dr. Marsh, the doctor I first went to see when my leg started hurting, the family that decorated our house. And I get a check from the Montgomerys, the family of Dr. Montgomery, the one who gave me a shot at Lost River and asked if there was "anything I wanted to talk to him about." And yes, I even get a check from Lydia's parents. (*Need to stop thinking about her, though . . . seriously . . . time to move on . . . but wait . . . maybe . . . if she got to know me a little bit more . . . NO . . .*) Once a month, Mom and I add up all the checks and mail them to Paul DiBello. Paul deposits them in my race account at the National Sports Center for the Disabled and sends each donor a tax-deductible receipt. Then I send them a thank-you note. We've got it down to a science.

Paul calls me and says that donors can send the checks directly to him and he'll put the deposits in my race account without me having to forward the checks. That way we can all save time on the paperwork, he says. But I've heard too many stories—team members who took me aside and told me never to trust Paul with money. They said that if you don't keep your own records, then Paul has total control of your money. And if he has control of your money, he has control over you.

But that's just being paranoid. He can't control me.

Paul also called to compliment me on my effectiveness as a fundraiser. He wants me to teach the rest of the team how to do something like this. It's simple, Paul. You just print a photo of yourself skiing on the outside of an envelope—make it full color, otherwise people won't open it—and enclose a letter about your dream, a piece of paper where people can put an X beside "YES! I want to make a donation!," and include a self-addressed, stamped envelope. Then you send them out and just sit back and wait for the donations. You have to trust that people will want to help.

I'm having lunch with Dad at a diner near his work. Back when Matt and I were kids, Dad would take us out on Special Times. The three of us played together almost every night—Nerf soccer in the hallway, baseball in the backyard—but Special Times were a chance for us to pair off, father and son. A Special Time would last for two hours, and we could do whatever we wanted with Dad. We would get three dollars from the entertainment budget, which we could spend on anything, even candy. I usually filled my two hours playing tennis against Dad, or playing tag with him on the playground, or, if I decided not to spend the money on sugar, putt-putt golf. We went on one Special Time per month. I used to wish months were shorter, more like weeks, so I could go on more Special Times. Thirty days seemed like an eternity to wait.

But now we're too old for Special Times, and Dad's busy with work. So this summer he and I have been doing lunch every couple of weeks.

"You're working really hard to be able to go to Colorado," Dad says.

"Yeah . . . well . . . I really want to make the Paralympics."

"Do you enjoy this part?"

"What do you mean?"

"The working out, the fund-raising. Do you enjoy it?"

"I don't know. I guess."

"It's just that you're going to give up a lot of years of your life for this goal. And if you make it, great. I hope you do, and I think you will," he says. "But God forbid if you get hurt or something, I don't want you to look back and think it was a waste of time."

"Uh . . . okay," I say.

"I'm not saying you shouldn't ski. I think it's great what you're doing. I'm just saying I hope you can learn to appreciate the journey. Because life isn't always about the destination."

I tell Dad thanks for the advice, but I know that it's advice I won't need, because I *will* make the Paralympics. Nothing can stop me, not getting hurt, or getting frustrated, or losing a lot of races, or anything else like that.

The last step is meeting with Mrs. Reynolds, Principal of Harrisonburg High School. We meet. We talk. Then I write her a formal proposal, which she approves. Next I write a proposal for Superintendent Ford, explaining how I will have enough credits to graduate this December, and I don't really need to be in school this spring, but I do need to be in Colorado, training so I can win a gold medal at the 2006 Paralympics in Turino, Italy. Dr. Ford sends back an official letter saying my request is approved. I can skip my final semester and still receive a diploma with the rest of the class.

So that's what I do. First semester finishes and I pack my bags and load them in the van. Mom is really sad, but I tell her not to be. It's not like I'm moving away forever. I'll be back in three months, when the season is over.

Dad drops me off at the airport, and I fly to Colorado to become a full-time ski racer.

24

Paul DiBello, our double-amputee team director, didn't actually buy us tickets for the 2002 Paralympic Opening Ceremony. He just arranged for the other coaches to bring us to Salt Lake City today. If we want to watch the event itself, we're on our own. So it's a good thing I'm friends with Ralph, because he has no problem getting a ticket for himself and for me. Free. I ask him how he did this.

"Confidence," he says.

Coffi'dense.

"Um . . . okay," I say. "Well, thanks!"

"You got it, Smoshes."

That's what he always calls me: Smoshes. I guess because it rhymes with Josh . . . sort of. Ralph invents nicknames for everyone— *everyone*. Even if he's never going to talk to them again. Like if you just met him on the ski lift, he'll have a nickname made up for you by the time you get off at the top of the mountain.

Our seats for the Opening Ceremony are up on the top row— but they were free, so I'm not complaining—and rain and snow falls on us and the fifty thousand other people in the Olympic (now Paralympic) stadium during the ceremony. People stare at Ralph and me. We are two guys of highly contrasting size and skin color wearing matching blue plastic ponchos and standing up in the very top row, each on our one leg, hopping and hollering while everyone

around us huddles together to keep warm. When the host team, the
U.S. team, finally marches into the stadium—last, the climax, after
all the other countries—that's when people *really* start staring at
Ralph and me.

"That's us in four years!" I yell.

"Hell yeah, Smoshes!"

HIH-ha-ha-ha.

"Woooooooooo!"

We embrace, hopping up and down on our single legs.

"Turino, baby!"

"Two thousand six here we come!"

Neither of us is wearing a prosthesis. Ralph never wears one. I
wear mine about half the time. It's good to wear for social occasions,
and times when I have to carry ski equipment. But when I know I
will have to do a lot of walking—like I am tonight in Salt Lake—I
stick with crutches, because they're much easier to use.

Before Salt Lake, Ralph and I were at a World Cup race in Canada, where we came in second to last and last, respectively. Not too
good. But about average for my season so far. It's been almost three
months since I finished high school and moved to Colorado. I've
been in four or five races, all with disappointing results, even though
I train six days a week. Whenever I get on the race course, as I come
down the mountain trying to remember all the information and tips
and techniques for ski racing that I've stuffed in my brain, my body
freezes and I lose faith in myself.

But being in this stadium with all these cheering people and fire-
works and teams of athletes marching in and music, I can forget
about the race results and remember the reason I moved out west in
the first place: down there on the field, those athletes are wearing the
uniform of their home nation.

When the ceremonies end and the stadium starts to clear out, I
feel a sense of purpose, as if my muscles are eager to engage in some
kind of movement. I need some time alone, so I tell Ralph I want to

go explore. We agree to meet later in the evening. I walk down the cement stairs, still wet—crutches, leg, crutches, leg—until I am on the ground level, looking down a tunnel that leads into brightness. The brightness is so complete that the tunnel itself, its two walls, floor, ceiling, blend together like a black hole. This is where the athletes—the *Paralympians*—walked an hour ago. I think about this. I want to walk there, too. I want to know how it feels. But there is a pair of guards at the end of the tunnel, silhouetted in the light. Do they have guns? Can they arrest me? I hear Mom in my mind, telling me not to risk it—*it will go on your permanent record, you won't get into college, you will work at McDonald's the rest of your life*—and then I hear something else, a single word: *coffi'dense*. So I march through the tunnel and in between the security guards— "Evening, gentlemen"—give them a nod. They nod back. And then I'm on the field, walking the same lap around the stadium that the Paralympians just did.

The rain has stopped, but there are still shallow pools of water everywhere, all of them just beginning to freeze over. The stadium is quiet except for the sound of the Paralympic torch burning a few stories up, making a sound like a flag whipping and waving in a gusty wind. I walk onto the center stage and look at tens of thousands of people, including Mom and Dad and Matt, and I am wearing a red-white-and-blue uniform. I wave to the crowd.

I think about everything I've done to get here, to make the Paralympic team, about all the times I've been at the gym and I've pushed my leg beyond exhaustion, and about all the hours I've spent reading books about skiing, about how there are days when I wish I were back home with my family instead of being seventeen years old, living in Colorado with teammates I don't really know. I think about all this, and about how it's all worth it now because I am standing in front of this roaring crowd, knowing that I did it, I finished, I made it, I was a cause and this is the effect and therefore there is order and meaning to the universe. And the best part is, since I've made the

Paralympics and since I've gotten this uniform, from now on, nothing else matters. No matter what happens to me, no matter how disappointing or sad things get, no matter if the rest of my life is a failure, no matter if people don't like me, no matter if I never get a hot girlfriend, I can always look back and say to myself, "It doesn't matter because I was a Paralympian. I represented my country. I made the team."

"Can I take your picture?"

The question snaps me out of my daydream and I find myself standing in front of fifty thousand empty seats.

"What?" I say.

"Can I take a picture of you standing on that stage?"

The voice comes from below me, on the ground level, where I see a man wearing a laminated badge around his neck and a plain black baseball cap on his head. A nylon bag is hanging from his shoulder. He holds a camera with both hands.

"Sorry, I'm not competing in the games," I say.

I'm not even supposed to be standing here.

"That's okay," he says, kneeling down so the torch is framed behind me.

"But hopefully I'll be there in 2006," I add. "So . . . um . . . you just want me here like this?"

"That's perfect."

I clench my jaw, squint a little. This photo will win awards.

"Tell you what," he says, shutter clicking. "If you make it in 2006, I will take your picture there, too."

I smile, despite my best efforts at jaw clenching and eye squinting. I just can't help it.

"It's a deal," I say. "I'll be there."

25

"**D**ance party!" Matt yells.

He cranks up the volume on Dad's Honda Accord and throws the passenger-side door open. I look in the backseat at Dad—I drove, Matt called shotgun—and I can tell that despite my father's best efforts to look "fun" and "spontaneous" in front of his teenage sons, he is obviously uncomfortable. First, because the radio is blasting *secular* music, meaning we are liable to hear swear words or drug references. Second, because we are in a crowded parking lot at the King's Dominion theme park, and his fifteen-year-old son, Matthew, is dancing wildly, failing his arms, and jumping up and down on the asphalt.

"Yeah, dance party!" I say. I hobble on my crutches around to Matt's side of the car and join in the dance party, albeit using more conservative and self-conscious movements.

With both of his sons now partaking in an act of apparent fun and spontaneity, Dad is forced to join in. He is about as awkward as I am, rocking side to side and moving his forearms like a jogger. I look at Matt and note that he is currently performing a spanking motion in the air in time with the music, a move whose sexual connotations I don't think Dad will pick up on. Matt smiles broadly and nods at me, thus affirming our shared knowledge of sexually suggestive dance moves. Ah, the sweet bond of brotherhood!

The last time I witnessed Matt's famously uninhibited dancing was at the Harrisonburg High School homecoming dance in the fall before I moved to Colorado. After Matt's Christian private school was shut down due to lack of enrollment, he was finally allowed to attend public school. Imagine! Matt at Public School!

The school secretary, and a lot of the teachers, too, called him "Josh" for the entire year, and all the others—the ones who recognized him as a unique person, a separate entity—just called him Josh's brother. He's not only living in my shadow, it's as if, to some people, he's not even living at all. Especially with the old people at church, and especially once I was out in Colorado during ski season. I guess without me standing beside him, the old people just recognized a Sundquist boy and defaulted to me.

"Hi Joshua, how you doing, son?" the old grandmothers would say to him every week after the second service.

Matt would always tell them he was doing quite well, thanks, especially because he got a new artificial leg that's just amazing and would they like to see it? Then he would pull up his pant leg to reveal a flawlessly designed leg complete with teenage male leg hair and perfectly bronzed, fleshlike skin. Yes, yes, he would tell them, the technology *has* come a long way recently. Sometimes the old people would ask him how the skiing was going, was he still training for the Paralympics? No, he would tell them; he'd quit skiing. He had recently been considering dropping out of high school, too.

Oh Matthew.

This used to be funny, just pure hilarity (I don't feel bad for the old people, to be honest, because that's sort of what you deserve if you can't tell two people apart when one of them is missing an entire leg), but more recently it hits a little close to the truth. The part about quitting skiing? Yeah, that part. It's not that I want to quit, exactly. It's just that I'm considering taking *a break*. Then I'll refocus and go for 2010. See, despite my glorious moment of imagination in Salt Lake City, my overall season in Colorado ended up being just one disappointment after another. I didn't place well at races. I barely improved at all in my training. In short, it looks like the path to 2006 can only lead to failure. *Then* those old people would be able to tell us apart. Look, there's Josh, the one who didn't qualify for the Paralympics after training for years, pouring himself into it 100 percent. And there's Matt, the one who made the soccer team at Harrisonburg High School his freshman year, the one who gets to wear a uniform and travel around the state playing center forward.

But for today, I will forget about all that. Today is fun. Today is roller-coasters. Today is King's Dominion with Matt and Dad.

Most theme parks allow people with disabilities to skip the line for roller-coasters. You just go through the exit gate and get right on. I used to think that was the greatest privilege in the world. I remember right after my amputation, when Make-A-Wish gave us a trip to Disneyland, how Mom and Dad would push me through the exit gate while I sat in a wheelchair, too tired from the chemo to walk around all day. We could skip the line like this and then choose any car to ride in. I always chose the front. They'd even let us go around twice if we wanted. And those privileges, back when I was ten years old, made everything—the sickness, the amputation, the cancer—almost seem worth it. We could *skip the lines*! At *Disneyland*!

But these days, given that I will turn eighteen next month, I am much more concerned with the stare I get from the guy at the front of the line when I walk through the exit and choose a car that happens to be the one he was next in line for. Sometimes he'll complain to the ride attendant, get into an argument. You think this kid is better than me? Just because he's missing a foot? What the hell!

Kind of awkward.

That's why when we decide to do a virtual reality ride today, we wait in the line like everybody else. Matt wants to skip, but I am the disabled one, so it's my call. And I'd rather wait.

We finally make it inside the virtual reality theater and snag three

seats in the front row. Front and center. We sit for about two minutes, seat belts fastened, eyes trained on the blank screen. The
anticipation—even though, growing up, I came here so many
times—grows in my stomach, expands. Maybe I'm getting old
enough that I shouldn't be excited about virtual reality anymore, but
I am. I don't think I'll ever grow out of it.

Then a girl in a King's Dominion uniform walks across the front
row to where we are sitting.

"I'm sorry, sir, you won't be able to participate in this experience,"
she says to me.

"Are you serious?" I ask.

Is this a joke? Did Matt put her up to this?

"Yes, it's unsafe."

"How is that possible? I'm wearing a seat belt."

And then: Would I like to talk to the manager? Yes, I would
please, and thank you. Two more minutes of seat belts and blank
screen. People are getting fidgety. You can hear it in the mumble-
mumble of the hundred or so voices in the theater. The first girl returns with a second girl. Neither of them is older than me. But they
are both wearing uniforms, no doubt about it. And the second girl
has a visor. A *manager's* visor.

She makes her opening statement:

"Sir, you won't be able to participate in this experience because
you are handicapped."

And I make mine:

"That doesn't make sense. The seat belt can hold me in just as
well as anyone else."

"Don't worry, you can still watch the movie. There's a bench on
the floor level for handicapped guests," she says, gesturing toward
what is indeed a flat, stable bench—the sort you might find in a
baseball dugout. It's identified helpfully by a blue handicapped sign
attached to the back.

"Are you serious? I've been on this ride at least ten times!" I say.

In my entire life, I've lost my temper only three or four times. When the doctors tore me off Mom before the operation. When Dad told me he'd force me back on chemo after they found the spots. When I finally got through to speak with a middle-school principal on the phone and she hung up on me mid-sentence. Only three or four times. That number is about to become four or five.

"I am really sorry, sir,"—*Stop calling me sir, I'm barely older than you*—"but you are going to have to sit on the bench or leave the theater."

"Are you serious?" I say, nearly shouting. The entire theater is listening now, and I want them to hear every word. I want to turn them against this manager, to incite a hundred-person riot of epic proportions.

"Yes, I am sorry."

"So you are kicking me out because I have one leg?" I yell, emphasis on *kicking me out* and *one leg*.

"No, as I said there is a bench available for—"

But I am not going to listen to her label me with the word "handicapped" again. Handicapped is quadriplegics who need feeding tubes. Handicapped is severe mental retardation with round-the-clock care. I am not fucking handicapped.

I pick up my crutches and I walk to the exit. It's a metal door, the kind with a wide horizontal bar you press down to unlock and swing open. I cock my arm and smash the bar with the bony part of my palm with enough force to crush a stack of bricks. The door flies open, and after the echo of the door hitting the limit of its hinges, the room is silent.

"He's *pissed*," someone whispers as I walk out.

I am outside. The sun is so bright it hurts my eyes. Along the sidewalk, down a hill, across a bridge, then up a hill. I stop in a plaza, surrounded by hundreds of happy people walking around, laughing, holding hands because they don't have to hold onto crutches in order to walk.

I wish this plaza were more crowded with visitors, more packed together. Crowds are my hiding place. Normally, when I stand alone with my crutches or on my artificial leg with its exposed titanium, I form an unnatural silhouette that sucks in every passing eye. But when I find myself in crowds, the mass of bodies shields me, and for a few glorious minutes I am just another part of the multitude, just another forgettable face floating among strangers.

Then Dad and Matt are right beside me. They've followed me. I look at Dad. I see his glasses, his hair parted and dropping down on both sides just over his ears. I take a deep breath, to sigh it out, to say without words, "Well, *that* was crazy, huh?" But instead of sighing, I exhale the breath into a sob. Dad puts his arms around me and I hide my face in his shoulder, tears bleeding into the cotton of his T-shirt. I am crying in the middle of this theme park in front of all these happy people. I open my eyes, lift my head enough to see Matt. Pain is written on his face. But it's the awkward, confusing sort of empathetic pain that makes you wonder if you should be doing something to help, and if so, what, exactly. We look at each other, sharing the same look as we did nearly ten years ago, roles reversed, when I walked in on him wrapping a belt around his neck and attaching it to our bunk bed. I remember seeing him standing there on the mattress of the lower bunk, the fabric of the belt taut beneath his jaw, and how we looked at each other, and I felt his hurt. But I didn't know how to make it go away.

I know that's how Matt feels today as I cry, looking at him. He doesn't know how to make it go away, either.

I close my eyes and a movie starts playing on the screen of my mind. It's a middle school where I gave a motivational speech. There is this kid in the back who raises his hand during a question-and-answer time.

"If you could choose whether you would lose your leg or not, what would you choose?" he asks.

I watch some of the other kids look at one another. Stupid question, they are thinking. Who would ever choose to have only one leg? They are sure I will say no. Then I turn and watch myself on-stage, looking up toward the ceiling, taking a breath, biting my lower lip.

"Yes, actually, I would choose it," I finally say. And I explain: "Having one leg is kind of difficult at first, but eventually you figure out how to do everything you could do before. And because I lost my leg, I've gotten to do so many cool things, like be on national TV and ski race and speak to you here today. And I've learned so much. I've become a stronger person."

The kid who asked the question, and all the other kids, and all the teachers, they all nod. This is profound stuff, they think. This is a mature, inspiring speaker whose presence is gracing our stage. He would *choose* to lose his leg because it has made him a *stronger person*. Wow.

The movie ends and I am back crying in Dad's arms, and I real-ize that was the most completely stupid thing I've ever said. How could I say I *wanted* only one leg? Is *this* what I wanted? Humiliation in front of my little brother and father and a hundred strangers in a theater at the hand of a visor-wearing, uniform-clad teenage theme park manager? I hate my life. I hate being inspirational. I hate being mature for my age. I hate all that shit.

We go to the front office, tell them the story. A Guest Services woman—that's what her name tag says, "Guest Services"—with too much makeup on her double chin makes a phone call and tells us they are very sorry, it was all a big misunderstanding. I am allowed to participate in that experience after all. So we walk back to the vir-tual reality ride and wait in line all over again. While we wait, I sit on the metal rail that marks the line, the one that has a sign reading, "No sitting on rail."

I have always thought I healed well. I got sent home from the hospital only five days after my amputation. It took just one week of physical therapy for me to learn to walk on an artificial leg. I finished chemotherapy exactly a year after I began it, because my immune system never got tired. But all that was just the physical healing, just the beginning, only the outer layer of what I can now see is an onion-like mass of healing issues and problems and side effects of all sorts, physical, mental, and who knows what else, that have to be peeled back to reach an inner, sweet core—if such a thing exists; I don't really know if it does anymore—of recovery.

We take the same three seats in the front row. I recognize a certain visor walking across the front row, coming toward me. I dig my heel into the linoleum floor.

But she didn't come for a fight.

"I am really sorry about that earlier," she says. "I didn't know amputees were allowed on. I hope you understand."

Normally I would just shrug and say, "Don't worry about it." That's what I would say, because I am a really nice guy. Or, I used to be. Before today. Before everything changed.

"Actually," I say, "that was one of the worst things that has ever happened to me."

And on the drive home that night, aftershocks and adrenaline still unsteadying my hands, I decide that, yes, I will take a break from skiing. I will focus on college. I will wait on the Paralympics, go in 2010, maybe. I just don't have a shot at making the 2006 team.

And so this is who I am when I arrive at The College of William and Mary in August: Not a ski racer. Not a motivational speaker. Instead, I am an unhealed, handicapped eighteen-year-old, victim of cancer, son of a mother whose cancer is expected to relapse, member of a family beaten down more times than I care to explain to the kids I meet in my dorm.

People always say college is the best four years of your life. But these people—they drink, have sex, join fraternities, skip class, do things I do not do. I go to class each morning, then sit at my desk and study until exactly five o'clock in the afternoon. Then I go to the student rec center and work out . . . but for what? Why do I need to get stronger? Why do I need to gain muscle? I go to bed by ten, have to put in earplugs because the rest of my dorm stays up another four or five hours. My roommate stays up, too, sometimes, so I have to wear one of those masks that block out all the brightness of the room.

At the start of Christmas break, I tell Mom and Dad not to send in my tuition for second semester. I'm not sure I'm going back. I pack my ski gear and fly on a cheap, early morning flight from Dulles airport to Denver International, then take the shuttle van up I-70 to Winter Park. I buckle my boot and step down on the heel piece of my ski and ride the lift to the top of the mountain. I sit down in the snow and watch the afternoon sun move west and begin to drop behind the treeless peaks of the Rocky Mountains across the valley from the Continental Divide. From here, I can see so much. I can see the Balcony House building where I first met Paul DiBello and Ralph Green in Paul's office, where in fact Paul DiBello is probably working right now, swearing at someone, no doubt. I can see Cranmer Trail, the first slope I ever skied here. I can see Winter Park's NASTAR course, nearly identical to the NASTAR course at Massanutten where I met the assistant coach of the Massanutten Junior Race Team that Sunday morning I skipped church to ski. And in the other direction I can see Route 40 as it winds through the valley toward Fraser, where Ralph lives, where I first had a spaghetti dinner at his apartment two years ago and he told me, as he had to do many times before I believed him and committed to it, that I needed to move here if I really wanted to make the Paralympic team.

Why am I at college? This is where I belong! In Colorado! In the snow! In the mountains! In the clouds! Forget college. I don't need to go. I already know what I want to do with my life: This. I want to ski. All I have to do is go down to the Balcony House right now, to Paul's office, and give him the word: I'm back. I'm staying for the

rest of the season. And I could do it, too. It wouldn't be very compli-
cated. I've brought my ski equipment with me. And money's no
problem. Of the fourteen thousand dollars I ended up raising last
year through my fund-raising letter, I've still got six left. So it's set-
tled. I will stay.

But then what? Train every day, chasing a uniform I'll never
wear? Get on the snow each morning, swinging my outriggers at
windmills? I need to face reality: I am not good enough. Last year
was a disaster. And Turino 2006 simply isn't going to happen, no
matter how hard I try. I will fail, and I already know how *that* feels.
I've been there, done that, let that happen, *let them see* that happen,
once, twice, with motivational speaking and with Lydia. Never
again. So, no, I won't ski. I will go back to college, where I am quite
sure I can graduate in four years with a bachelor's degree in something or other. No failure.

"The hell if I'm going to let you use your race account money for a
fucking ski vacation!" Paul says.

He's his normal happy, cheerful self, sitting behind the desk and
looking at me with eyes set just above that same old sawed-off nasal
apparatus.

"What do you mean 'ski vacation'?" I ask.

"This! What the hell else would you call it?"

"I came out to see if I wanted to train this season."

"And?"

"I told you. I'm going to wait till after college and then train for
2010."

He slams his desk with both fists, with all six or seven—it de-
pends on how you count the stubs—fingers. "Bullshit!" he shouts.
"If you aren't training for 2006, this is just a ski vacation, because
you, Sundquist, have quit!"

"I haven't quit. I've just pushed back my time line."

"Two thousand six is your time line. That's what you raised your money for. If you aren't training for it, then you've quit and I'm going to send back your money."

My six thousand dollars?

"Wait—what? You can't do that."

"Listen, Sundquist. You've got two options. Number one, you keep training for 2006. Number two, you stop training, I divide up the six thousand dollars four hundred ways and send it back to all your donors in Harrisonburg with a nice little letter about how you quit because you don't have what it takes."

What? He can't . . . he wouldn't . . . Would he? Yes, he would. He's Paul DiBello. He would love that. He'd probably take the time to personally handwrite the four hundred letters using his own mangled fingers, each letter worded for maximum humiliation, each mailed with the intention of ruining my reputation back home forever.

"You can't do that."

"Try me."

Then I fall back to the same line of defense that has been used by otherwise intimidated boys since the dawn of spoken language: "My Dad's going to come after you." I go on to tell Paul DiBello exactly what my Dad will come after him with, which is specifically what my Dad keeps in the top drawer of his dresser: a calculator. Yeah, my Dad is an *accountant*. But if Paul DiBello is impressed—and he should be, because this is a money question, a numbers question, and Dad is good at anything to do with numbers—he doesn't show it. In fact, he doesn't say anything at all.

"You won't get away with this," I say eventually, to fill the silence.

I go outside and call Dad on a pay phone, give him the rundown. He's upset. Like I hoped he would be. I had also sort of hoped he would offer to get on the next plane to Colorado, so he could fight Paul with his calculator or, if necessary, his fists. But no such offer is made. Instead, Dad talks about some IRS mumbo-jumbo and says Paul is wrong.

"Do you know the CFO?" he asks.

"For the National Sports Center for the Disabled?"

"Right. Do you know him?"

"Her. Yeah, I do."

And I hope, Dad, that you are impressed at how I know what "CFO" stands for.

"Do you trust her?"

"Yes."

Oh, I get it! Great idea, Dad! You'll call the CFO! Have a talk with her, financial professional to financial professional! Get this all straightened out!

"You should talk to her," Dad says.

"Me?"

"You know her, right?"

"Oh, okay. Yeah. Right, I know her. I will talk to her."

I thank Dad for his help, hang up. He's busy, I know. He's got a job. He can't just come out here and solve all my problems for me, stand in front of me and block Paul DiBello from hurting me while I sit in a chair and cry and hold on to Mom. I'm eighteen years old, after all. And besides, being my father is not Dad's only job in life. He's a regular human being, too, with regular human-being problems of his own to deal with. My father—a regular human being.

I try to see the CFO, but she's busy, in a meeting. *Why are people always in meetings?* So I will just have to figure this out on my own. Paul gave me two options. Option one, I could stay out here and train. But if I do that, I'm training for something completely impossible. I will spend the next three years working toward the Paralympics and then, in the end, not make it. But if I go with option two and return to college, Paul will send my money back to all those donors with his accompanying letter of disgrace. That would be . . . I can't even describe it. That can't happen. Won't happen.

So it's lose-lose, failure-failure. Either I invest the next three years in training and racing, and then fail in 2006, or I invest the next three years in college, and Paul writes a letter to four hundred people telling them I am a quitter. Either way, I lose.

I don't sleep much that night. I can't stop thinking about Paul—about his imposing figure, his mangled body.

I once asked Paul what *happened* to him. He told me he was ice-climbing in a ravine with his best friend when a storm came out of nowhere. They tried to get out, but his friend lost a hold and Paul watched him fall and disappear into the blizzard. Paul didn't know how far his friend had fallen or whether he was even still alive, and there would be no way to carry another body while climbing an ice cliff in a snowstorm. So Paul said a silent goodbye to his best friend and climbed out alone.

The blizzard was so thick Paul couldn't see which direction to walk in. So he headed directly into the wind until he literally ran into a building. It was locked, so Paul knocked down the door and collapsed on top of it. Turns out it was a ranger station. When they discovered him passed out there on the floor, the frostbite had already gotten both his legs and most of his fingers and face. Everything would have to be amputated. A few days later, when they found his friend, his broken bones were frozen stiff.

After the amputations, Paul quit his job and became a ski racer. He eventually won ten world championships and a pile of Paralympic medals. Then he started this team.

"I will offer you a compromise," I tell Paul the next morning.

"I'm listening," he says.

Here goes.

"I will keep racing, but only a little. I'll do one race per year. That way I keep my points from getting an inactivity penalty and my FIS license stays valid. I could still potentially qualify for 2006."

There. Done. Will he go for it?

"All right. I'll play your game."

"It's not a game, Paul. It's a fair compromise."

"Whatever, Sundquist. We both know you'll never get the race results you need for the 2006 team by competing once a year."

"Maybe not, but I would stay ranked and licensed. I could still make the 2006 Paralympics . . . theoretically, at least . . . so the intended purpose of the money would stay in the picture."

"Whatever, Sundquist."

He waves his deformed hand in the air as if brushing crumbs off a table and then looks down at his papers.

"Thanks Paul," I say after he's agreed to my compromise.

I stand up and walk out. It's a victory. One race per year is no big deal if I do it over Christmas break. It'll take only two or three days out of the entire year, and it will be just enough to keep Paul DiBello happy. And if he's happy, he won't send my money back to my donors.

Of course, when I am home during the summers I will probably run into some of the people who gave me money, and they'll want to know how my training for the 2006 Paralympics is going.

"I've decided to wait and go for 2010 instead," I'll say.

Will I really go for 2010? Who knows? Probably not. But by then I will have graduated college and moved far away and won't ever have to see any of those people. They'll just assume I made it, or maybe they'll forget about me altogether. The bottom line is if they do remember me, it won't be as a failure or a quitter. Not a failure, because I won't have trained for 2006 and failed. Not a quitter, because they won't have received a letter from Paul DiBello telling them so.

It's perfect.

Well, sort of. The only problem is there's this other voice, heard by no one else, that says if I go back to finish my freshman year of college instead of staying here to ski, I am a quitter *and* a failure. It has been whispering this to me all day and shows no signs of letting up.

26

"And what is this appointment about?" the secretary asks over the phone.

"Well, I guess . . . depression?" I reply.

I say this in the form of a question, as if I am hoping she will offer an answer. She does not, at least not directly.

"How's two o'clock?" she asks.

The next day I arrive early. Of course. I do that a lot now. I used to be so busy, always running late, always chasing my red lines and uniforms and hot girlfriends who would date me very soon. I watched the clock, packed as much as I could into each hour. Now I show up twenty minutes early because I don't really have anything better to do.

The now embodied secretary pushes a clipboard across the check-in desk and smiles at me the way people at church did after Mom was diagnosed with cancer. I take the clipboard and sit down in the waiting room, noticing how everyone else seems to have come to the Student Health Center in pairs, or, in the case of one girl, even in a trio—one sick girl and two friends to comfort her—whereas I have an entire loveseat to myself. I set my backpack on the empty cushion to fill the void.

A long time ago—I'm a sophomore now, so I guess three years ago, when I was still giving motivational speeches—I would've looked around a room like this, looked at each person, and guessed as to what I could teach him or her about life. *That guy right there . . .*

yeah . . . probably needs some goals. And that girl . . . she probably doesn't value herself enough. And I would be tempted to stand up on this loveseat, to balance on the cushions while I gave them a motivational speech to solve all of their problems, because I had life figured out and they didn't.

That was a long time ago.

On the clipboard is a list of "yes or no" boxes beside questions such as "Have you lost interest in things you previously enjoyed?" and "Do you have trouble staying focused on everyday tasks?" and "Do you have trouble sleeping?"

I check yes on almost all of them. The sleep question especially hits home. I remember when I used to envy those people who could get by on just one or two hours each night. They can be so productive! They can work two full-time jobs instead of one! They are living twice as much as I am! I used to wish God had created *my* body like that. I wished He had, and I wanted to know why He hadn't. When I arrived in Heaven I was going to ask Him. I was going to say, "Why'd I have to waste all that time sleeping while other people lived more each day than I did because they didn't need to sleep? Why did I slumber whilest the insomniac Bill Clinton got to walk around having extramarital sex for twenty-three hours per day? No fair!"

But not anymore. Now I wish I could wake up each morning just long enough to take a multivitamin and check my email, then go back to bed until the next day. I'd sleep a little bit longer each time, and someday maybe I'd disappear completely into my dreams. No more synapses of phantom brain pain, no more guilt about who I was supposed to be in the year 2006, no lying in bed looking ahead at . . . nothing. No more. Just sleep.

In fact, there is only one box on the clipboard sheet I mark as no: "Have you ever considered causing physical harm to yourself?" I check no because even though marking no is kind of a lie, and I never lie, if I told the truth, the doctor would go directly to his office and call Mom and Dad. And then they would think themselves failures as parents. I want them to be able to go on feeling proud living their illusion of having successfully raised a son—a well-adjusted cancer survivor, an amputee getting good grades at a reputable college with a bright future full of white picket fences and home-schooled grandchildren—not a loser of a kid who can't ski race or get a girlfriend or even keep his own thoughts under control.

I can still hear Dad, ten years ago in the minivan after dinner at Country Cookin, his voice cracking into starts and stops as if transmitting Morse code, saying, "I'm sorry, Joshua, I wish they could amputate my leg instead." I didn't understand it then, but now I know that a child with loving parents never suffers alone. The parents feel all the pain their son or daughter does, perhaps even more. So, even though Mom and Dad never kept secrets from me—and I appreciate that, I really do—I'm not going to let them find out about this. For their own good.

I carry the prescription slip around in my back pocket for a few days. It feels like I've stuffed a block of lead in my wallet. I want to get it filled—I need to—but I just can't bring myself to go to the pharmacy. First, because antidepressants are for losers, for people who haven't read self-help books and taken control of their destinies, as I have. Second, I am on Mom and Dad's medical insurance policy, so they'd find out, and that would—let's not mince words here—suck. And third, because it's the last line of defense. If antidepressants don't work, there's nothing else. It's over. (That is, unless I go into therapy, but they don't even let losers of my level into therapy. Nope. It's strictly open to *ultra-super*-losers.)

I hold out for as many days as I can stand it—*it* being that presence of no presence, where thinking itself, the very process of whatever it is exactly that synaptic nerve endings do up there, is painful. No more. Please. Stop. So I call Dad, tell him about the grayness.

And now he calls me every day, asks about it. By name: The grayness. *Why didn't I just call it depression?* Every time I hear Dad say that word, my secret word that I previously used only in the privacy of my own mind to describe the emotionless space between black and white where I live, it makes me shiver, as if I'm naked.

And then I find out that I'm going to be an ultra-super-loser, too, because Dad says he's glad to pay for the prescription, but he and Mom talked about it and—*oh, great! Thanks Dad! Why don't you put it in the church bulletin while you're at it? Maybe send out a letter to my four-hundred donors?*—they decided that if they pay for a prescription, they'll want me to be in therapy, too. That's the deal. All right, fine. Ultra-super-loser-Dome, here I come.

"I like those shoes," I say.

"Thanks," says Tim. I don't know his last name. *Are therapists doctors? Should I call him Doctor Tim?*

"Yeah, I like those," I say again.

They are brown dress shoes made with soft leather, like on a leather couch.

"My wife's parents live up in Pennsylvania," Tim says. "And we go up and visit them every year for Thanksgiving. There's this great big store there with all sorts of shoes. It's like a warehouse. And they just have the most fabulous prices. So most years at Thanksgiving, I buy a new pair."

"Thanksgiving's coming up next month, huh?"

"Yep. Seems like summer just ended, doesn't it?"

"It does, yeah."

I think to myself: I hope I won't get to see this year's pair of New Thanksgiving Shoes. I hope by next month to be done with weekly therapy sessions and returned to civilian life.

I glance at the clock above Tim's desk. Almost thirty seconds. Mom and Dad are paying $120 an hour for this guy, so they've just spent a dollar on our conversation about . . . his shoes. Yikes. They're nice shoes . . . but not *that* nice.

"So why are you here?" Tim asks.

I was hoping he would not ask this. I already described my symptoms, lasting as they have for some eight months, to his secretary over the phone. (I'm becoming well versed in these divulge-personal-life-to-receptionist conversations.) Couldn't she just have passed the message along? I was hoping I would come in here today and he'd say, "All right, here's how you fix yourself. Step one, step two, step three." That's what all my self-help books used to do. They never asked *why* you were reading them. They just gave you the solutions to all your problems.

But Tim asked, so I guess I will have to tell. I spend the next three sessions, the next three weeks—and Mom and Dad's next $360—telling Tim why I am here, telling him the events that have led me to this place, to this feeling, or rather, lack of feeling. We move in reverse chronological order, like rewinding a movie. I tell him about the grayness (and I use that word to describe it, too, because Tim is my therapist, and he needs to know), about how recently when I talk to people, I'm not paying attention, and they say things like "Josh? Josh? Are you listening?" because my mind has floated back into that gray expanse of space, about how I sit in class and, while everyone else seems content to be a student and learn things, I worry about the craziest things, like whether I am dying, and whether I am living—you know, like, *really* living—life to the carpe-diem fullest, until my chest gets tight and I can barely breathe, and I have to go to the hospital, and I tell him about two weeks ago, when I finally got my prescription for Wellbutrin, the assistant pharmacist was the girl from my Political Philosophy class and how whenever I see her now she asks, "How are you *doing*?" with such grave concern that I'm sure everyone within earshot can figure out my recent medical history, and I want to sue her for some kind of assistant pharmacist confidentiality breach.

And then we're on our fourth session. Tim, wearing his brand-new shoes: How long has all this been going on? Me, with the same shoes as always: Since freshman year of college, I guess. Well, I started having some of the grayness my senior year of high school. And then I have to tell him about when I cried at King's Dominion, and then about this guy with one leg from Brooklyn who had something I didn't, and then about when Mom couldn't nurse Anna, and then about this girl who called me back one time and one time only. And I will never let that happen again.

"Why not?"

"I just can't."

"Why?"

"Because you only live once. I don't have time to fail."

27

That weekend I get a call on my cell phone. The number's not in my phone book.

"Hello?"

"Yo Smoshes! What's popping?"

"Yo!" I say, in spite of myself. "Not much. What's up with you?"

"Chilling, chilling."

"Where'd you find my number?"

"I hear you finally get a cell, so I ask some people till I get your digits."

. . . axe some people

Coming from anyone else, this would have sounded like the confession of a serial killer.

"Oh nice," I say. "Hey, I saw your picture in *Ski Racing* magazine a couple of months ago. Was that at Mount Hood?"

"Yeah, son. We train there for a month last summer."

. . . train dare fo a munt las summah.

"It's, like, a glacier, right? In Oregon?"

"Yeah, man."

"For real, you looked sweet. I can't believe how far you were leaned into that turn!"

"Ha! Yeah I be skiing fast."

"And congrats."

"For what?"

"For making the U.S. team!"

"Thanks, man."

"That's awesome . . ." I say, remembering that photo I saw in the magazine, the one of Ralph angled so far his arm was almost touching the snow. Perfect balance. But what I remember most from that photo was the red, white, and blue he was wearing. Ralph got the uniform. *That could have been me.*

"Actually, 'ats why I call you today, Smoshes."

"Oh yeah?"

"Yeah, man. Jason retire. People say Monte goan retire, too."

Jason, Monte. These are names of one-legged skiers—three-trackers—on the U.S. team. If they retire, there won't be many left, which is good for the younger three-trackers who are trying to make the team. That's because the U.S. Disabled Ski Team and the U.S. Paralympic Team—the U.S. team being named every year, the Paralympic Team every four years—have quotas to fulfill in their makeup, like affirmative action for different disabilities. Normally three-trackers are the disabled skiing equivalent of the white male: ubiquitous, undesirable. Supply exceeds demand. Blind skiers and skiers with cerebral palsy, however, are the perennial minorities, the slots that are always difficult to fill. But if what Ralph is saying is true, then space might open up for one-legged skiers, just in time for—*really? maybe?*—the Paralympics, two years away.

But let's be real, two years is not enough time to train. And why am I smiling right now? Why am I having a conversation I can actually pay attention to? I almost forgot—I'm *depressed.*

The next time I go to see Tim, he says there is something we discussed last time he wants to "spend more time exploring," as if this is all some kind of exciting spelunking adventure.

"All right," I say. "What was that?"

Yeah, and maybe we'll find some cool stalagmites and stalactites while we are at it. (Ha! Good metaphor. I can't believe I remembered those words, "stalagmites" and "stalactites," from way back when we used to go on homeschool field trips to . . .)

"Sorry," I say. "Can you say that last part over again?"

"Sure," Tim says, raising his eyebrows. He looks back down at his yellow legal pad. "You said, 'You only live once. I don't have time to fail.' What did you mean by that?"

"Just what I said."

"Why? Why don't you have time to fail?"

"It's just something I always tell myself."

"Always?"

"Well, for a long time."

"How long, would you say?"

"Probably like ever since . . . I was nine years old."

"When you had cancer?"

"Yes."

"Why did cancer make you not have time to fail?"

I look at the floor. Then I look at Tim again.

"Back when I had cancer, there was this kid Johnny. I shared a room with him sometimes when I was getting chemo. But Johnny's parents never stayed with him during his treatments. They just dropped him off and went home because they were like pretty poor and had to work. It was real sad."

"That *is* sad," Tim says. "I had a similar friend growing up. He lived across the street from me, with his grandmother. We used to play checkers. I loved checkers."

Tim always does this, interrupting my therapy to tell me something about himself. I think it's supposed to help me feel like we are friends, like we are revealing things in turn from our respective histories, like our conversations are a two-way street. But in what kind of friendship does one person talk about his most stalagmite-covered recesses of memory while the other person reveals, you know, his favorite childhood board game? And who charges $120 an hour to be your friend—unless, of course, this person is offering a little bit more than friendship? Please, Tim. This is *therapy*.

"What happened to Johnny?" Tim asks, signaling that we are finished with this particular foray into friendship-building.

"He died."

"I'm sorry to hear that."

"Yeah."

"How did that make you feel?"

Really? Did you really just ask me that?

I chuckle at the cliché. But then I think about Johnny and I feel, well, sad.

"It was tough, real tough," I say.

"Life is tough."

"Yeah it is."

"You still think about Johnny?"

"All the time."

"And?"

"And what?"

"How does that make you feel?"

I shift on the couch. It's a normal couch, like what you'd have in your living room, not the Freudian dentist chair I expected the first time I came here.

Tim lifts his eyebrows. He does that a lot.

"This is going to sound stupid," I say, "but sometimes I feel like he's staring down at me from Heaven with all those other kids who died while I was in the hospital. They are counting on me to live my life to the fullest, and to reach one hundred percent of my . . . potential, in everything I do."

"What if you don't reach one hundred percent?"

"Then I let Johnny down. Then he would want to scream at me."

"What exactly would he scream?"

I've thought about this before. I know exactly what he would scream.

"Well, pardon my language here . . ."

"Okay."

"He would scream, Josh, what the fuck are you doing? I am dead! You are alive! You got a second chance at life, I didn't! You've got no right to waste your life being ordinary! You don't have time to sit around! You don't have time to fail!"

Tim nods. "So you have to succeed, because otherwise you let Johnny and those other kids down?"

"Yeah . . . I guess."

"What if you could succeed even if you failed?"

I just look at him.

"What if," Tim continues, "you did your best, and that was enough? You gave one hundred percent effort, and even if you didn't reach one hundred percent success, you just accepted it, because there's nothing you can do to change what's already happened?"

I think: That is the stupidest thing I've ever heard, Tim! You either reach one hundred percent or you don't! You either succeed or you fail! This is common sense!

One morning a few days later—days that I fill with journaling and nighttime walks and the occasional bit of studying—I am taking a shower, surveying our disgustingly grungy bathroom. My roommate and I are in a stalemate with our suitemates, with everyone holding out on cleaning in an epic test of stamina in the face of increasing filth. Who will break? Who will be the one to clean it? I look at the shower, examining its caked grime and soap residue, assorted hairs, crusty washcloths draped over the curtain rod, and the cracked shampoo bottle that seems to be leaking an ooze of congealed milk.

I am a neat, clean person. I do not like things this way. In fact, I've been thinking about taking a weekend to scrub the bathroom, throw away everything empty and broken and make it shine again.

But I know, realistically, it wouldn't stay clean for more than a few hours. So this morning I wonder if maybe I should just leave it be, because I can still get a pretty decent shower even in a messy, far-less-than-perfect bathroom like this one. After all, I am not a health inspector. I am a Christian. I live by grace. This morning I look around again and notice the warm running water, the functioning drain, the sturdy towel rack.

Winter has come. It's a Thursday night, and snow is pouring down on the campus. I get an idea.

Like every good university, The College of William and Mary has a rite of passage for its students. And like every good rite of passage for students, this one involves public nudity. Specifically, streaking across the Sunken Gardens, a grassy field enclosed on the long ends by bushes and divided into square sections by parallel sidewalks. Tonight, with tomorrow's classes already canceled, there is a massive snowball fight—five, maybe six hundred students—in the Sunken Gardens.

The perfect night.

I return to my dorm and round up a few of the semi-friends and acquaintances I've made in between bouts of grayness here at college: Graham, my freshman roommate, and Paul, who lived on the third floor last year, and Brett, the most liberal member of my Bible study group, liberal being sort of a prerequisite for this activity. Ten minutes later, I'm walking through the night with this crew to the Sunken Gardens, all of us wearing sweaters and gym shorts with no underwear. The other guys shiver. Me? I still follow the tradition I developed in Colorado of wearing shorts every day, regardless of weather. People always ask me about this—they tell me I look cold, say I should put on some pants. But I wear whatever I feel like wearing. It just so happens that I always feel like wearing shorts.

As the crew walks toward the gardens, I hesitate—start to walk more slowly. In all these years no one, besides my parents and a few doctors, has ever seen *the scar*. I never took group showers at Boy Scout camp. I've never even changed clothes here at college with my roommate in the room.

Five or six hundred people? What will they say? Will they be repulsed, disgusted by the seven inches of smooth pigmentation that runs from my left hip down to the end of my butt cheek? Will they whisper when I walk by them in the cafeteria tomorrow and next week and next year, whisper about what they *saw* tonight? But this is college. And the spots on my lungs didn't kill me. And I got a second chance at life, and it hasn't been perfect, no, not even close, but I will live it as best I can—succeeding, failing, streaking, whatever.

So I lead the group to the Sunken Gardens, and we drop our clothes in a pile in the snow and tear across the field. I'm fast on my crutches, but not as fast as my friends, all of them with two legs. They run out ahead of me and get pummeled by snowballs. When *I* come through the crowd, though, the snowballs stop flying. Arms hang at sides, snowballs still gripped in hands. It is so quiet I can hear my rapid breathing and the dry crunch of the snow beneath my one shoe and the crutches. The snowball fight has ended because . . . they are staring at me. They are staring at *the scar*! But as gusts of wind create goose bumps the size of chickenpox all over my body, I begin to worry that everyone may be staring at another part of my anatomy, which in the cold has shriveled up to approximately the size of a Vienna sausage.

"Hey look!" someone yells. "It's a girl!"

People cheer.

I look down, aghast. It has shrunk down to nothing! They have mistaken me for a girl!

Just then, an actual girl runs by, also naked. *Whew! False alarm . . . don't stare . . . look straight ahead . . .*

Just then my right crutch tip hits the brick sidewalk on a patch of snow that has been packed into ice. The world stops. I lose my crutches and my three limbs splay out in the snow and I slide several inches on my bare front side. The crowd gasps, literally gasps collectively and so loudly I can hear it. I gather my crutches and stand up. There is a moment where we just regard each other, this crowd and I—the crowd, horrified at the painful sight it has just witnessed, and me, standing there in the center of the crowd, naked, the front of my body rubbed bright red. I can hear my own eyelids blinking.

I raise my fist in the air.

"Yeah streaking!" I yell.

The crowd erupts into shrieks of affirmation.

"Yeah!"

"Right on!"

"Let's all get wasted!"

A few weeks later I get an email from a middle-school principal. He's heard about the speeches I used to give, and he tracked me down here at college to see if I would do a presentation for his students. I hit Reply and start to type an email about how the speeches were a long time ago, how I'm not into all that anymore—and then I think, well, wait, maybe . . .

And so, in the spring, I find myself taking the stage in front of a small auditorium packed with three hundred seventh-graders. *Here we go.* I start with a couple of funny stories about having one leg— that resident who tried to take a pulse from my prosthesis, and the time a girl looked down at it and asked, "Is the foot fake, too?"

The students laugh.

Then I transition.

"I didn't come here today to tell you how to live your life or give you answers or advice about your problems," I say, "because I'm just like you. I'm still trying to figure things out."

I take a few steps across the stage.

"But there are two things about life that I'm sure are true, and those are the two things I want to talk to you about today."

I hold up one finger.

"First thing. Repeat after me. Life is tough."

"Life is tough," the three hundred voices echo.

I hold up two fingers.

"That's the bad news. The second part is the good news. Repeat after me. Life is beautiful."

"Life is beautiful," they repeat.

"Good job," I say. "That was . . . that was perfect."

28

When I arrive at Winter Park in December, I go straight to Paul DiBello's office to find out our training schedule. My adrenaline starts to flow, Pavlov style (*ding-ding*), at the thought of standing in front of that desk. And that adrenaline, combined with the fact that it takes several days to adjust to the eight-thousand-foot altitude at the Winter Park base, results in my being out of breath when I enter the office. But Paul's not there. I find one of the assistant coaches.

"Where's Paul?" I ask, gasping a little.

"You okay?"

"Yeah, fine, thanks."

"You didn't hear?"

"Hear what?"

"Paul's appendix burst. He's been in the hospital for several months."

"Really?"

"He almost died."

"Wow."

That phrase—*he almost died*—reminds me of a decision I made: I will not go to Paul DiBello's funeral. I decided this last summer when I went to train on a glacier at Mount Hood, Oregon, the only place in North America where you can ski race all summer. My three months of training was going to cost upward of ten thousand dollars, but it wasn't until after I moved to Oregon that I found out Paul wasn't going to let me use my race account money to pay for it. I would have to persuade my parents to loan me the money . . . or something. This was when I decided I would not attend Paul's funeral.

Even so, I would never be one to wish a painful hospital stay on anyone, not even Paul. So I'm sorry to hear today about his appendix, I really am. But I'm glad that he won't be around to bother me this year.

Unfortunately, I won't be seeing much of Ralph this season, either, because after he made the U.S. team, he left Winter Park and moved to Vail. I finally catch up with him a few weeks into the season, at a race in Colorado.

"So why you back?" he asks me as we ride the lift.

"What do you mean?" I ask.

"You quit, Smoshes. Now you back. Wus up with dat?"

Why am I back, Ralph Green? How much of the story do you want to know? Do you want to know about last year, about when I walked the campus at night and looked up at the stars and felt my new worldview and the daily three hundred milligrams of Wellbutrin XL and Tim my new-shoed therapist, all flowing through my veins, filling me with the full spectrum of Technicolor emotions—red orange yellow green blue violet—that had been absent for so long? Do you want to know about how the Paralympics, seen through this prism, was no longer a binary, a zero or a one, an either-I-make-it-or-I-don't, but was now an irresistible magnetic strip of a red line ahead of me somewhere, and no matter how improbable it was that I would actually cross that line, this chance would be enough to make it worth trying? It was enough, because *I* was enough. Either way. I was enough. I just needed some kind of red line to *chase,* that's all.

And Ralph, let me tell you about when I walked the campus asking myself if it would be *worth it* to start racing again, start aiming for the Paralympics once more. Would it be worth it if I didn't make it and my four hundred donors hated me for failing? Would it be worth it if I had to take a leave of absence from college to move back to a ski resort in Colorado, leaving my friends and also veering off the white-picket-fence path to the sure disapproval of my parents and all other gainfully employed adults? Would it be worth it if I had to spend every cent of the money left in my ski racing account and then go into even more debt to pay for my training? Would it be worth it if I had to return to the cold mountain air every day, air that's frostbitten me before and would surely do it again, where I might bruise ligament and tendon and marrow? Would it be worth it if I had to get up early to wax my skis and stay up late to study training videos and then lie in bed worrying about whether I was doing all I could to pursue the team, or whether there was something I was still missing in my regimen?

I thought about all these things during my walks. And you know what happened after that, Ralph? When I called Paul DiBello? What he said when I asked him my percentage chance of making the 2006 Paralympics, if I made a comeback and started training and racing full time again? One in a million. Not even 1 percent! I should've stayed in the sport while I was still on track, he said, back in 2002, he said, back when I quit. Now it's 2004, and I'm telling you it's impossible. I appreciate your enthusiasm but I've coached for thirty fucking years and I just want you to be realistic. And you know what I said? Paul you may have coached for a long time but you've never coached an athlete like me. Really! My exact words! I said Paul even if the chances are less than 1 percent, even if they are actually one in a million, like you say, I can accept those odds because I know I will put in 100 percent effort. And if I do that I can accept any percentage chance of making the team because I will have no regrets. And Paul said Sundquist you can do whatever you want. It's your life. I'm just letting you know.

And Ralph, I don't care what Paul says, because it's all different now. I used to think skiing would make me famous and rich. Now I know that it will do nothing for the former and take me farther from the latter. But like I said, it's different now. Now my favorite daydream has nothing to do with fame or fortune. No, now it takes place in a well-appointed lounge in Italy where I gather in 2006 with my whole family and best friends and I raise a glass and propose a toast: *To dreams—sometimes, every once in a while, they really do come true* . . . then I take a sip and try not to spill any on my Paralympic uniform. My dream of that perfect moment is what inspires me now.

But Ralph, you probably don't want to know all that, do you? You asked why I came back, but you don't want to know the complete answer.

So I say, "Because I love ski racing."

After I return from the race, I get a call from Dad. It's a Bad News Call, I can hear it in his voice. Six years ago he was the one who told us about Mom's cancer. What's interesting is I don't think these roles would work in reverse; if Dad ever got cancer, I think he'd still be the one to tell us, not Mom. I bet I'd hear it from Dad if Matt got sick, too, or Luke or Anna. This must tough for Dad, being the liver of the family, filtering all the bad news through himself.

"Mom has been having pain," he says.

I don't want to jump to conclusions. But I do.

"Okay . . ."

"She went to the doctor."

I don't say anything.

What is this, Dad? Some kind of dramatic pause? Spit it out!

"The cancer is back."

The cancer is back. I am strangely calm. The news is sad. Definitely sad. But at the same time, it's sort of a relief, an end to the anticipation that has been hanging over all of us. I have felt it whenever

I've gone home during breaks. Every morning Mom goes on a walk. To stay strong. A few hours later, the mail carrier arrives with magazines and newsletter updates about the latest in cancer research. Three times a day Mom eats meals that are not simply vegetarian, not simply vegan, but composed entirely of raw vegetables, raw nuts, and herbal supplements. All this was meant to delay the inevitable relapse, to push it further into the future. But to delay the pain of relapse also meant to stretch the pain of anticipation, and like so many things in life, the anticipation of impending pain was at times so heavy that I couldn't help but wonder sometimes if the event itself would turn out to be a lighter burden than the anxiety it caused, both for Mom and for the rest of the family.

"So what does it mean?" I ask.

Dad can tell me very little. They'll watch it for now, won't do anything until the cancer grows bigger. A lymphoma like Mom's becomes increasingly resistant to chemotherapy through a sort of survival-of-the-fittest among cancer cells, so you don't want to waste the early effectiveness of treatment on a small tumor. That's why we are entering a holding period, an incubation. Plus, later she may also qualify for an experimental drug trial. It would be the only chance of a cure.

That afternoon I sit on the ski lift, my vision obscured by salinized condensation on the inner lens of my goggles. How old is Anna now? Seven? Seven years old?

God, if You will give me one favor, please let Mom live long enough so that Anna grows up to remember the color in her mother's eyes.

And how long until the 2006 Paralympics? Just over a year?

And God, if You want to give me a second favor, please let Mom live long enough to see her son wear the uniform. Maybe even let her be well enough to come see me wearing it in Italy, if I walk into that stadium.

She probably won't be around for 2010. So 2006 is not just the best shot for her to see me, it's the only shot.

Sports psychology books will tell you that to reach peak performance, you have to believe so strongly in your chances of victory that it seems inevitable to you and everyone around you. But for me, such a belief would contradict every available data point from my past race history. So, instead, I just try to believe that it's possible. Because if it's possible, then there's hope, and if there's hope, it's worth my best shot. That's why I get a bracelet, why I put it on my wrist. It says, "Believe." I'm not going to take it off until the 2006 U.S. Paralympic Team has been officially selected.

The main thing I have going for me is that I'm physically stronger this season than I ever have been before. During the fall, when I was still at school, I was working out all the time. At the gym, I would do squats to develop strength—free squats, standing on my one leg with the seven-foot-long barbell balanced across my shoulders, plates stacked on each side, two hundred pounds, for reps. On other days, usually at night, I would climb the fence around the football stadium. I would set my crutches at the bottom of the student section and then hop to the top row, and then back down again, and I'd keep making these laps until on one hop my toes didn't clear the next step and I landed on the cement stairs, my hands breaking the fall. I'd rest for exactly thirty seconds and then do another set, repeating the whole cycle until I felt I could look back on the workout without regrets. That was how I developed agility. For balance, I would go to the woods at the edge of campus, to the ropes course, and I would stand for as long as I could on a guy-wire tightrope stretched between two trees.

The competitive ski racing season covers the winter and most of the spring, and then training at Mount Hood is available all summer. That leaves a gap in the fall—the time I was at school—when you are off snow and therefore end up losing the feel for your ski boot. That's a problem, because in ski racing, your boot is everything. It connects you both to your ski and to the snow. It's your center of balance, the place where all your weight and the vectors of your turn come together into one fundamental nexus of force—centripetal, centrifugal, G—all the forces of momentum. Your boot is also your steering wheel for driving around each gate, so you want it to be very sensitive to movement in your leg. You accomplish this by creating the snuggest possible fit. When I got my new boot last year, I started with a shell three sizes too small. I skied on it for two or three days, until the bruises and blisters were apparent enough on my foot that a boot fitter could heat up the plastic shell in those spots and punch them out, leaving little pockets of relief the size and shape of a nickel.

The nerves in your foot build up resistance to the discomfort of your racing boot throughout the course of a season—I'm not sure how this works, but that's just what happens—so to make sure I never lost that conditioning during the off-snow gap in the fall, I bought a special in-line skate with a binding on it, so you could attach a ski boot to the wheels. I would wear this three-foot-long device up the elevator of large parking decks. I'd take the elevator up, and then roll down each level, avoiding cars and speed bumps and dragging the rubber of my crutch tips when I got off balance.

That was my physical training. To prepare my mind, I watched an old VHS recording of the 2002 Paralympic ski races in Salt Lake until the videotape wore out, the frames flashing haphazardly on the screen. I read every book I could find—autobiographies by ski racers such as Picabo Street and Phil Mahre, "How to Ski race" instruction manuals, and books about physics, too, about those vectors and forces that come into play when you turn around a gate.

That's what I did to prepare in the off-season. And after making it to Colorado in the winter, I started training as hard as I could. But I've learned that it's not simply about training more. It's about training more in the right way. And not only the right way, the right way for *me*, for my own strengths and style. I've decided that this means taking fewer practice course runs than a lot of ski racers do, and instead just skiing the mountain to develop my feel for the snow. I like to leave my outriggers in the locker room and ski with regular ski poles, making turns where I lean over so far my hips nearly drag in the snow. Skiing with poles leaves no room for error. With outriggers, you can lean on them if you get off-balance. With one ski and poles, your balance has to be perfect, or you fall. When I do use outriggers, I like to go in the woods, ski through the trees, down the rock faces. And when I ski training courses, usually a few runs each morning, I do them at maximum intensity. I try to treat them like a real race—no goofing around, no holding back. I inspect the course. I do stretches. I wear my race suit. I want to be physically adapted to the feelings of the race suit and the adrenaline and everything else I will feel on race day. In this way, every day of training is a race day simulation. Like Coach K told me so many years ago, if I can do great in practice, in training, then I can be amazing when it comes to my game time, because I will use the excitement of the real thing to ski even better.

That's the other reason I like to go out and ski by myself. I like to imagine my game time and practice my victory celebration. I always start with spoken commentary:

"Here's Josh Sundquist, legendary champion, in the gate. He's getting ready to take his final run for the gold."

And then I ski down the hill, smashing imaginary gates. I get into a tuck and carry my speed across the finish line, and as I throw my ski sideways, sending up a rooster tail of snow, I look at the scoreboard and see my name beside where it says, "1st." Then I lift my arm in the air and I pump it up and down, revving the crowd to a thunderous ovation.

I've never actually skied in front of an audience before—most disabled races have just five or six spectators—but I like the thought of it, and the tingles always remain in my spine long after that crowd and scoreboard have disappeared.

Dad calls me again a month into the season. More Bad News. Today it's about Matt. He's run away.

"He's what?" I ask.

"He's run away," Dad says.

"To where?"

"We don't know. That's the whole problem."

"Why?"

Dad explains. Matt—who was elected Student Council president a few months ago—was helping some friends from school who wanted to set up a Gay-Straight Alliance Club. He's not gay, but he wanted to show his support, so he put his name behind it. Mom heard about the club and, without knowing her son was helping start it, brought her Public School Moms Prayer Group to Principal Reynolds's office for a meeting. Mom and her friends opposed the group, of course, thought it would undermine the moral fabric of their children's education and all that. Word of this meeting got back to Matt, and he flipped. Mom was trying to ruin his Student Council presidency behind his back. She was a terrible mother. She didn't love him. She had never loved him.

And then Matt disappeared.

"Dad, he didn't really run away," I say.

"How do you know?"

"Running away is like when the kid leaves town with someone he met online and you put his face on a milk carton. I'm sure Matt is just at a friend's house."

"Well regardless your mother is quite distraught."

The only time Dad ever uses that term to identify Mom—*your mother*—is when he doesn't know what to do, as if by describing her in relation to me (*your* mother) rather than himself or the family in general (*my* wife or Mom), he is suggesting that I might be the one responsible for solving the problem.

"Everything's going to be fine, Dad," I say.

At least, I think so. Or I hope so. For the last couple of years, I've felt as if there were two Matts, a set of twins posing as a single individual, a brother of mine. There is the Matt who can be dropped into any social environment, hostile or friendly, and within ten minutes of hitting the ground be best friends with everyone within a fifty-foot diameter. That's the Matt who dances with Miss America and leads everyone in the YMCA dance onstage at Children's Miracle Network parties at age seven. That's the Matt who went from home-schooler to winner by a landslide of the Student Council presidency at public school. And then there's the *other* side of Matt, the one who says devastating things to his terminally ill mother and then runs away. The one who says he might not even go to college next year, who will always fight the system. He's the one who didn't get to go to Lost River, the one who had only four words played on *The Brad Huddleston Morning Show*.

What's clear is that these two Matts are fighting for control over my brother's life. What's not clear to me is which one will come out on top.

The talk with Dad sends me back to skiing for the afternoon. Riding the lift silently through the trees I listen to the peculiar quiet that you can hear when you're surrounded by snow, a quiet that you can actually feel in your ears, like sonar. All skiers know this sound. It's as if the snow absorbs the faint white noise and reverb of everyday life.

And all at once I am sure, so sure, that God is real. There is no other explanation for existence. And if He is real, I feel equally confident that He, too, is listening to the snow right now, and furthermore, He is listening to my thoughts, just like Mom always said.

Am I doing this right, God? Am I living right? You want me to ski, don't you? I ski because I love to ski, and I love to ski, I think, because You made me that way. Right?

And am I supposed to train so hard? Mom always said that you should do your work as unto the Lord, by which she meant to make sure that we vacuumed and mopped very thoroughly. But it's more than that, isn't it, God? It's the fact that You've given me this new day to live, this body that still breathes and pulses with life, this body that has faced death and has overcome. How could I not train hard? How could I accept anything less? When I train, I must train hard, because I train as unto You.

But does single-mindedly pursuing the sport I love make me selfish? Should I instead be making sacrifices for You, God, sacrifices for the least of these, for the poor in spirit? Maybe I should be a missionary, or a pastor, invest my talents and store up my treasure in Heaven. God, if You want me to do something else, I beg you to give me the desire, because I cannot give up what I love, as many Christians seem to do, out of some arbitrary, masochistic ideal of puritan sacrifice and spiritual discipline. I love skiing too much. I hope You are all right with that.

And what about others? Am I doing that right? When I was little I was so concerned about telling everyone about Jesus. I felt obligated to be like Dad, always pointing the unchurched and unsaved and un-Christian toward the straight-and-narrow path to Heaven. I would sit with strangers on ski lifts like this one and devise ways to drop Jesus casually into the conversation, as if He were the weather, and then listen for a nibble to indicate spiritual hunger in my liftmate's soul. If, on the other hand, I lacked the courage and said nothing to guide the conversation toward spirituality, I always felt guilty afterward. But God, I've long since lost my sensitivity to that guilt, and therefore I don't make the effort to evangelize anymore. It's not that I don't think Your son is important. I do. Definitely. He's everything. It's just that I don't think I have the right or the authority to prescribe a particular spiritual path to other human beings. That's not what You want from me, is it? You wouldn't want me to tell Ralph that according to the theology of the church where I grew up, he's going to Hell, do you? I hope not, because I can't. I just can't do it. Ralph's relationship with You is none of my business. I'm sorry, God.

And speaking of Hell, what about me? Am I breaking too many rules, God? I kissed a girl—all right, *made out* with a girl—for the first time this past semester. Was that wrong? Mom would say I shouldn't kiss a girl until I am ready to marry her. You don't mind kissing, do you, God?

And speaking of Mom, why is she sick, God? I don't even know what to say to You about her cancer. What can I say that hasn't already been said for thousands of years, since the days when Job demanded You answer his queries and account for his suffering?

And . . . one more thing. Am I a good son? Are Mom and Dad going to be proud of me for ski racing, for doing my best to finish strong even if I fail in my pursuit of 2006? Is giving them the opportunity to feel this pride what it means to honor my father and mother? I hope so. And am I a good brother? A good example to Anna and Luke? To Matt? To be honest, though, God, I feel that more often I look up to Matt, not vice versa, because despite the stress he puts on Mom and Dad, I have to admire his freedom, his abandonment of rules, and his pursuit of pure passion.

29

I look to my left, at the two racers in the other lanes. In the far left position is Clay Fox, one-legged ski racer, member of the U.S. Disabled Ski Team, and a veteran of the sport. Two years ago he finished the season as the disabled World Cup champion in slalom, meaning he was the fastest disabled slalom skier on the planet.

In the middle position is Toby Kane, one-legged ski racer and member of the Australian Disabled Ski Team. Earlier this season he won his first World Cup race. Won. A World Cup race. Two months ago.

And in the far right position is . . . me. I've got excellent credentials, too: In my first slalom race, I fell five times. I've finished last place in the majority of my international competitions. Really impressive stuff.

So probably the biggest mystery is how I am standing in the starting gate, because this heat is the finals, which means I actually beat some pretty fast racers in the first three rounds to advance to this point. That's big news, since I've never really beaten anyone—at least not anyone decent—before today. But then again, it's been since high school that I've competed in a race like this. In contrast to a normal ski race, where each competitor goes through the course one at a time, the Wells Fargo Bank Cup is a three-way, head-to-head slalom. There are three identical courses placed parallel to one another, about ten feet apart, and all three racers ski down at the same time.

"Racers ready in one minute," the timekeeper says. I slide up to the start. There are three cattle gates—like the ones they use to release a cowboy on top of a bronco at a rodeo—that will swing open simultaneously, allowing each of us onto his course. After that, the first one across the finish line at the bottom is the winner.

And the winner, I know—all three of us know—will get a check written out in his name for a thousand dollars. A ton of money. That's important, because last summer, when Paul DiBello wouldn't let me use my race account to train at Mount Hood, I blew through all of my life savings and started borrowing from Mom and Dad. At the rate I'm spending, I will be ten or even twenty thousand dollars in debt by the time the Paralympic team is named next year. In other words, I really need that one thousand dollars.

That money is the most important thing riding on this race. The results themselves don't actually matter, at least not in terms of world rankings, because this is not a sanctioned race; it's an annual fund-raiser for the Winter Park Disabled Ski Team, started a few years back by none other than Paul DiBello. It's got his muddied fingerprints all over it—big money on the line, the best racers in the world, and plenty of danger, because with the three courses so close together, if a racer crashes, he could end up taking one or both of his competitors to the hospital with him. Ralph actually got hurt in this race a couple years ago, an injury that cost him a month in recovery time—that's why he's sitting this one out today, at the bottom, in the crowd. Paul's been released from the hospital, so I assume he's down there, too. After all, this race is his legacy.

That's another thing about this race: the crowd. There are about three hundred people down there who helped raise money for the program. Three hundred people, many of them locals from Winter Park, many of them people I know, people who are pulling for me in this matchup. What these people don't understand is just how unlikely, just how *crazy* it would be for me to win this race. It would mean rocketing from relative obscurity to beat two of the top racers in the world and take home one of the biggest cash prizes in the sport of disabled ski racing.

And that's why this race *does* matter, because even though it won't affect my ranking on paper, even though it's not even a "real" race, next week I am going to Austria and Switzerland for my first European World Cup series. It will be the last set of major international races I compete in before the Paralympic team is selected next year. In other words, my race results in Europe will probably determine whether I make the 2006 team. Winning here today—though a virtual impossibility—would mean carrying the momentum of a stupendous upset into that make-or-break European World Cup series.

"Thirty seconds," says the timekeeper.

Could I really beat these guys?

Last night I made a deck of flash cards. On each card, I wrote the name of one of the racers registered for this race. Then I dealt the cards face up on the kitchen table, shuffled, and dealt again, imagining with the turn of every card what it would be like to beat that person in a head-to-head slalom race today. I did this until the process was hardwired. I would see a name and my mind would instantly auto-respond with "Re: Josh's Victory, Attachment: Victory_Image. jpg." The Clay Fox flash card, namesake of the racer in the far left lane, was the hardest to program in this way. I just couldn't believe I might be able to beat him.

And let's be real . . . I can't. Clay Fox? And Toby Kane, too? Versus me? No way. I will probably fall, probably make a mistake, probably embarrass myself. Yep, probably so.

I rotate my gloved hand and feel the bracelet snug against my race suit. *Believe.* Not that it's likely. That it's possible. *Is it possible?*

I pray.

Dear God, if You want to help me out here . . .

My normal pre-race mental routine begins.

Keep your shoulders level. Always bend your knee, stay loose, never stiffen your leg. Push against the front of your boot. Angle your hips out-side the—

And then:

What's that noise?

"Ten seconds."

I can hear a rhythm . . . it's from the crowd, the three hundred people at the bottom of the course . . . but what are they saying? I can't understand it.

"Five seconds."

With five seconds left, I am usually still reviewing my list of rules, still practicing them in my mind. But today I turn off my clattering self so I can sense the words rolling off the snow, through my helmet. *Is that really what they are chanting?* The sound is faint. But it is unmistakable.

Josh, Josh, Josh . . .

I feel excitement forcibly expanding my lungs, as if the crowd is giving me mouth-to-mouth resuscitation. *Game time.*

It all goes quiet, and I watch through my goggles as the timers count down beside my starting gate. Five, four, three, two—

I don't wait to see *one*. Instead, I push off my outriggers before the gate opens so I am moving with full momentum toward the metal gate that has still not swung open . . . *please please swing open now, now, now* . . . and just as my hips start to brush it—*pop*—it rotates out and I drop down the starting ramp and toward the first turn.

Thwack!

My first gate.

Thwack thwack!

Toby and Clay's.

I blaze through each turn, my shin guard hitting the gates low so they bend first at the base, like catapults, before whipping over and pounding the snow.

Thwack thwack thwack!

They're even with me, now pulling ahead, generating speed on each turn.

Thwack thwack . . . thwack!

Toby, Clay . . . Josh!

We roll up on the final crest—six gates left—and the crowd comes into view. All three hundred people enter my peripheral vision and from there flow straight into my bloodstream. And then, as if the future is a movie set on fast-forward, I see a preview of the last six turns. I see myself zipping around each turn and then across the finish line ahead of Clay and Toby. *That's it!* The movie has taught me how to win, told me what I need to do to get there first. *I see it!* No mechanical instruction, no strategy. The movie itself *is* the victory. I only have to enter it, to act it out.

And then I'm back on the crest.

I flow into the last six gates, letting the earth pull me toward its center of gravity, letting the dual blades of my ski cut a path so I flow over the frozen two parts hydrogen, one part oxygen—*shing, shing, shing.*

I hit the last three gates with such speed that I'm sure I've bruised my shin.

As I stretch my outriggers to trip the laser eighteen inches above the red line painted across the snow, I glance left and see Clay Fox and Toby Kane . . . *several feet behind me.*

I won!

I throw my ski sideways in the finish coral and pump my fist in the air, up and down. *I won a ski race!* The sound of the wind against my helmet sucks down with a *whoosh*, and I can hear applause and cheers louder and happier than any I've ever known. *The frostbite and the lactic acid and the bounced checks and the*—my Winter Park teammates rush around me, touching my raised arm, stepping on my ski, tripping over one another—*for here, right now*—I let out a scream—*because I will have this always, no matter what*—and I smile wide, my jaw pried apart as if by its own free will. *And—I almost forgot what this will mean . . . Will I make it? Can I make it now? Can I carry this race to Europe next week and to Italy . . . to 2006 . . . next year?*

Before I've even caught my breath, I hear the voice of someone from channel-something in Denver:

". . . a few questions?"

"Sure."

"How does this feel?"

"It's incredible. I've been training hard and I've never had a race like—and I finally—yeah, like, wow."

"Josh, early on, things didn't look good for you. How did you come from behind like that?"

Still breathing hard.

"Ha, ha ha—I don't know. No secrets, really. I just saw that I could win, and I let go on the last few turns, you know, just let it all go."

30

I think of that race I won. A year has passed since then. So much can happen in a year—good things, bad things. So many things.

Last month, Erik, the race director who eventually replaced Paul DiBello after his appendix burst, called me into his office. I thought he wanted to tell me that the Paralympic team had been named, and that it was time for me to head home. I walked inside—the building had been remodeled, with Erik having had the walls around Paul's old office torn down and put in couches for the team to lounge about on—and sat down. Erik told me he'd just learned the qualification criteria for making the Paralympics. The top twenty in the United States, he said, would be named to The Team.

I nodded. This was his way of telling me that I hadn't made it, just as we'd always expected, that it was finally time for me to pack up and head back to Virginia, to say goodbye to ski racing. I nodded. I had done my best. No regrets. I had finished. Not quite the way I had always hoped, but I had finished nonetheless. Just out of curiosity, though, I had to ask.

"What am I ranked?"

"As of this morning, you are number twenty," Erik said.

"Wait—what?"

Erik smiled.

"Do you mean?" I stammered. "Do you mean that if the team was named today, I would be on it?"

"That's right."

"Weird." That's all I said: weird. It was so unexpected, such a complete shock, that my first thoughts were entirely logistical in nature: Did I have time to spend the entire month in Italy? Would anyone be willing to buy expensive plane tickets to come watch? *Weird.*

Then I went outside and skied the trees, a steep section with rocks and moguls, and I shredded them until halfway down the mountain, when I just fell into the hill and started laughing. All those people! All the four hundred donors who had given me money, and the sponsors who had donated equipment, and the people at college whom I told I was leaving to *train for the Paralympics*, which must've sounded completely ridiculous—and all that mental energy, years of forcing myself to do things I didn't feel like doing. Money spent on training. Friday nights spent at the gym. Late-night and early-morning flights across the country and the Atlantic. My parents, my family, even my brother Matt, praying for me back home. Redeemed. Vindicated. I lay there in the woods until the snow began to melt into the backside of my ski jacket and pants.

It took a few tries before I could call home without crying. I'd dial a few numbers, then hang up. I had to work my way up to it, adding a number each time until I'd dialed all the digits.

"Hi Dad," I said.

"Hi Joshua."

"You know how you've been saving up your frequent-flier miles for your whole life? For, like, a special occasion?" I asked.

"Yes, mmm-hmm."

"I was thinking you might want to use them next month."

"Oh really?"

"Yep."

"What for?"

"To go on a trip to Europe."

"Why Europe?"

"I thought you might want to go to Italy."

There was a long pause.

"To Turino, Italy?" Dad asked.

"Yeah. Turino, Italy," I said.

Dad replied with the strongest language he could, using phrases like "Oh my goodness," which is arguably a euphemism for "Oh my God."

Exactly one month after that conversation and exactly one year after I won that head-to-head ski race, I find myself in this tunnel. The tunnel leads into brightness. The brightness is so complete that the tunnel itself, its two walls, floor, ceiling, blend together like a black hole. This is where the athletes—the *Paralympians*—walk into the stadium. I want to walk there, too. I want to know how it feels. And in just a moment, I will.

We walk toward the light, and I begin to make out the shapes of a mass of people through the opening in the passageway. I've been here before, thousands of times, in my mind. Ever since I stood in that empty stadium four years ago, I've been traveling ahead to come to this place, this stadium, to see it packed with people, as it is now, to hear it reverberating with applause, as it is now. And every time I've imagined being here, I've worn a uniform, just as I do now.

"We make it, Smoshes! I always be telling you we goan make it!"

"Yeah, Ralph. We made it."

Back in the staging area, they didn't tell us how to line up—no alphabetical order by last name or anything—so naturally Ralph Green jumped in the front of the line, just a few spots behind our flag bearer. And of course I jumped in the next position, right behind Ralph Green.

We reach the end of the tunnel so that the light from the stadium pours into our eyes as we hear "Stati Uniti d'America!" and the sight of thirty thousand people packed into the arena overwhelms us.

"Hell yeah!" Ralph yells. "HIH-ha-ha-ha!"

"Oh," I say, quietly.

We walk down the center stage, the United States Paralympic Team forming a long line of the one-legged, the one-armed, the user of wheelchair. I consider reaching up to wave to the crowd, but doing so would involve potential disaster. I was under the impression that a tailor at the Olympic Training Center in Colorado Springs was supposed to hem my Opening Ceremony pants, but apparently he or she didn't get that particular memo, so I have to use one hand to walk with my crutches, while the other maintains a vise grip on a ridiculously large waistband.

This is the uniform I've been waiting for? They could've thrown in a belt, or at least some underwear, in case my hand slips.

As we walk down from the stage and I get a closer view of the crowd, I notice how many of the people in it are disabled. I wonder if maybe after the ceremonies a few will sneak onto this stage, get their picture taken. Maybe they'll start training and make it to Vancouver in 2010. They'll be the next link in this chain of inspiration, this chain of hope, that I'm now a part of.

This chain of hope is much like the prayer chain I grew up with, except that it's based not only on faith in God, but also on faith in one another, faith in ourselves, faith in our dreams. It's a chain composed of all the people in this stadium, who are cheering for us now as they've cheered for us for so many years. For each athlete, all the links of the chain are here, in this stadium, whether in person or in spirit. There is a mother who cared, a father who protected, a brother who loved, a Dr. Dunsmore who healed, a Lydia who disappointed, a Ralph who challenged, a Paul who infuriated, and a Johnny who inspired.

On the bus ride back to the Village that night, I think of one of the people I wish was here, here in person: Matthew. But I think Matthew—Matt, I mean—would have been here if he could.

The last time I saw him was at start of the winter, at Christmas. Late that night, after midnight, when I had just slipped under the covers on my old bed at Mom and Dad's house, I heard his voice.

"Get up," he said.

"What?"

"Yo we're going to hang out."

"Dude I'm sleeping." I kept my eyes closed.

"Hey check this out," he said.

I opened my eyes to discover a bare bottom twelve inches in front of my face.

"Ha! You got poned!" he said.

I laughed. *Why am I laughing? I'm trying to sleep here.*

"Whatever. I'm going to sleep."

"I'm Josh and I'm a loser," Matt said in his mocking voice.

Yeah, well . . . I guess . . . you only live once.

"Fine. But not for too long. I've got to fly back to Colorado tomorrow."

We decided to visit a big new church building on top of a hill. Some kind of Brethren congregation, I think.

"I've been wanting to get on top of this roof," Matt explained on the way. "I think we can get on it somewhere."

"Really? I remember it being pretty tall."

"Uh-oh, sounds like *somebody's* a little grouchy about being woken up."

It is unclear why I find it so funny when he mocks me.

We parked in the far corner of the lot. First we tried Matt's idea of ascending via the heating and cooling unit. Failure. I saw another route and pointed it out to him. He followed it, hand over foot, supported via windowsills and conveniently obtrusive brickwork.

"Hand me your crutches," he whispered from above me. It was one of those loud whispers, probably louder than normal speech. "I'll hold them up here for you."

"Thanks."

I tossed him my crutches, one at a time, and then ascended, albeit using more arm strength and fewer legs than he did. Matt handed me my crutches. I have really expensive crutch tips—like forty dollars a pop—for occasions such as this one. Not roofs specifically but rather, inclines in general. We walked the forty-degree slant of the roof, the polymer of my crutch tips stretching to grip the shingles, until we reached the base of the steeple. Matt, apparently satisfied with the distance he had dragged me from my bed, sat down. He was wearing his normal wardrobe of thrift-store clothes, assembled in such a way that the outfit somehow said "vintage" rather than "old-fashioned."

I couldn't help but notice that from where we were sitting, up there beside that steeple, I could see another building less than a mile away, the one where we spent every single Sunday morning growing up, the one where I once saw a kid with a bowl cut and a lime-green travel soccer team uniform.

I turned to Matt.

"How is it?" I asked.

"What?"

"College! Everything in Boston!"

"It's amazing, man."

"Are the people, you know, snobby?"

"Some are. But most aren't. People realize that it's like totally amazing they got there," he said.

"Dad said you're running for vice-president of the student body next year."

"I'm thinking about it."

"That's awesome."

He looked down, ran his fingers along the bent shingles glued over the apex of the roof.

"I've met a lot of people. Even at freshman orientation, people were telling me I should run for president—of the student body, I mean."

"You think you will?" I asked.

"Yeah, maybe junior year. I want to get in there and change things, you know?"

"Fight the system?"

"Yeah."

"I bet people are so surprised when you tell them," I say. "Like people around here in Harrisonburg. You weren't always . . . well, I mean—*Harvard*, you know?"

"Yeah, I know . . ."

We all know. It was a total shock. He applied on a whim, as part of a sort of what-if proposition with himself. When he got the letter, he sent them an email: Dear Admissions, I wanted to let you know you have accidentally sent me an acceptance letter. No, they wrote back, there's no mistake. We're pleased to welcome you to the class of 2009.

"I still don't really get it, though. What changed for you in high school?" I asked. "I mean . . . you weren't always . . . you know . . . *on track* . . ."

"Soccer, mostly. Like when I got on The Stars. That made me focus, get things together."

Ah, yes, The Stars. One of Virginia's premiere travel soccer teams. Matt tried out, made the team his junior year of high school.

I never got the chance to wear the uniform of a travel soccer team, but Matt did. And in it he found grace. And sitting on that roof I realized this is why Matt and my stories are really the same, because although we ultimately played different sports, it was in those sports that we found our earthly salvation.

Matt spoke again.

"There was always a side of me that was, like, mature, though. I had to grow up early."

"What do you mean?"

Matt looked up past the steeple for a few beats. His hair was long and unkempt, according to his style of the last several years. Kind of the opposite of how he asked Mom to cut it during the year when I was on chemo.

"You know, when Nana passed away, I was the only one in the room with her. I saw her last breath and then I ran into the sunroom, and you were lying on their couch watching the cartoon version of *The Three Musketeers*. You remember?"

"Yeah."

"I ran outside and told Mom and Papa that Nana had just died, and I will never forget the look on Papa's face. After he had changed her diapers and all for like four years, he steps outside for one minute and then he's not by his wife's side when she passes. I always felt like I stole that moment from him."

"Wow."

"I was ten. It was never the same after that."

What could one say to a story like this?

Then it was quiet. It was the kind of quiet you get late at night on the edge of a small town—the occasional urban noise, like a car driving by, melted together with the kinds of sounds you might expect to hear when camping—cicadas, crickets, the wind.

Suddenly he said, "You know I almost dropped out of Harvard this first semester?"

"No . . . why?"

"Because Mom went back on treatment. I have this new axiom in life, that you have to appreciate what you have before it's gone. So I was going to come back and help take care of her. I even went in and told the Dean's Office I was thinking about leaving."

I nodded. A Matthew who would consider coming home to help

his mother is a Matthew I had not seen for many years. The Parable of the Prodigal Son is recorded in the gospel of Luke, but in our family, it seems to be found in the story of Matthew. I knew that story started with me, though. All the bad parts, I mean. I sat there, on the roof, wanting to apologize for it all: His mere four words on *The Brad Huddleston Morning Show*, his absence at Lost River, the shadow of my story that he grew up under. I just didn't know how to say it.

"I guess it was pretty—crazy for you when you were little, huh?" was all I managed.

Matt looked at me. Maybe he knew what I was trying to say.

"It was tough, yeah," he said. "But you know—I always think that the reason I won the student council election in high school, and the reason my interviewer at Harvard liked me . . . and even why people tell me I should run for office at Harvard . . . is because of everything that happened. You remember, right? When you had cancer? I had to go from house to house, staying with a different family from our church almost every day. Do you think I'd be able to relate to so many different types of people if that hadn't happened?"

Up on that roof, being above most of the lights of our town, the sky looked darker than usual. This made the stars, when we looked up at them, seem brighter.

Back in the Village I find several brand-new duffel bags on my bed, these in addition to the ones from the Olympic Training Center. I unzip them and find that my collection of uniform gear now includes two waterproof ski parkas, two micro-fleeces, a variety of winter hats in several colors, two pairs of gloves, sweatpants in both cotton and polyester, short-sleeve T-shirts with the team logo, long-sleeve T-shirts with the team logo, jerseys, a pullover with a zipper, several windbreakers, two sweaters (one of wool and one of a cotton-cashmere blend), long underwear, a vest, a pair of sneakers, two pairs of boots, multiple scarves, a few baseball caps, a retro-style warm-up jacket, all manner of socks, a ring, a watch, a puffy down jacket, a fleece blanket, a woven blanket, and a pair of sunglasses, not to mention the pants with the oversize waistband, a white leather jacket, and a beret (actually, three berets—one red, one white, one blue) from the Opening Ceremony uniform. Every item—including even the pack of Kleenexes, the many key chains, the deck of playing cards, and other Olympic-licensed trinkets—is red or white or blue, or all three.

In the outside pockets of one of my bags I find a strip of polished brown leather with snaps on the ends. The center of the band is embossed with the Olympic rings.

"Wow," I say aloud.

I slide off my rubber bracelet, the one that says, "Believe," and replace it with the leather one, snapping it into place so that the rings face outward.

Living in the Olympic Village is amazing. Not perfect, though—contractors were trying to complete it until the minute the Olympics started last month, so there are still leaks and odd smells in the unfinished underground hallways that connect the dorm buildings with the central cafeteria and gathering complex. Then again, it's hard to beat the perks—free food 24/7, a free coffee bar, free DVD rentals, a brand-new gym, an Internet lounge, and more than the FDA-recommended lifetime dosage of Paralympic footage pouring out of flat-screen TVs everywhere.

Best of all are the Olympic-themed Coca-Cola machines in all the buildings. Each athlete has a Coca-Cola bottle shaped key chain with a wireless chip inside. You just wave the key chain in front of the machine and the red lights switch from "$3.00" to "Free." Then you press the button of your choice, and you hear the rumble of plastic in the bowels of the machine, and then—*poof*—like magic, a cold twenty-ounce beverage drops down. I choose Powerade, the official sports drink of the Olympic and Paralympic games.

I usually get the flavor that comes in the commemorative gold bottle. I am not sure what this flavor is exactly, but the taste is also something commemorative—someone said it was watermelon, but I'm not sure—and very sugary. There's nothing better than walking around in the shadows of the Italian alps after most people's bedtimes, wearing a pair of shorts, a U.S. team jacket, and drinking a free Powerade packed with sugar, like candy, even though it's not Friday.

It's so great I drink ten to fifteen commemorative twenty-ounce bottles per day. I adhere to this diet until the second-to-last day of the games, when I am struck by debilitating stomach cramps. At first I blame the abundant pasta (this being Italy), but when on a whim I try switching from Powerade to water for a few hours, my beleaguered gastrointestinal system makes a full recovery.

My slalom race takes place on the last day of the Games. That night we sit at a table in a little Italian restaurant outside the Village.

"To drink?" our waiter asks. He has an accent, but it's understandable enough.

"A glass of red wine, please," I say.

I'm twenty-one, after all. So I can drink (although, I hear the drinking age here is, like, three).

"That sounds nice, Giovanni," Dad says, glancing at our waiter's nametag. "I'll have a glass as well."

I look at Dad. *Wine? Dad, drinking wine?*

Then I remember a story Dad shared with me last year. He was at church, telling an acquaintance about how Mom's cancer had returned. She'd been approved for a promising experimental treatment and had had an invasive biopsy to get a tissue sample to make a custom cancer vaccine. But four months into the preparatory chemo cycles, they discovered that she had a rare DNA sequence—present in only one third of 1 percent of the population—which rendered her incompatible with the treatment.

This acquaintance, this Christian, said to Dad, Well you know, brother, God is good.

But Dad did not reply with his usual "All the time." Instead he asked, what do you mean by that? I mean, omniscient, yes. All-powerful, yes. By what do you mean by *good*?

And the acquaintance put his hand on Dad's shoulder and said, brother, let me put it this way. All our wives are going to die sooner or later. It's just that yours might end up going a little sooner than the rest of us.

I think that's when Dad knew that it was about time to resign from being an elder of our church. Not because he'd lost faith in God's love for humanity, but because he had gained faith in his own love for his family. He wanted to spend less time in church committee meetings and more time at the family kitchen table.

The waiter comes back with two wine goblets and a glass of water.

"Grazie," I say, feeling very Italian.

Dad and I order a pizza.

"And for you, madam?"

"I'll just have a slice of their pizza," says Mom.

Pizza? Mom? What's going on with my parents today?

But things are different now, I guess. Before Mom relapsed, it was like she was trying to outrun death by eating her rabbit food—sprouts and broccoli leaves and wheatgrass—and drinking her blue-green algae juice every day. Now that the cancer's come back and then gone away again, the experimental treatment a bust but traditional chemo still having eliminated most of the tumor, it's like she's been given bonus time. So she's not running anymore. She's living.

"And also a side salad, please," she says.

Well, sort of living.

"So, who's this guy you're staying with here?" I ask.

"Guido," Dad says.

"And you found him online?"

"Yes. Mom did."

"Free?"

"We're giving him money for food."

"Nice work," I say, sarcastically. "Saving up for my college?"

"Hey we still have to put Luke and Anna through school!" Mom says, elbowing me and smirking.

"Right, sorry. I forgot about them."

We talk about my slalom race this morning. I tell Mom and Dad what it's like to be standing in that ski gate, a television camera in your face, the timekeeper counting down the last five seconds before the most important race of your life. You try to keep your mind clear. Don't focus on technique. Don't worry about falling. Just think about that red line at the bottom, about getting there as fast as you possibly can.

And then you push off—*this is my moment*—and fly down the course, barely able to stay ahead of the gates, trying to push as close as you can to the edge of that cliff without flying off it and crashing. You barely make it across the finish line, and when you slow down, the wind stops blowing in your helmet and you can hear the crowd screaming. *Four thousand people.* If you end with a big, slow arc in front of the stands in the finish arena, pumping your fist in the air, a wave of applause will follow you across the spectator stands. It's magic.

But I don't tell Mom and Dad about the next part, when you turn around and look at the scoreboard on the Jumbotron, praying that it will be like you imagined it, like it is in the movies, a Cinderella story. Instead, you see your name next to "34th." And then you think to yourself, *What am I doing here? Why was I named to the team? I am a complete total absolute embarrassment to this uniform.*

Even though I don't tell them about it, I think they can see the disappointment in my eyes when I remember. They look at each other.

"Actually, Dad made some calculations, and you did pretty well," Mom says.

"Well, I beat Ralph. I was happy about that," I say.

"That's not what she's talking about," Dad says. "Your world ranking before the Paralympics was fifty-fourth. You finished today at thirty-fourth. That means you placed twenty spots higher than your ranking would predict! That's outstanding!"

Dad. Always the numbers person.

But I already thought about that, Dad. After the race I got the official results and examined them carefully. It turns out that I finished thirty-fourth because so many people crashed this morning. My actual FIS points result—a measurement of how many seconds slower I was than the best racers in the competition—is right on par with my fifty-fourth-in-the-world ranking. So you're wrong, Dad. My performance was average for me.

For a moment, I consider telling you so. I should always tell the truth, right? No matter what? But then I look at you, and at Mom, and you both just look so proud of your thirty-fourth-in-the-world son. And how many parents can say they saw their child compete in the Olympics or Paralympics? What right do I have to steal your joy tonight?

After all, truth is not always a virtue when it is pursued for its own sake or, worse, simply to make its teller feel morally superior. That's the problem with those who let the rules of religion overshadow its spirit—which is, of course, love. And grace. In other words, there are times when telling an outright lie may be the most loving thing a person can do.

So I smile. As if I've just realized for the first time, thanks to your insight, Dad, that my race today was fantastic. As if I am proud of my thirty-fourth-place finish. As if I am satisfied with my performance. As if you and Mom have brought me joy—which in fact you have, not with these calculations, but simply with your presence in Italy at Opening Ceremony last week and at my race today.

"Wow," I say. "You're right. Thirty-fourth *is* twenty spots better than my ranking!"

Then Dad and Mom look at each other, beaming.

The pizza arrives. It's different from the kind you get in America, and like most things European, the difference is primarily one of scale. That means, in the case of pizza, less dough, less sauce, less cheese. But good. Really good.

"Hey I have something for you guys," I say, reaching into my backpack. "Some gifts. Here."

I hand Mom a U.S. team coat. It's white, cut straight and slim in the sleeves. And I give Dad a blue polyester warm-up jacket that zips up the front.

"No, I can't take this," Mom says, stuffing it into the backpack I've just pulled it out of.

Many people say things like this only to be polite. Not Mom. She's totally serious.

"You have to," I say. "I'm not taking it back."

I toss it in her lap.

"Why would you give us part of your uniform? You worked so hard for it!"

"You all are the reason I got here. This is as much your victory as it is mine."

"Maybe I could just borrow it for a few days and then return it?"

"No, Mom, keep it. Besides, I'm giving almost everything away. I want to mail a piece of my uniform or a souvenir or something from here to everyone back home who's ever helped me or donated money to my training."

"That's going to be *really* expensive for postage!" Mom exclaims, her eyes expanding.

"It's all right, Linda," Dad says, patting her hand. "That's something those people will keep forever."

"Exactly," I say. "I'll figure out the money later. Like I said, you know, a person doesn't go to the Paralympics by themselves. You bring everyone with you, like, at least in spirit. So all those people should get a piece of the experience."

After dinner, walking back to the Village, we run into Erik, the new Winter Park Disabled Ski Team coach. I've already decided that I am going to give him my U.S. team vest.

"Can you please take a photo of us, Erik?" Dad asks.

"Absolutely."

I put my arms around Mom and Dad, standing with the sun setting behind us, a pink sky set behind the treeless, snow-covered Alps. We are all three wearing some part of my uniform.

We say our thanks and goodbyes to Erik and continue walking.

"You've come a long way since you were nine years old," Dad says.

"I think we all have," I say.

Dad nods. "You know, we've never really told you this, but you almost didn't make it."

"What are you talking about?"

Dad tells me that the day the spots showed up on my lungs, one year after I finished chemo, when Dr. Dunsmore called him and cried on the phone, she said I had only three to six months to live. And that Sunday, the day I skipped church because I was too ashamed of the apparent relapse, Pastor Smuland scrapped the sermon he had prepared and told the entire congregation my prognosis. Then he preached a message about the glory that awaited me in Heaven.

"It's a miracle you're alive, Joshua," Mom says.

"It's a miracle *you're* alive," I say, putting an arm around her.

Little did Pastor Smuland know, back when he preached that message. Little did he know about the glory that still awaited me— that awaited us—here on earth, today in Italy, just now in that photo. Cancer can never erase that picture.

Acknowledgments

This is firstly a story about my family, and thus I am indebted to them not only for so freely allowing me to share intimate details of our history, but for the part each member has played in creating the story itself. I am especially grateful for the boundless love my parents have poured into my life. They are as near to perfect as human beings have come in the last two millennium. Our family has weathered much, and more storms will undoubtedly arise. My only prayer is that when they do, Mom, Dad, Matt, Luke, Anna, and I can face them together, and that Dad will not try to substitute his free biscuits for blueberry pancakes.

I wrote this book with the goal of creating a readable narrative, not an exhaustive recounting of the events of my life. The benefits in readability, however, come at the expense of credit, namely credit deserved by the many individuals who have played important roles in my story that did not fit in these pages. I would like to acknowledge some of those people now.

Our lives are our relationships, and I have been blessed with many that shaped the stories I wrote about in this book. I want to acknowledge my friends from William and Mary, especially Brad and the rest of Lodge Four, including Danny, Graham, Paul, Brett, and Kyle, as well as FCA, Harrison House, Monroe, and my boys from Friday Afternoon Group, most notably Bill Warwick. I wish to acknowledge my relationship with God as the sustaining force behind my victories of the past and my hope for the future. I'd like to acknowledge all the girls I've ever liked. You know who you are. Let me know if you change your mind. I want to acknowledge Harrisonburg High School for tolerating my hubris and Covenant Presbyterian Church for giving me all my best friends growing up. In fact, without this church family (especially Dr. Smuland, the Fords, the Marshes, the Barnes, Robert Strickler, and the Pearsons), I don't think my biological family would've survived the ordeals described in this book.

Thanks to Alice Curtin, my assistant and my cohort in gluten-free eating, for everything.

Thanks to Paul Cirone, Molly Friedrich, Jacobia Dahm, and Lucy Friedrich at the Friedrich Agency for believing in my manuscript. I will never forget listening to Paul's voicemail, saying he loved the sample pages. I was in Detroit Metro Airport, crying.

I am incredibly grateful to Josh Kendall for giving me the chance to tell my story, and I am truly honored to work with an editor of your talent and intelligence. Thanks to Maggie Riggs, Wendy Wolf, Carolyn Coleburn, Noirin Lucas, Jenna Dolan, and to the rest of Viking for your passion for this project.

Thanks to the UVA Children's Hospital for saving my life. When you are a child, it's difficult to understand people's actions, even when those actions are meant for your own good. Looking back now, though, I know and appreciate that I received nothing short of the best possible care from my entire team of nurses and doctors. The kindness and support we received from the likes of Dr. Kim Dunsmore and Dr. Raj Malik, in particular, cannot be put into words, and the same goes for Ginger, Teresa, Pat, Cheryl, Kim, and the CMN crew including Martha and Robert. If I ever have a sick child, I will take him or her to UVA.

My career as a ski racer would never have happened had it not been for Mark Andrews and Therapeutic Adventures, Sandy and the Massanutten Junior Race Team, the NSCD, NASC, Willy J, and

Erik Petersen, as well as sponsorships from Head, Uvex, and American Eagle. I want to acknowledge the Nuttings and their Nut House for giving me a home and a hot tub in Colorado, and Linda Tobin for spearheading my fundraising. I wish to acknowledge my many Winter Park and Paralympic teammates and coaches, all of whom I will never forget, and all of whom will be justified in their inevitable doubts as to whether my short and lackluster skiing career deserves to be recorded in a book.

Let me also take this opportunity to publicly acknowledge the incredible generosity of the many families, individuals, and organizations who donated to my training fund when I first started ski racing. Your gifts were and are astounding in their magnitude. My most profound satisfaction in life is the knowledge that your generosity ultimately paid off, that you sacrificed to give a boy's dream a fighting chance, and that eventually we made it, together, to Turino. I wish to acknowledge in particular the stunning generosity of both the Sease families, James Rollo, the Montgomerys, the Cupps, Wayne Harper, the Cochrans (and thanks for the bedroom!), the Alvises, the Krauses, Shickel Corporation, the Whittens, the Andersons, Douglas Houff, Bruce Elliott, the Rouses, John Holloran, Tom Sowers, the Parishes, Valley Blox, and the Millers.

I am so grateful for the support I received from Catherine Bowman, Pettit's Landscaping, Robert Van Winkle, Don Farley, Lindsey Funeral Homes, Golden China Restaurant, Steven Sodikoff at Steven Toyota, Patricia Doss, the Jacksons, the Honorable John Paul, Appalachian Physical Therapy, Enterprise Food Service, Zane Showker, Bill Neff Enterprises, John Crist, Nolan McHone, David Lee, Margot's Decorating Outlet, Miller and Jameson, the Shrums, Dayton Interiors, the Hunters, Bostic and Bostic, Harrisonburg Refrigeration Service, Rockingham Mutual Insurance Company, Francis Bell, Jr., the Gunns, Nationwide Truckers Permit Service, Bob Wade Auto World, the Bompianis, the Kaylors, the Heaths, the Lantzes, Kunz Appliance Service Center, Carolyn Frank, Butch

Strauwderman, Verstandig Broadcasting, Park View Auto Sales, Cecil Gilkerson, Paul Yoder, University Motors, Walt Sowers, Charles Wampler, David Garber Jewelry, the Lees, the Adamsons, Flowers by Rose, the Gillespies, the Tiptons, the Jellums, Susan Sweeten, the Smiths, the Martins, Dave Eshleman, Sherwin Jacobs, Gary Stiteler, the Bradfields, John Walsh, Verna Rodes, the Metzgers, Dr. George Weidig, Mensel Dean, Carlyle Whitelow, the Whittens, Bill Long, Carl Harman, Frank Miller, the Bradshow Garrison, the Downtown Prayer Luncheon, the McIntyers, the Johnsons, Steve Bird, the Hoovers, the Forsyths, Ivan Letner, Gerald Hopkins, Dr. Alan Cason, Rockingham Rotary Club, First Assembly of God, Exterior Distributors, Kiser Auto Sales, and James Wheatley.

Several people opened doors so I could pursue ski racing without falling too far behind scholastically. Thank you to Mrs. Reynolds and Dr. Ford for letting me go pursue my dream during high school. Thanks to Dr. Clemens, Dr. Holmes, Dr. Szykman, and Dr. Pease for generously allowing me the flexibility to take classes from Colorado and even Italy. Thanks especially to Sam Sadler. Were it not for your intervention to grant me housing on campus, I don't think I would've skied that final year.

The pages of this book have matured thanks to feedback from a ridiculously large number of people. I'd like to especially acknowledge the constructive criticism of Emily Chau, Bruce Horovitz, Valerie Kibler, Scott Moyers, and Rob "Uncle Wonderful" Rouse, and the encouragement of Clay Clemens, Juanell Teague, and David Kopp. Thanks to Anthony King for his assistance with AAVE. Thanks to Pebbles for late nights compiling reader comments. Finally, let me offer my sincere gratitude to my other readers of the full length draft who so generously shared their insights and opinions, including Aaron Taylor, Aimee Donley, Al Brenner, Alan Clark, Alberto Lopez, Alex Roviezzo, Alex Sorensen, Ali Schneider, Alix Auck, Allison Sudtelgte, Alyson Hall, Amanda Odell, Angela Bohrer, Anna Thomas, Anne-Marie Totah, Anthony King, Arielle

Borowski, Ashley Braziel, Ashlie Kramer, Beth Tormaschy, Betty Whitley, Bob Schreck, Brenda Hill, Brian Huynh, Brian Allen, Briana Hanny, Briana Morgan, Bridgit Breker, Brittany Abber, Brittany Cleem, Bryce Hites, Bryce Dupes, Carly Allison, Catherine Hagar, Catherine Kasler, Cathy Lavoie, Caytlin Buckel, Chelsea Couto, Chelsea Westermann, Chris Fisher, Christopher Bywaletz, Christopher Holden, CJ Reid, Clint Noethlich, Cody Hayes, Colleen Monahan Dobbs, Cortney Feickert, Dana Tuggle, Daniel Kao, Danielle Chudolij, Danya Counts, David Erwin, Donn Raseman, Doug Johnson, Elizabeth Watts, Emily Clark, Emily Lumpkin, Emily Padget, Eric Hudson, Eric Jacobson, Erin Kane, Evan Shelan, Felicitas Nungaray-Vera, Hallie Weber, Hannah Clark, Hannah Ahn, Holly Higgins, Hwayeon Seo, Izza Soubiane, Jacob Holloway, Jake Ridenour, James Hiett, Jane Canepa, Jeena Schmit, Jeff Nava, Jenn Bobzin, Joan Massie, Joanne Hora, Joelle Rickard, Joline O'Hara, William Rupp, Joseph DeFulio, and Josh Luo. And many thanks to the readers of the sample pages: Shannay Witte, Jeff Meissner, Vickie Johnson, Kelly Pierce, Ruth Johnson, Mary Strickler, Maxine Hauck, Chris Fisher, Sharon Sayler, Jennifer Booth-Jones, Kathleen DeFloria, Louis Abbey, Joanne Wrasse, Shauna Scott, Kristen Rempel, Freda Douglas, Victoria Cheslik, Elizabeth Mangano, Kevin Baumgarn, Stephanie Miller, Bob Harris, Glenda Ryder, Janet Young, Kathy Stan, Michael Cossette, Terri Kruse, Julie Pollard, Vanessa Swindell, Bob Jacobs, Nancy White, Shawna Besancon, Kristin Moran, Julia Perkins, Tanja Haylock, Caren Sloane, Brenda Hill, Lisa Hunt, Diane Wilson, Regina Overton, Neil Spiller, Dana Tuggle, Mike Rollo, Kelli Harrington, Betty Whitley, Sami Strong, Brandi Meeks, Jackie Walby, Susan Marman, Kristi Meidinger, La Rae Piotrowski, Ali Schneider, Karen Thompson, Karen Underdahl, Pam Wilz, Terri Deichert, Jim Fahy, Joy Fisher, Donna Fricke, Lexi Friedt, Jolene Gress, Petrina Haag, Butch Hrouda, Julie Jahner, Stacey Kovash, Rosella Perdaems, Peggy Rolle, Marleen Schnaidt, Dorothy Zeller, Krista Warbis, Elena

Malysheva, Lois Myran, Maralee Kubas, Curt Pierce, Beth Tormaschy, Lora Voegele, Cheryl Wehri, Fawnah White, Tod Winter, Abby Arseneau, Andrea Rivera, Emily Fava, Julia Cassel, Camille Squires, Ben Goggin, Jaclyn Harwood, Donn Raseman, Elaine Van Effen, Linda Conner, Lori Abichandani, Samantha Hall, Ali Towers, Kathy Eckley, Theodore Ni, Nina Crutchfield, Alan Clark, Nelson Zhou, Joshua Weiss, Alexandra Rivera, Jerald Severson, Jay Byoun, Tommy Gasbarro, Al Brenner, Amy Carruth, Belal Akhtar, Tyler Urban, Becca Newkirk, Nada Elrafei, Dane Wallace, Crystal Marshall, Shaun Browning, Bianca Edwards, Brenna Clark, Neva Nobles, Kim Billings, Susan Spencer, Larry Sebastian, Patricia Kirby, Kane Young, Anthony King, Carlean Jundt, and Matt Negaard.